Trademark Counterfeiting, Product Piracy,
and the Billion Dollar Threat
to the U.S. Economy

Trademark Counterfeiting, Product Piracy, and the Billion Dollar Threat to the U.S. Economy

Paul R. Paradise

Q

QUORUM BOOKS
Westport, Connecticut • London

Library of Congress Cataloging-in-Publication Data

Paradise, Paul R., 1950–
    Trademark counterfeiting, product piracy, and the billion dollar
threat to the U.S. economy / Paul R. Paradise.
        p.   cm.
    Includes bibliographical references and index.
    ISBN 1–56720–250–0 (alk. paper)
    1. Intellectual property—United States.   2. Trademark
infringement—United States.   3. Product counterfeiting—United
States.   4. Piracy (Copyright)—United States.   5. Intellectual
property—Economic aspects—United States.   I. Title.
KF2980.P37   1999
346.7304'88—dc21   99–10410

British Library Cataloguing in Publication Data is available.

Library of Congress Catalog Card Number: 99–10410
ISBN: 1–56720–250–0

First published in 1999

Quorum Books, 88 Post Road West, Westport, CT 06881
An imprint of Greenwood Publishing Group, Inc.
www.quorumbooks.com

Printed in the United States of America

The paper used in this book complies with the
Permanent Paper Standard issued by the National
Information Standards Organization (Z39.48–1984).

10 9 8 7 6 5 4 3 2 1

Every reasonable effort has been made to trace the owners of copyright materials in this
book, but in some instances this has proven impossible. The author and publisher will
be glad to receive information leading to more complete acknowledgments in subsequent
printings of the book and in the meantime extend their apologies for any omissions.

Contents

Preface

During 1995 and 1996 the United States nearly imposed trade sanctions on the People's Republic of China for the piracy of U.S.-owned copyrights for music, computer software, and motion pictures by the Chinese. Only the signing of an agreement by the Chinese in both years regarding greater protection of intellectual property avoided an all-out trade war.

The trade dispute underscored how serious a problem the counterfeiting of trademarks and the piracy of copyrights and patents had become. Under the old English common law, the crime was called "palming off." What the counterfeiter does is to steal the goodwill and brand name recognition inherent in a brand or trademark by attaching a counterfeit brand to his product and palming it off as the genuine article. Stealing the brand is as old as human commerce, but in modern times, the globalization of the economy and advances in technology have led to an explosion in counterfeit products. Prescription pills, automobile and airplane parts, heart pumps, garments, and a multitude of consumer products have been counterfeited and palmed off as the real product.

In modern times, the U.S. business community has become the principal victim of the explosive growth of counterfeit products. Product counterfeiting is a business crime. The emergence of the United States as the dominant world economy has had the unfortunate consequence of making its products the ones most often counterfeited. According to the International AntiCounterfeiting Coalition (IACC), an international trade group based in Washington, D.C., the U.S. economy lost $200 billion in 1995 due to counterfeit products. This figure is nearly twice the figure for the European Common Market, with estimated losses in revenues of $135 billion in 1995.

Much of the counterfeiting explosion began in the years after World War II in the developing countries. Initially, the problem was small and localized. By the 1970s, the situation had become too great to ignore. Companies and trade groups have fought back by lobbying for stronger protection of intellectual property, recommending trade sanctions, and by public education. In the United States, fifteen companies banded together in 1978 to form the IACC, which lobbied for passage of the Trademark Counterfeiting Act of 1984, the first federal law addressing the crime. Within a few years, the IACC's membership had risen to include over 300 corporations.

This book examines product counterfeiting from the perspective of U.S. industry. The industries discussed in the book are ones that have a serious counterfeiting problem, notably: entertainment, automobile, airplane, pharmaceutical, and apparel.

Acknowledgments

Trademark Counterfeiting, Product Piracy, and the Billion Dollar Threat to the U.S. Economy originally began as a series of articles. I was encouraged to continue with the writing by the publishers of *P.I.*, *Electronics Now*, *World and I*, and *Soundtrack Journal*. They published articles that would later be incorporated into the present book. I am especially indebted to private investigator David Woods and the publisher of *P.I.* for "Designer Counterfeiting," which appeared in the Spring 1992 issue of *P.I.* and would eventually be the stepping-stone for everything that followed.

Many other people offered generous support and assistance in the preparation of this book. I am especially indebted to Stephanie Mitchell and the general counsel's office at the Office of the United States Trade Representative (USTR) for reviewing the chapter in this book on the trade dispute with the Chinese.

I would like to thank the Recording Industry Association of America (RIAA), the International AntiCounterfeiting Coalition (IACC), and the Business Software Alliance (BSA) for the considerable assistance these trade groups provided me with. I interviewed numerous people in this book and I would like to thank each and every one for their time and comments. Finally, I would like to thank my father, who kept this project afloat financially during a difficult time.

1

Trademark Counterfeiting

Trademark counterfeiting? Most people have never heard of the term, although they may be familiar with names such as imitation, knockoff, replica, look-alike, counterfeit, and fake.

Under the English common law, trademark counterfeiting was called palming off. What the counterfeiter does is to "palm off" a counterfeit product as the genuine product by a ruse as to source of origin. The counterfeiter usurps the goodwill and brand-name recognition inherent in a trademark by attaching a counterfeit trademark to his product. "Palming off" is often used to refer to trademark counterfeiting to this day. Illegal actions may also include the counterfeiting of the packaging, referred to as the trade dress. In France, the term "contrefaçon" refers to any form of intellectual property infringement, while the term "piraterie" is closer to the English meaning of counterfeiting. The term "l'imitation illicite" refers to the creation of an approximate copy of another's mark. In Germany, the expressions "markenpiraterie" and "produktpiraterie" encompass both the meaning of the English word counterfeiting and infringement.

Trademark counterfeiting is not to be confused with the counterfeiting of money, nor with industrial piracy, which involves the theft of trade secrets. Trademark counterfeiting refers to the unauthorized reproduction or counterfeiting of trademarks, while the terms product or commercial counterfeiting are broader and include the counterfeiting or piracy of intellectual property.[1] Although intellectual property rights include several types of protection such as patents, copyrights, trademarks, trade secrets, design protection, plant variety protection, and others, commercial counterfeiting primarily involves patents, copyrights, and trademarks.

Product counterfeiting has a long history, but since the 1970s losses have escalated alarmingly. President Clinton threatened to impose $1.8 billion in trade sanctions in 1995 and $2 billion in trade sanctions in 1996 against the People's Republic of China for the pirating of American-made products—notably recorded music and computer software. Only the signing of an agreement in both years prevented an all-out trade war.

The trade dispute with China focused international attention on what had become an epidemic in commercial counterfeiting. Long considered a crime involving only the counterfeiting of jeans and watches, the list of products expanded to also include heart pumps, automobile and airplane parts, prescription pills, and countless other products.

In addition to palming off, commercial counterfeiting may involve illegal duplication and actual theft; these primarily involve products protected by copyright and by patent.

Although all counterfeiting involves duplication to some degree, illegal duplication is largely a problem caused by technological invention and for the most part involves only copyrights. Under copyright law, the copyright owner has the exclusive right to distribute his creative works. The unauthorized duplication and distribution of another's creative work in the absence of a licensing agreement or other authorization is illegal.

The earliest form of illegal duplication involved book piracy. Prior to the invention of the printing press, book piracy was impossible. Books were reproduced by hand, and it took years to produce a copy. With the invention of the printing press in the late 1400s, the need for a copyright—or right to produce copies—became necessary. In modern times, high-speed duplicators have made music, computer software, and motion picture piracy an inexpensive and lucrative, illegal business venture.

A notable copyright pirate was Isaac Zafrani, who set up an international organization selling pirated motion picture video cassettes in 1979.[2] Zafrani's main business expense was the purchase price of fifty high-speed video cassette duplicators. Operating out of Panama, Zafrani set up the duplicators in the "slave" position, so that the machines worked nonstop duplicating copies of American-made videos. Zafrani's illegal enterprise was engaging in back-to-back video copying, which is the most prevalent type of video cassette piracy. In the United States, an estimated 10 percent of the nation's 25,000 to 30,000 video retail outlets deal in pirated video cassettes.

Zafrani hired traveling salesmen to sell the illegal copies in the remote villages of South America. Zafrani's operation sold in bulk to freighters passing through the Panama Canal. Before he was apprehended, business had become so lucrative that Zafrani had opened up a European office.

Actual theft involves copyrighted works and patented inventions. Despite their intangible nature, they can be stolen in their entirety. Simply put: when a pirate steals a sound recording, a computer program, or the chemical composition of a pharmaceutical—he has stolen the product. The pirated product may or may not have the quality of the legitimate product—but the inventiveness, the creativity, and the research costs that make the product unique have been stolen. The loss is much greater than the loss involving trademarks: when a counterfeiter attaches a counterfeit mark to a product, the theft is limited to the goodwill and brand recognition.

Technological advances have made actual theft the fastest-growing type of commercial counterfeiting. With the advent of digital technology, pirates can make actual copies of computer software, recorded music, and motion pictures with no loss of quality in successive generations of copies.

In the latter half of the twentieth century, copyrights are suffering the greatest losses, in part because of the many new products that have been invented, such as the analog cassette, video cassette, compact disc (CD), and many other products, and because of advances in the means of distribution. Although trademark counterfeiting was widespread in China throughout the 1990s, the trade dispute that was investigated by the U.S. Trade Representative (USTR) in 1994–1996 involved works protected by copyright: sound recordings, computer software, and motion pictures.

The distribution of works protected by copyright has been revolutionized by the invention of cable television, which involves satellite transmission, and by the Internet, which can involve the digital transmission of copyrighted works such as computer programs, video games, and sound recordings. Previously, the piracy of copyrighted works required the possession of a legitimate product in a fixed or tangible form (i.e., a book or a music cassette), but these technological advances in the commercial distribution of copyrighted works have offered new avenues for product piracy in intangible form (i.e., cable programming).

Cable piracy, also called signal theft, involves the actual theft of copyrighted material. The birth of the cable industry is attributed to Jerry Levin, who reinvented the cable television industry when he proposed that the service be distributed by satellite. Satellite transmission of cable programming transformed Time Warner's Home Box Office (HBO) into a cable giant. The cable pirate, who hooks up illegally, is stealing television programming, which is protected by copyright. In the United States, an estimated one in four cable viewers does so illegally; the problem is worse outside the United States, where entire countries engage in signal theft.

The ultimate triumph of digital technology is the Internet, where everyone is connected to a cyber universe by computer, modem, and telephone line. In the twenty-first century, electronic commerce by way of the Internet is expected to reinvent the way people purchase products. The Internet offers perhaps the ultimate avenue for a counterfeiter, who can e-mail a pirated computer program or music recording anywhere in the world, and keep his identity a secret.

THE IMPORTANCE OF INTELLECTUAL PROPERTY

No matter how vast a company's portfolio of physical and financial assets, its portfolio of intangible assets known as brands is even more valuable. Indeed, the goodwill, brand-name recognition, and quality associated with the trademark Quaker Oats ® are as important as the product itself. John Stuart, former chairman of Quaker Oats, once said, "If this business were to be split up, I would be glad to take the brands, trademarks, and goodwill and you could have all the bricks and mortars—and I would fare better than you."

Because of their intangible nature, placing a monetary value on intellectual property did not occur until modern times. Reckitt and Colman, the food conglomerate, was the first to put a value on its trademarks in 1985. Other corporations followed. Today, every major corporation places a monetary value on its brands, which, like other property, can be bought and sold.

Since the mid-1970s, the biggest development in the U.S. business landscape has been the change from a manufacturing economy to a service economy. This change has made intellectual property the most valuable commodity of the U.S. economy.

"Intellectual property [IP] is the seed of economic prosperity," says Professor James P. Chandler, president of the National Intellectual Property Law Institute. "Look around you—a chair, a car, these are physical products that are grounded in IP law."[3]

According to Professor Chandler, American-made intellectual property constitutes 80 percent of all intellectual property in the world. He cites a study completed by former Vice President Dan Quayle, who chaired an economic council for President Bush. In the study, the volume of American intellectual property was compared to the volume produced by the rest of the world. Quayle's study group found that the United States produced more IP than the rest of the world combined and ten times more IP than any other single country.

Today, most countries recognize that trade in intellectual property is the foundation of a country's wealth. Previously, world commerce dealt only with trade in goods, not intellectual property. Strong IP protection is very important in the global economy chain, where goods are manufactured in many countries (see Figure 1.1).

"Intellectual property is to the twentieth century what coal was to the nineteenth century," says John Bliss, president of the International

Figure 1.1
Basic Outline of Intellectual Property Protection

	Trademark	Copyright	Patent
Protectable Subject matter	Any sign or combination of signs	Literary and artistic work (incl. computer prog.)	Inventions in all fields of technology
Requirement for protection	Cabable of distinguishing (optional: visually perceptible)	Presented as a literary work	novelty involve inventive step capable of industrial application
Method of Protection	Registration Use in commerce	Creation	Filing
Scope of Protection	Prevent others from using similar signs for similar goods in course of trade if liklihood of confusion	Right to authorize or prohibit commercial rental	Prevents others from making, using, offering for sale, importing for these purposes that product or a product obtained directly by a patented process
Term of Protection	10 year periods renewable indifinitely	author's lifetime plus 50 years	20 years from filing date
How to maintain protection	Requirement of use Renewal of registration		Renewal every year
Other conventions to comply with	The Paris Convention (1967)	The Berne Convention (1971)	The Paris Convention (1967)

Source: The Counterfeiting Intelligence Bureau (CIB).

AntiCounterfeiting Coalition (IACC), a trade group based in Washington, D.C. "IP has become like a natural resource. It is every bit as valuable, if not more valuable, than personal property."

The chief threat to the U.S. economy is the counterfeiting of its intellectual property. Before continuing with the discussion of product counterfeiting, copyrights, trademarks, and patents will be defined, and a short review of the major laws governing all three will be presented.

Trademarks [U.S. Code, Title 15, Chapter 22]: A word, design, symbol, device, or combination used by a manufacturer or merchant to identify his goods and distinguish them from others. Trademarks include brand names identifying goods, service marks identifying services, certification marks identifying goods or services meeting certain standards, and collective marks identifying goods, services, or members of a collective organization.

Copyrights [U.S. Code, Title 17]: An original work of authorship that meets the criteria of originality, tangible form, and fixation. A copyright goes to the form of expression, rather than to the subject matter of the writing. Works of authorship includes literary works; musical works, including any accompanying words; dramatic works, including any accompanying music; pantomimes and choreographic works; pictorial, graphic, and sculptural works; motion pictures and other audiovisual works; sound records; and computer programs.

Patents [U.S. Code, Title 35]: A grant of a property right by the government to the inventor of an original invention that meets the criteria of novelty, unobviousness, and utility. Three types of patents are recognized: utility patent, design patent, and plant patent. Countries differed as to whether a patent is awarded to the inventor who is the first-to-file or the first-to-invent, but under the Trade Related Aspects of Intellectual Property Rights (TRIPS) of the General Agreement on Tariffs and Trade (GATT), patent offices are required to award patents on a first-to-file basis. In the United States the right conferred by the patent grant extends throughout the United States and its territories and possessions, and it is a "right to exclude others from making, using, or selling" the invention.

Trademark Act of 1946 (Lanham Act)

In passing the Lanham Act (the Act), Congress recognized the extended use of trademarks and decided "public policy requires [they] receive nationally the greatest protection that can be given them." Although trademarks need not be federally registered to be protected, the Act entitles trademark owners to register their marks in the U.S. Patent and Trademark Office (USPTO), if goods bearing the mark have been shipped in interstate or foreign commerce, or if services under the mark are either subject to federal regulation or have been rendered in more than one state.

Federal registration offers substantial advantages: (1) it serves as notice nationwide of the registrant's ownership claim in the mark; (2) it serves as evidence of the registrant's exclusive ownership rights in the mark (shifting the burden of proving otherwise to anyone challenging those rights); (3) it gives federal courts jurisdiction to hear infringement claims, counterfeiting claims, and related state unfair competition claims; (4) it precludes states from requiring modifications in the display of the registered mark; (5) it can be used as a basis for trademark registration in some foreign countries; and (6) it can be recorded with the U S. Customs Service to prevent importation of infringing foreign goods.

Eligibility and Procedure

Certain aspects of a trademark may prevent its being eligible for registration. For example, the mark may be descriptive, or include immoral, deceptive, or scandalous matter, or matter that disparages or falsely suggests a connection with persons, institutions, beliefs, or national symbols. Further, marks that include flags or other governmental insignia cannot be registered. Also, marks that include names, portraits, or signatures of living individuals will be refused registration without the individual's written consent. Finally, a mark may so resemble a registered mark that registration will be barred. Matters of substance, including whether there is ownership of the mark and use as a mark, may also be the basis for refusal of registration.

The USPTO examines all trademark applications. If it determines the trademark is entitled to registration, the mark is published in the USPTO's *Official Gazette*. Persons believing they will be damaged by the registration may file an opposition with the USPTO within thirty days of publication.

If all requirements are met and no problems arise, a certificate of registration is issued. At this point, one of the following trademark registration notices may be used (usually near the right shoulder of the mark) to notify the public that the mark is registered: "Registered U.S. Patent and Trademark Office," "Reg. U.S. Pat. & Tm. Off," or the letter R enclosed within a circle. Notice is not mandatory; however, profits and damages cannot be recovered under federal law unless it is used or the infringer actually knew of the registration. Use of a trademark registration notice before the mark is registered is inappropriate and may prevent the owner from obtaining relief against an infringer. The informal symbols TM (for trademark) or SM (for service mark) may be used with unregistered marks to indicate a claim of common law trademark rights.

Remedies against Infringement and Counterfeiting

Trademark infringement exists when any person, without the consent of the trademark registrant/owner, uses the same or a confusingly similar mark, on the same or closely related goods or services, in the same geographical area or, in some cases, within a natural area of expansion.

Registrants/owners may bring a civil action against infringers. The remedies available (under federal law and most state laws) are: (a) an injunction against future infringement; (b) the infringer's profits; (c) damages for past infringement (which may be trebled under federal law); (d) destruction of all materials bearing the infringing mark; and (e) court costs and, in exceptional cases, reasonable attorney's fees.

Criminal penalties and stiffer civil remedies are available under federal law (and some state laws) for *intentionally* dealing in goods or services *knowingly* using a counterfeit mark. Federal criminal penalties include: (a) fines for individuals up to $2,000,000 ($5,000,000 for subsequent offenses), or imprisonment not exceeding ten years (twenty years for subsequent offenses), or both; and fines for corporations or partnerships up to $5,000,000 ($15,000,000 for subsequent offenses); and (b) destruction of articles bearing the counterfeit mark. Federal civil remedies include: (a) seizure, *without notice*, of the goods, counterfeit marks, means of making the marks, and relevant business records; and (b) *mandatory* treble damages and attorney's fees (including investigator's fees).

Continuity of Trademark Rights

Common law trademark rights continue indefinitely as long as the mark is properly used and not abandoned. To maintain a federal trademark registration, however, a declaration that the mark is still used in interstate or foreign commerce must be filed during the sixth year after registration, and if first registered after November 16, 1989, the registration must be renewed every ten years, or every twenty years, if filed prior to November 16, 1989. A petition to cancel a registration may be filed by anyone who believes he is or will be damaged by the registration. These petitions must generally be filed within five years of the registration. Except under certain circumstances, once a mark has been in continuous use for five consecutive years subsequent to registration (and is still in such use), the right of the registrant to use the registered mark in commerce for the specified goods or services will become incontestable.

Copyright Act of 1976

Federal Copyright Protection

The Copyright Act (the Act) seeks to promote literary and artistic creativity in the United States. To achieve this, the Act grants authors/creators exclusive rights to (1) reproduce their works, (2) distribute the reproductions, (3) display and perform the work publicly, (4) prepare derivative works, and (5) authorize others to do these things.

To receive copyright protection, the creation must be *original*, and either a literary, musical, or dramatic work; pantomime or choreographic work; pictorial, graphic, or sculptural work (including the nonutilitarian design features of useful articles); motion picture or other audiovisual work; sound recording; computer program; or compilation or derivation of preexisting works.

Federal copyright protection *automatically* begins as soon as a work is created *and* fixed in tangible form (written down or recorded on tape). Unfixed works (extemporaneous speeches; unrecorded live performances) may be protected by state law since they are not covered by the Act.

Maintaining Copyright Protection

Prior to the effective date of the Berne Convention Implementation Act of 1988 (March 1, 1989), work that was publicly distributed *must* have had a copyright notice affixed to it to prevent loss of federal protection. Copyright notice comprises: (a) the letter "C" enclosed within a circle, the word "Copyright," or the abbreviation "Copr.," (b) the year of first publication, and (c) the name of the copyright owner. Notice may be omitted on certain articles such as jewelry, stationery, and other such works. The notice advises others of the rights claimed. As to the works distributed before March 1, 1989, the omission of or error in the notice will not invalidate the copyright if (a) few copies are involved, (b) the copyright is registered within five years, *and* reasonable effort is made to add the notice to all publicly distributed works once the omission/error is discovered, *or* (c) the omission/error violated an express written condition for distribution. Now, notice of copyright is not required; however, omission of notice provides a defendant with additional defenses in an infringement trial.

There are other requirements under the Act that copyright owners must meet. For instance, there is a deposit requirement, which provides that within three months after a work is published with notice in the United States, two complete copies of the best edition must be deposited in the U.S. Copyright Office. Failure to do so also does not invalidate a copyright; however, if the Register of Copyrights makes a written demand for the deposit, failure to deposit within three months after this demand can result in a fine up to $250, plus the retail price of the work, plus $2,500 if the failure is willful or repeated.

Federal Registration of Copyrights

To register copyrights in published or unpublished works, an application, two complete copies of the best edition of the work, and a $20 fee must be filed in the Copyright Office. Although failure to register does not invalidate a copyright, prompt registration is advisable since: (a) it is a prerequisite to suing an infringer; (b) damages and attorneys' fees *cannot* be recovered for infringements beginning before registration (unless registration occurs within three months after first publication); (c) a certificate of registration issued before or within five years of publication is evidence of a valid copyright; (d) certificates may be recorded with U.S. Customs to prevent importations of infringing works; (e) registration is required to renew copyrights in works published before 1978; and (f) registration preserves the copyright information on the work.

Works created on or after January 1, 1978 have copyright protection for the author's (or surviving joint author's) lifetime plus 50 years. A "work made for hire," or an anonymous or pseudonymous work is protected for the shorter of 75 years from publication or 100 years from creation.

For works created before 1978, the period of copyright depends on certain factors. If unpublished and protected by state common law copyright, the work automatically becomes federally protected in 1978, and is guaranteed federal copyright protection for 25 years, plus an additional 25 years if the work is published during the initial 25-year period. (Note: special rules apply to sound recordings created before February 15, 1972.) Works protected by federal copyright before 1978 are protected for 28 years from publication (or from registration if unpublished), with possible renewal for an additional 47 years.

Copyright Infringement

Copyright infringement generally occurs when there is unauthorized use or copying of a copyrighted work. Copyright owners must prove that (1) the alleged infringer had access to the work, and (2) there is "substantial similarity" to the owner's work. Such a showing generally shifts to the alleged infringer the burden of showing independent creation.

There are several limitations on the exclusive rights of a copyright owner. For example, the following activities are *not* copyright infringements: (1) use of the basic idea expressed in a work; (2) "fair use" of a work (such as use for purposes of criticism, comment, news reporting, teaching, scholarship, or research); (3) independent creation of an identical work; (4) sale or limited public display of a *lawfully* made copy or phonorecord of a work by the owner of the copy or phonorecord; (5) use under one of the four compulsory licenses[4]; (6) importation of specified quantities of copies by an importer for *private* use; and (7) copying or adapting a computer program as an essential step in utilizing it in conjunction with a machine or for archival purposes. These are only some activities that are *not* copyright infringements.

Remedies for Copyright Infringement

Copyright infringement that is willful *and* for profit is a federal crime for which a court is *required* to order: (1) a fine of not more than $100,000, or imprisonment not exceeding one year, or both (penalties are generally much greater for reproducing or distributing infringing phonorecords of sound recordings or copies of motion pictures [or other audiovisual works], depending on the number of copies, the period of infringement, and the number of offenses); and (2) seizure, forfeiture, and destruction of all infringing reproductions and all equipment used in their manufacture.

There are also civil remedies for private parties (including the holders of any exclusive rights in copyrighted works). They include (1) injunctions against future infringements; (2) impounding and destruction of all infringing copies and articles used to make them; (3) actual damages suffered by the copyright owner; (4) any additional profits of the infringer; (5) instead of actual damages and profits and at the copyright owner's election, statutory damages for all infringements beginning from $500 to $20,000 (subject to reduction or increase); and (6) court costs and a reasonable attorney's fee.

Criminal Penalties

Under the 1976 Act computer piracy—no matter how egregious—was never more than a misdemeanor copyright violation. At that time, the computer software industry was in its infancy. By 1989, the computer software industry estimated that illegal copying amounted to an industry loss of $1.6 billion. In 1992, the 1976 Act was amended to provide harsher criminal penalties. Originally introduced to deal with the growing problem of computer piracy, the statute was broadened to include all works protected by copyright. Under the new provisions, an infringement becomes a felony based on a combination of the number of infringing copies or phonorecords made or distributed, and their retail value. The penalty is up to five years' imprisonment, or a fine, or both, if the offense consists of the reproduction or distribution of at least ten copies or phonorecords of one or more copyrighted works, with a retail value of more than $2,500, during a 180-day period. A second or subsequent offense can result in imprisonment of up to ten years.

The Patent Act

Patentable Inventions

The Patent Act authorizes the U.S. government to provide, subject to certain conditions and requirements, three types of patents. A "utility patent" (also called a "functional patent") can be obtained by anyone who invents or discovers a new and useful *process* (chemical, mechanical, or electrical procedure), *machine* (mechanism with moving parts), *article of manufacture* (man-made product), or *composition of matter* (chemical compound, combination, or mixture). A "design patent" can be obtained by anyone who invents a new, original, and ornamental design for an article of manufacture (for example, the "Flying Lady" sculpture on the Rolls-Royce automobile hood), and a "plant patent" can be obtained by anyone who invents or discovers and asexually reproduces any distinct and new variety of plant, including newly found seedlings.

A patentable invention is normally owned by the first person to conceive it if he/she works with reasonable diligence to reduce it to practice or to file a U.S. patent application. Inventors should always evidence their conception by making a "disclosure record." This can be a simple written description and sketch of the invention that is dated and signed by the inventor and a witness capable of understanding the invention. Normally, only the actual individual inventor can apply for a patent. However, any joint inventors are required to sign the application or the resulting patent will be invalid. Errors in an application arising without deceptive intention usually may be corrected.

To be patentable, an invention or discovery must meet at least the following criteria: (1) *novelty* in that the item was not previously (a) known to or used by others in the United States, or (b) patented or described in a printed publication anywhere in the world; (2) *unobviousness* to a person having ordinary skill in the relevant art; and (3) *utility* in that the item has a useful purpose, actually works, and is not frivolous or immoral. The government thoroughly examines inventions for patentability, and reexamination may be sought at any time to raise a substantial new issue of patentability.

Patent Protection

Unless a patentable invention can be kept secret for many years, patent applications should be filed as soon as possible. Patents protect against innocent infringements, and are the *only* way to protect an invention that is no longer secret. Finally, a patent will be unobtainable if, among other things, more than one year before filing the application, the invention is described in a publication, patented, or offered for sale in the United States.

After a patent application has been filed, the informal legend "patent applied for" or "patent pending" frequently is used on the articles or processes and in advertisements for them. After a patent has been issued, the legend "patent" or "pat." and the number of the patent is usually used. This notice is not mandatory but may be necessary to get damages from an infringer. Use of an improper patent notice is punishable by fine.

Duration and Assignment of Patents

A utility or plant patent generally lasts seventeen years from the date the patent is issued. However, the term can expire earlier if specified maintenance fees are not paid three and one-half years, seven and one-half years, and eleven and one-half years after issuance of the patent (plus a six-month grace period). The term can also be extended up to five years for certain patents on human and animal drugs, medical devices, and food and color additives to restore some of the patent life lost during the product's premarket approval process. A design patent lasts fourteen years from the date the patent is issued. Since patents *cannot* be renewed and are publicly disclosed when issued, anyone can make, use, or sell in the United States devices embodying the formerly patented invention once the patent has expired or been declared invalid.

Written assignments of the entire patent or a part interest may be made and filed in the Patent and Trademark Office either with or after the filing of an application. Agreements may also be made requiring the assignment of future inventions and patents. Small businesses and nonprofit organizations may elect to own inventions made under government grants; however, the government retains a nonexclusive royalty-free license and often gives U.S. industry a preference in the use of such inventions.

Trade Related Aspects of Intellectual Property (TRIPS)

On December 8, 1994, President Clinton signed implementing legislation conforming U.S. patent laws to the TRIPS Agreement of the General Agreement on Tariffs and Trade (GATT). TRIPS requires patent offices to award patents regardless of where the product is invented or produced, with the result that the USPTO must treat inventive activities in any World Trade Organization (WTO) member country the same as in the United States.

Previously, a U.S. patent had exclusive rights for seventeen years from the date of issue. Under TRIPS, U.S. patent law was changed. Patent applications filed on or after June 8, 1995 have a term of twenty years from the date of filing in the United States. Patent applications filed before June 8, 1995 have a term of seventeen years from issue *or* twenty years from filing, whichever is longer.

Patent Infringement and Remedies

Valid patents that have not been the subject of inequitable or unlawful conduct protect against unauthorized manufacture, use, or sale in the United States of all devices embodying the invention or of components intended for assembly abroad into such devices, whether they were copies from authorized devices or resulted from an independent act of invention. However, patent infringements suits or arbitration proceedings are brought cautiously since they are generally expensive and often bring an attack against the patent's validity.

Although there are no criminal penalties for patent infringement under federal law, the following civil remedies are available: (1) an injunction against future infringement; and (2) compensatory damages (at least equal to a reasonable royalty), which may be trebled. For infringement of a design patent, the infringer's profits (not less than $250) may also be available. It is important to note that damages may only be recovered for infringement during the six years preceding the filing of a lawsuit and only if the infringer was notified of the infringement and continued to infringe. Notice may be presumed if the patented article bore a patent notice.

COMMON LAW BACKGROUND

Undoubtedly the first brand names were cattle brands. The word "brand" comes from the Anglo-Saxon verb "to burn." In ancient times, many articles of commerce were branded, including slaves. Brand names indicate ownership and also serve as a personal mark, and hence a means to identify the individual.

In the Middle Ages, the use of trademarks as indicators of goodwill and quality was established with the rise of the guilds in Europe. A guild is a collection of artisans engaged in commerce. The early guilds each had a distinctive guild mark. The use of guild marks became widespread. Eventually, trademark registration systems of various kinds developed in Europe. In 1374, an ordinance of Amiens required every smith to use a mark different from every other mark on his metal work to identify the maker. Counterfeiting was rampant. In 1282, a law was passed in Parma that forbade artisans engaged in the manufacture of steel or iron articles, such as knives and swords, to use the same or similar mark as that of any other guild member. The penalty was £10 for each offense.

In medieval France, trademarks were regarded as property and protected against infringement by civil remedies.

Bread was a widely counterfeited product. In the Middle Ages the diet of the common man consisted almost entirely of bread, ale, and cheese. The breads came in many varieties. The exact proportion for each variety of bread was determined by the government, and changed each year, depending upon how bountiful the wheat harvest had been. In 1202, King John of England proclaimed the Assize of Bread, making it illegal for bakers to adulterate their bread by mixing in beans or other substitutes. Violators were put into the pillory. In 1266, the English Parliament enacted a law requiring every baker to have a mark of his own for each type of bread. Bread counterfeiting remained a problem for hundreds of years.

The reigning monarchs took trademark counterfeiting very seriously. The king's seal was widely used in commerce and counterfeiting was considered a capital offense. In the fourteenth century, the Elector of Palatine pronounced an edict stating that any innkeeper caught selling spurious wine would be punished by hanging. Under a royal edict of Charles IX in 1564, imitators of marks were placed in the same category as counterfeiters of money and executed.

Book piracy flourished in England during the fifteenth and sixteenth centuries. England was in a state of constant religious and political warfare and the books were aimed at the warring Protestant and Catholic factions. The government's attempts to try to stem the pirate trade played an important role in the development of modern copyright law.

In the late 1800s, England was faced with a counterfeiting problem that was a harbinger of the problem the United States would encounter a hundred years later. In the late 1990s, the United States had emerged as an industrial and a cultural leader, but had a serious counterfeiting problem with its trading partners in East Asia. In the late 1890s, England was an industrial leader and a cultural leader, but had a serious problem with the English-speaking colonies, notably the United States, over the widespread pirating of English copyrights and patents.

There is one important difference between the piracy situation in England in the late 1800s and the situation in the United States in the late 1900s. The United States was an isolationist in the late 1800s, and as such, not a big trader. The Asian countries, on the other hand, were members of a global economy; the effect of their piracy was more widely felt.

During the years following the Revolutionary War, the United States freely pirated pharmaceuticals, books, and sheet music. The Americans, along with the Canadians and Australians, were notorious pirates of English printed sheet music during the late 1800s.[5] This was the period of the British music hall, which popularized new songs and gave birth to a generation of songwriters. Most middle-class English families at the time could afford pianos. Many families got caught up in the songs of the era and played them at home.

In 1881, the Music Publishers Association was founded in England. This organization played a leading role in fighting the piracy of printed sheet music in England and abroad. The Association estimated that 90 percent of printed sheet music coming into England from America consisted of pirated reprints of English copyrights. This deplorable situation was an outgrowth of the market in the United States, which was almost entirely pirate. There was little that could be done about the situation in the United States. The former colony was not a signatory to any international copyright convention, and copyright protection was afforded only to American nationals.

In response to the widespread music piracy by the United States, the Secretary of the Music Publishers Association sent a letter to the English Postmaster General's Office and offered to send their own experts to assist in the identification of pirated music. The Association also wrote to all steamship companies traveling between England and America, and asked for their assistance in stopping the flow of pirated sheet music. To tackle the domestic market for pirated sheet music, the English enacted stronger legislation that allowed for a seizure without warrant of pirated copies of any music composition upon request in writing by the owner of the work. To assist in a seizure, the Music Publishers Association established its own internal force of established agents, including fifty ex-policemen and upwards of one thousand volunteer helpers.

In a celebrated case, Chappel & Co., a music publisher, brought suit against the company of James Fisher & Co. for music piracy in 1905. James Fisher & Co. was founded in January 1904, but used several false names to circumvent the authorities. One of the owners was James Frederick Willets, who was known in various circles as the "Pirate King." Willets was the secretary of a group called the People's Music Publishing Co., which was founded on the lofty, but illegal goal of bringing music cheaply to the masses by way of piracy.

Chappel & Co., a major music publisher at the time, had a serious piracy problem. Chappel had published thousands of copyrighted popular musical works, but nearly all of them had been pirated abroad or pirated at home in England. After stronger legislation was enacted, Chappel seized 300,000 illegal copies of its copyrighted works and two million belonging to other publishers in the years leading up to the case against Willets and James Fisher & Co. The case subsequently became known as "The Great Conspiracy Case." During the trial, 200 exhibits were entered and over fifty witnesses called by the prosecution. The defense had neither witnesses nor exhibits. When it was over, the prosecution had won a minor victory. Willets received nine months without hard labor; the others received smaller sentences.

The Constitution of the United States provided for rights in patents and copyrights, but not trademarks. In 1791, a petition by Samuel Breck and other Boston sail makers was sent to the Second Congress asking for the exclusive right to use certain marks for designating their sailcloth. Jefferson reported to Congress that it would "contribute to fidelity in the execution of manufacturing, to secure to every manufacturer, an exclusive right to some mark on its wares, proper to itself."[6]

Jefferson recommended a system of registration at the various district courts. Until passage of the Trademark Act of 1870, this was the procedure followed by merchants who wanted formal protection for their marks and labels. The Trademark Act of 1870 grounded trademark protection in Article 1 of the Constitution, otherwise referred to as the copyright clause.

Under the 1870 Act there was no mention of trademark counterfeiting. The period following the end of the Civil War was marked by lawlessness, particularly in the South, whose legal and governmental institutions had been shattered. In 1876, four hundred leading merchants and manufacturers petitioned Congress to enact criminal sanctions against trademark counterfeiters.

In response to the petition, Congress amended the 1870 Act to make trademark counterfeiting a crime. The legislation would be short-lived.

In the case *U.S. v. Steffens*, 100 US 82 (1879), the Supreme Court held that Article 1 of the Constitution could not serve as a basis of authority and therefore the Trademark Act of 1870 was unconstitutional.

The Supreme Court's ruling was prescient. Trademarks are neither creative works nor inventions; they are indicators of source or origin, and function only within a business environment. The *Steffens* decision led to the drafting and passage of the Trademark Act of 1881. Under the 1881 Act and all subsequent Trademark Acts, use in interstate commerce is the basis for registration of trademarks.

The congressional record is unclear, but for reasons lost to time, the trademark counterfeiting provision of the 1870 Trademark Act was not incorporated into the 1881 Trademark Act. Nor was it incorporated into any subsequent Trademark Act. The 1946 Trademark Act, referred to as the Lanham Act, makes no mention of trademark counterfeiting. As such the remedies for trademark counterfeiting are the same as for trademark infringement; generally, a civil suit for damages.

Unlike the industrialized countries of Europe, the United States was the only industrialized country without a substantive body of law addressing the problem of product counterfeiting at the start of the twentieth century.

The absence of any criminal penalties would ultimately cost U.S. companies billions of dollars starting in the late 1970s, when trademark counterfeiting began to escalate. The lack of any criminal remedies meant that prosecutors could do little. If the illegal manufacturer was large enough—engaged in interstate transportation, or connected to organized crime, or part of a network that was distributing and manufacturing counterfeit merchandise—a prosecutor could use various legal remedies relating to criminal conduct to arrest the pirates and seize the illegal merchandise. Otherwise, there was little that could be done.

Faced with a growing trademark counterfeiting problem, U.S. businesses could do little. The commencement of a civil suit for monetary damages was an insufficient remedy to halt a fraudulent business entity that was engaging in commercial counterfeiting. Civil suits are slow, often taking years to come to trial. By that time, the counterfeiter would have destroyed his business documents and moved, never bothering to show up in court. Seemingly, the only civil remedy was an injunction.

The absence of any criminal penalties for trademark counterfeiting meant that a commercial counterfeiter could offer for sale products that were patently unsafe without risk. Prescription drugs, automobile and airplane parts, heart pumps, baby food, shampoos, and many other products have been palmed off as the genuine product over the years. In the words of one judge, the list of products that can be counterfeited is "limited only by the human imagination."

President Reagan signed the Trademark Counterfeiting Act into law in 1984, after lobbying by industry groups, notably the International AntiCounterfeiting Coalition (IACC). The IACC was formed in 1978 by the Levi Strauss Co. and 15 other companies that were seriously endangered by commercial counterfeiting. By 1985, its membership had grown to more than 300 major corporations, associations, and professional firms worldwide.

Many of the basic elements of the 1984 Act can be found in the 1876 counterfeiting amendment, which was seemingly lost by oversight. The 1876 amendment provided for a fine of up to $1,000 and imprisonment for up to two years for anyone who sold or dealt in counterfeit marks. The amendment provided for search warrants to be issued upon the written request of a trademark owner.

Criminal penalties under the 1984 Act signed by President Reagan call for a fine of up to $100,000 and a prison sentence of up to five years, plus an award of treble attorney's fees to an aggrieved trademark owner. The 1984 Act was amended and provides for a fine of up to $2,000,000 or imprisonment for up to ten years, or both. Companies can be fined up to $5 million.

In addition to criminal penalties, remedies in a civil action were bolstered. One of the principal weapons in the fight against trademark coun-

2

The Worldwide Threat

How big of a problem is commercial counterfeiting? Estimates vary, but losses have escalated alarmingly since the mid-1970s. The IACC places overall losses for U.S. industries in 1995 at a whopping $200 billion—up substantially from $86 billion in 1988. According to the Counterfeiting Intelligence Bureau (CIB) in England, an estimated 5 to 7 percent of all products on the market are counterfeit. The CIB estimates that the United States lost 120,000 jobs and Europe lost 100,000 jobs per year during a ten-year period ending in 1997. The Centre for Exploitation of Science and Technology, which placed the rate of counterfeiting at 7 percent in 1991, estimates that the world piracy rate may be as high as 10 percent today.[1]

ORGANIZED CRIME

There are several reasons for the huge upswing in counterfeiting losses. One reason is that organized crime is becoming more involved in commercial counterfeiting. Why are criminals selling counterfeit watches and designer jeans? Because it is lucrative, and the crime is not likely to draw attention or significant jail time. "Trademark counterfeiting has become a core activity for organized crime because of the big rewards and low risk of prosecution," said a spokesperson for the Institute of Trading Standards Administration in Britain.

In 1991, David Thai, who was formerly the gang leader for the Vietnamese gang Born to Kill (BTK), confessed to earning over $13 million from the sale of counterfeit watches. Operating out of Canal Street, the huge illegal CD production and distribution operation based in Milan. The Mafia-backed production plant was producing twenty-four million illegal CDs each year. The CDs were exported all over Europe, and were imported by the Irish terrorist groups.

"The monetary value of pirate, and especially counterfeit, CDs has attracted professional international criminals who are also involved in other serious crimes, such as the distribution of drugs," says Mike Edwards, director of operations for the International Federation of the Phonographic Industries (IFPI), based in London.

"Beginning in the early 1990s, it became apparent during IFPI investigations involving European CD pirates that we were up against sophisticated criminals. For example, we were astonished to find after one successful action against a pirate that the police had been keeping the individual in question under surveillance. The defendant was involved in the CD business as a legitimate front for his drug smuggling and distribution activities. On another occasion, police action netted thousands of pirate compilation CDs, several kilos of cocaine and a loaded automatic rifle. Fortunately, the superior firepower of the police on that occasion prevented any serious incident."

In Hong Kong, the movie industry, which produces martial arts and gangster movies, was hit hard as a result of the trade dispute between the United States and China in the mid-1990s. Many of the pirates moved to Hong Kong and set up underground CD plants. Organized crime, otherwise known as triads, infiltrated the lucrative pirate market. Criminals vied to control production, and sought to coerce leading film stars to work in their productions. Film executives were murdered. By 1998, the pirate market controlled an estimated 40 percent of the Hong Kong movie industry.[4]

In addition to the influx of organized crime, advances in technology and the increased globalization of the economy have made product counterfeiting an easy start-up business and contributed to the growing losses.

TECHNOLOGICAL ADVANCES

Technological advances have added fuel to the explosion in product counterfeiting. Until modern times, pirates roamed the high seas searching for merchant ships to plunder. Modern-day pirates have the advantages of fax machines, computers, overnight mail, trucks, cellular phones, and e-mail.

Overnight mail has ushered in a revolution in shipping and has been used with devastating effect by the modern trademark counterfeiter. For example, during the 1980s the American Amusement Machine Association (AAMA) had a serious problem with counterfeit coin-operated video games. Most of what makes a video game unique is contained in several ROM chips on the printed circuit board. Once the counterfeiter duplicates the information on these chips, he can produce pirated copies of the legitimate game. The typical counterfeiter is a small to mid-sized computer company that illegally manufactures printed circuit boards and ships the boards by overnight mail, which is quick and usually passes through customs. After the AAMA developed a customs enforcement program, the counterfeiting problem was curtailed.

The Motion Picture Association of America (MPAA), a trade group that represents many of the major motion picture companies, often finds that counterfeiters purchase a legitimate copy of a popular video in the United States and ship it overnight to a foreign country, where the legitimate video is used as a master. Thousands of copies are duplicated and offered for sale before the MPAA's member companies can offer the legitimate in video the same country.

In 1998, illegal video CDs (VCDs) of the movie *Titanic* were available for $2 in Singapore, within two weeks after release of the motion picture in the United States. According to Lowell Strong, the head of antipiracy operations for the MPAA in Singapore, the picture quality of the VCDs was poor. Strong believes that the pirates obtained copies of the movie in the United States by sneaking a camcorder into a movie theater and taping it from the movie screen. A single copy obtained with a camcorder and shipped by overnight mail would have been enough to begin production.

In 1993, the Sara Lee Corporation, whose subsidiaries make Champion clothing, Coach leather goods, and Aris Isotoner gloves, reported a sharp increase in unusually high-quality counterfeits. At nearly the same time, Dooney & Burke, manufacturer of leather bags and wallets, began to discover high-quality counterfeits that sell for nearly the same price as the legitimate product and are sold in small shops around the country.[5] The explosion in high-quality counterfeits has been seen in Europe as well. According to Peter Lowe, assistant director of the CIB, high-quality counterfeits in the apparel industry have been seen in department stores throughout the United Kingdom.

The appearance of very high-quality counterfeits or "cyber-fakes" is the result of advances in computer technology that allow counterfeiters to embroider and reproduce exactly all of the design qualities of the legitimate products, including the trademarked label. By leasing a twelve-head Tajima embroidery system, a counterfeiter can replicate stitched logos, and sell the product as the legitimate, rather than as a "knockoff."

The invention of the compact disc has made music piracy an international problem, according to Edwards of the IFPI. "Whereas in the past, cassette piracy has generally been a purely national problem, with pirate cassettes being manufactured and sold in the same country, and usually in the same region of the same country, CD piracy is international. Pirate CDs have been known to be manufactured in Taiwan, transshipped through Malaysia, air freighted via Belgium to Paraguay, from where they are intended to be smuggled into Brazil and Argentina."

GLOBALIZATION OF THE ECONOMY

Experts often cite the globalization of the economy as a major reason for the explosion in counterfeit goods. This globalization has been made possible by advances in shipping and communications and has ushered in a world market in which most consumer products are manufactured in many different countries. A television purchased in the United States may have been manufactured in Mexico; the electronic parts may have been shipped to Mexico by Japan. This type of global chain has been a boon to many developing countries in Latin America and Asia, which can participate in a global market.

Product counterfeiting is a crime with a long history, but the globalization of the economy has allowed the modern-day counterfeiter to unload his illegal goods in nearly any country, particularly countries with little intellectual property protection. Often, the counterfeit goods are shipped through customs.

The Counterfeiting Intelligence Bureau (CIB) was established in 1985 by the International Chamber of Commerce to meet what had become an international problem in trademark counterfeiting. With world headquarters in England, the CIB is a nonprofit organization representing large multinational companies, trade associations, law firms, and technology producers around the world.

The CIB has created two worldwide networks to assist its members: Counterforce, which is a network of intellectual property law firms in 57 countries that specialize in product counterfeiting; and Countertech, which is a network of high-technology companies that manufacture anticounterfeiting security devices such as holograms. By the end of 1987, the CIB had undertaken over 500 investigations in more than 35 countries of counterfeit products ranging from wall coverings and furniture to alcoholic beverages and pharmaceuticals. By the year 2000, the CIB hopes to establish the Global Anti-counterfeiting Group, which will be an international alliance of all the main anticounterfeiting organizations.

Globalization has presented a counterfeiting problem of serious dimensions for the U.S. business community, which is the primary victim of product counterfeiting. The paradigm case evidencing the impact of globalization was the trade dispute between the United States and the People's Republic of China that began on June 30, 1994. In 1994, as part of China's rush to private enterprise, there was an explosion of counterfeit products—notably software and music compact discs (CDs). Much of the illegal product was initially traced to an estimated twenty-nine CD plants, many of which were located in Guangdong Province, a special economic zone. According to J. C. Giouw, regional director of the IFPI in Hong Kong, the pirates controlled an estimated 90 percent of the market in 1994. The CD plants had an estimated yearly output of 75 million CDs. In less than two years, the CD plants had usurped most of the legitimate market in much of East Asia, and illegal products were showing up in Western markets.

"The CDs coming from China were showing up around the world," says Frank Creighton, vice president of investigations for the Recording Industry Association of America (RIAA), a trade group that represents 90 percent of the U.S. music industry. "It became a worldwide situation. We saw pirate and bootleg CDs involving Western music, Indian music, Asian music, and nearly every type of music in the world market. The CDs were showing up in Europe, the United States, and even in Paraguay."

Popular Western artists included the Beatles, Bob Dylan, Nirvana, and Pearl Jam. Cantonese pop (also called "Canto-pop") stars, with a wide audience throughout East Asia, were widely pirated. What was so disturbing about the trade dispute with the Chinese was the speed with which an international black market was established. Despite the threat of trade sanctions in 1995 and 1996, Chinese piracy remained widespread.

Much of the modern counterfeiting problem involves the developing countries. To exercise control over the worst offenders, the United States enacted the Trade and Tariff Act of 1984, which authorized the President to restrict or deny favorable tariff treatment under the Generalized System of Preferences (GSP).

Most of the developing countries have benefited by trading with the United States under the GSP. The GSP provides for preferential duty-free entry to 149 designated beneficiary countries and territories. The program was instituted on January 1, 1976, and was authorized under the Trade Act of 1974 for a ten-year period. The program is administered by the U.S. Trade Representative (USTR), who derives much of his power under the Trade Act of 1974. The intent of the GSP is to encourage the economic development of Third World countries by allowing them to trade duty-free with the United States.

The GSP has worked especially well in East Asia, because the countries in this region have a long history of trading among one another. The GSP has assisted this centuries-old trading pattern, often referred to as the overseas Chinese. During turbulent times in China, the rich business class was forced to relocate to other countries in Asia, while continuing to trade with China. As a result of this migration, the Chinese represent a wealthy minority in many Asian countries, with ties to other Chinese throughout Asia and mainland China. The overseas Chinese have been written about in several books, notably *Lords of the Rim* by Sterling Seagrave.

The reapproachment with China by President Nixon in the early 1970s paved the way for economic growth in East Asia. The United States has benefited by increased trade with the East Asian countries and attained a position of influence in East Asia that would have been unimaginable at the end of the Vietnam War. America's influence in this region is based on trade and goodwill, and represents a turnaround from the foreign policy ashes that brought the country to war in this region.

The downside to this success story is that all of the East Asian countries have been notorious pirates of American intellectual property (see Figure 2.1). The close trading ties that these countries maintain among themselves and with the United States have made commercial counterfeiting a booming business.

The authorization for the GSP was renewed through July 4, 1993 by the Trade and Tariff Act of 1984, which hinged GSP treatment for developing countries to intellectual property protection. Under the 1984 Trade and Tariff Act the President was authorized to consider whether countries are providing adequate protection for U.S. intellectual property, and to restrict or deny GSP benefits where such protection is inadequate or to take retaliatory action by restricting imports.

U.S. businesses, besieged by a wave of counterfeiting in Asia and Latin America, lobbied hard for passage of the 1984 Trade and Tariff Act. On June 25, 1985, the IACC and other industry groups testified at public hearings conducted by the USTR as part of a general review of the GSP. The public hearings were called for under the 1984 Trade and Tariff Act. IACC testimony was presented by a panel of witnesses, including Jim Bikoff, who was then president of the IACC, Rob Spiegelman of Jordache, Frank Wang of the law firm of Lee & Li, and Bob Sherwood of Pfizer, who submitted a written statement.

IACC president Bikoff led off with a call for immediate action against Taiwan, Korea, Singapore, the Philippines, Mexico, and Brazil, because of their failure to protect IP rights. Bikoff stated, "The countries deriving the most benefit from the GSP program are the very countries where U.S. intellectual property rights have to a large extent not been respected or enforced." Frank Wang discussed the IP climate in the People's Republic of China, and the difficulties encountered in securing adequate protection and enforcement of intellectual property.

"Until the 1984 Trade and Tariff Act was passed, the U.S. could not go after another country for failure to protect U.S. intellectual property," says Carol Risher, vice president of copyrights and new technology for

Figure 2.1
Notorious East and Southeast Asian Pirate Countries

- Japan. At one time in the early 1980s virtually 80 percent of the home video market in Japan was pirate. The tide was turned due to the efforts of the Motion Picture Association of America (MPAA), which launched a massive public education and enforcement effort. By the late 1980s, the pirate market had shrunk to about 40 percent, and some retailers were voluntarily turning in pirate products. Japan is currently a leading computer pirate. The BSA estimates losses to computer piracy in Japan at over $2 billion.

- Singapore. Nicknamed the "world capital of piracy" in 1984. In just a two-year period, after passage of an improved copyright law in 1987 and effective enforcement, losses shrank from $385 million in 1984 to $10 million in 1988.

- Taiwan. Once a major book pirate, then a computer software pirate. Under threat of trade sanctions, the Taiwanese cracked down, after the USTR initiated a Special 301 investigation in 1992.

- South Korea. Formerly a major book pirate, and still a major computer pirate, despite being the target of a Special 301 investigation in 1991. The BSA estimated that it lost nearly $550 million in 1994.

- Thailand. In January 1989, President Reagan denied duty-free entry into the United States of $165 million in Thai imports under the GSP due to the failure to protect U.S. copyrighted works. Although GSP benefits were restored, in April 1992, the USTR placed Thailand on the Priority Watch List for pirating music recordings. The BSA estimated the piracy rate at 98 percent in 1994.

- Indonesia. A major pirate in the early 1980s. In 1985, bilateral trade negotiations were undertaken with the European Commission and the United States against Indonesian piracy. In 1986, the IIPA filed a petition under the 1974 Trade Act to deny GSP benefits to Indonesia unless improvements were made. The BSA placed the computer piracy rate at 99 percent in 1994.

the Association of American Publishers (AAP). "After that, the U.S. had the leverage of the U.S. market. We could say to a country that unless they provided adequate and effective protection for American intellectual property, we were not going to trade with them."

By 1984 the United States had been in a long-running battle to protect its intellectual property rights in East Asia. In 1985, the International Intellectual Property Alliance (IIPA) submitted its Ten Country Report[6] to the USTR on the worst IP offenders. The IIPA is an umbrella trade organization that represents many other trade groups protected by copyright, including the Recording Industry Association of America (RIAA), the National Music Publishers' Association (NMPA), the Association of American Publishers (AAP), and others that collectively represent over 1,600 industries. Heading the list of IP violators were Singapore, Indonesia, Taiwan, and Korea (the other countries were Nigeria, Philippines, Brazil, Malaysia, Thailand, and Egypt). In its Twelve Country Report[7] submitted to the USTR in April, 1989, the People's Republic of China, Saudi Arabia, and India were added to the list of IP violators.

In response to the growing counterfeiting threat, Congress passed the Omnibus Trade and Competitiveness Act of 1988, which enhanced the USTR's powers to protect U.S. intellectual property rights. The Act provides for an overall strategy for the protection of IP. The USTR is required to initiate investigations of countries denying adequate protection and has the authority to impose trade sanctions.

Although the United States has threatened to rescind GSP benefits many times since enactment of the 1984 Trade and Tariff Act, and the USTR has conducted numerous investigations as required by the Omnibus Trade and Competitiveness Act of 1988, the counterfeiting and piracy of U.S. American intellectual property remains widespread in most developing countries. The most notorious pirate has been the People's Republic of China, which has been the beneficiary of favorable tariff treatment as a Most Favored Nation (MFN).

GRAY MARKET GOODS

The globalization of the economy has placed a strain on customs inspectors around the world. The flow of material entering the ports of entry in most industrialized nations allows customs inspectors to examine only a small percentage of the goods. As a result, most counterfeit merchandise passes right through customs.

In the United States, customs examiners usually inspect about 5 percent of the goods entering the country. The examiners are on the lookout for contraband, contaminated food products, diseased animals, and a myriad assortment of goods that are either illegal or pose a danger to the public. With such a vast flow of goods, shipping counterfeit goods that resemble the legitimate product into the country is relatively easy. In Antwerp, Europe's second largest port, 2,000 to 3,000 containers pass through the port each day, but as late as 1996, there were only six customs inspectors, who were able to inspect only one of every hundred containers. In late 1994, French manufacturers and customs officials launched "Operation Père Noel" to stem the flow of brand-name goods passing through the country's borders; under a new French law, customs officers can confiscate counterfeit goods and levy fines without having to go first to a judge.[8]

Most bootleg music recordings are manufactured in Europe and shipped into the United States through U.S. Customs. To fool customs inspectors, the recordings are shipped without cover art or anything else that would identify it as illegal. One of the most infamous bootlegs (called a boot in the pirate trade) was Prince's *Black Album*. After recording the album, Prince decided that he did not want the album released; however, someone obtained a master of the album and released it illegally in Europe. The album was shipped back into the United States with a label that said "Christopher: The Complete Sessions." Most fans of Prince know that Christopher is an alias that the rock star uses, but the ruse fooled customs inspection. Bootleg copies of the *Black Album* appeared in the Netherlands in 1988.[9] The unauthorized album was eventually released into the legitimate market.

Customs inspectors are further hampered by gray market goods. Also called parallel imports, gray market goods are goods that are legitimately manufactured overseas, but are exported by the overseas manufacturer to compete with the legitimate manufacturer's goods. Gray market goods are difficult to stamp out, because they bear a legitimate trademark. Parallel imports are a multi-billion-dollar problem for manufacturers of cameras, perfumes, and many other products.

In the United States, the gray market problem was dealt a blow in June 1989 when the U.S. Supreme Court held that retailers could buy trademarked foreign-made watches, cameras, perfumes, and other goods from independent distributors overseas.[10] Because of this ruling, distributors could sell the parallel imports in the United States at lower prices, over the objections of the legitimate companies and their authorized distributors.

To get around the 1989 Supreme Court ruling, many manufacturers tried copyrighting the packaging on their goods. Under copyright law, the copyright holder has the exclusive right to distribute copies of his work; hence by copyrighting the packaging on their goods, the legitimate manufacturers could bring suit in court for copyright infringement.

The Coalition to Protect the Integrity of American Trademarks (CO-PIAT), a trade group that represents many perfume and watch manufacturers, pioneered the use of this legal strategy in the case *Parfums Givency, Inc. v. Drug Emporium, Inc.*, 38 F.3d 477 (9th Cir. 1994).[11] The initial success of the strategy of copyrighting the packaging was dealt a blow in March 1998, when the U.S. Supreme Court ruled that American manufacturers could not use copyright law to protect their goods.[12]

LACK OF INTELLECTUAL PROPERTY LAWS

In many developing countries, where there are weak intellectual property laws and the near absence of enforcement, counterfeit merchandise is openly sold. The worst offender is the People's Republic of China, but in places like Tepito, Mexico, where two-thirds of all of the pirated music cassettes in Mexico are produced, there are streets named after classical music composers. Thousands of miles away in what was formerly Soviet Russia, pirated music and video cassettes are openly sold. In Cairo, many local video clubs allow customers to rent counterfeit video cassettes before their release date in Egypt by the legitimate manufacturer. In war-torn Africa, itinerant vendors travel from village to village and sell medications that are in many instances counterfeit.

The lack of intellectual property protection and lack of effective enforcement has been a driving force behind the piracy problem in East Asia and other developing countries. In what has become a familiar pattern, the pirates establish a stronghold in a region or country with weak IP laws and lax enforcement. When IP laws are strengthened and an enforcement campaign is initiated, the pirates move to another region and resume production.

In the early 1970s, Hong Kong was the largest music pirate in East Asia. To eliminate the problem in Hong Kong, the IFPI set up a regional office in the early 1970s. When the problem in Hong Kong was under control, the piracy problem in the region shifted to Singapore, which was labeled the "world capital of piracy" in 1984. After the piracy problem in Singapore had been eliminated, Indonesia became a major pirate, then Malaysia and Thailand. Each time the pirates in East Asia moved to another country, the IFPI and the MPAA countered by establishing a regional office in the same country as the pirates. During the 1980s, the MPAA set up regional offices in Japan, where over 80 percent of the market was pirate, and in Singapore. The purpose of the IFPI and MPAA regional offices was to lobby for stronger legislation and to establish an effective antipiracy campaign.

By the early 1990s, the IFPI had declared that music piracy in East Asia had been brought under control. Success was short-lived. Within a few years, Taiwan had become the center of music and software piracy. After the Taiwanese government cracked down, the pirates moved to the People's Republic of China, which became the region's main pirate. After the piracy situation in the PRC had been brought under control, the piracy problem shifted to Hong Kong and Macau, and reappeared in other East Asian countries, notably Singapore, Indonesia, and Malaysia.

The shift from one region to another in response to a piracy crackdown has been seen in many areas besides East Asia. For well over a decade the primary source of bootleg music in the world was Italy and Germany, both of which had lax copyright laws. This situation changed in late 1994 when the General Agreement on Tariffs and Trade (GATT) was ratified. As signatories to the GATT, Italy and Germany had to amend their copyright laws. Underground organizations in these countries that produced bootleg music moved briefly to Luxembourg, which was late in amending its copyright laws. Finally, Luxembourg amended its copyright laws, with the result that many of the larger bootleg organizations were put out of business.

The shifting from one region to another has been seen by the RIAA in its battle in the United States against music piracy. As part of its antipiracy campaign, the RIAA lobbies for stronger legislation, in addition to carrying out raids and surveillance. During the early 1980s, the RIAA's antipiracy campaign was concentrated in the Carolinas. When that part of the country had been put under control, the antipiracy campaign shifted to California, and then to the New York metropolitan area.

This shift from one location to another in response to a stepped-up antipiracy campaign has been seen with street peddlers. Street peddlers are the most numerous and difficult link in the counterfeiting chain to eradicate. Suing them in court is of little use, since the vendors have few assets. Criminal penalties are usually limited to a small fine.

"If you ask a street vendor what's hot, he'll tell you the search warrants are out today for Gucci and Louis Vuitton," says John Bliss, president of the IACC. "Despite the fact that these guys are on the streets, they're pretty sophisticated. They react swiftly and predictably to true criminal threats. In states where a strong felony statute is enacted, you see counterfeiters migrating to contiguous areas that don't have strong legislation on the books. When a strong felony statute was enacted in New York, the corresponding rates of crime increased in Philadelphia, Boston, and in the state of New Jersey."

The counterfeiting situation is worst in countries where IP protection is poor and the government is unstable. The collapse of Soviet Russia created a piracy situation of serious dimensions in the early 1990s. Under the Communist system, the state had a monopoly in music, films, and publishing. However, beginning in the 1970s, an underground market for Western music and books began to develop. With the collapse of the Soviet regime in 1991, government control ceased. One notable pirate, Andrei Tropilo, who was an underground music producer beginning in the 1970s, sold eleven million records in 1992 without paying a cent to the legitimate copyright holders.[13] Without a copyright law in force, the legitimate copyright holders could do nothing to stop Tropilo. An estimated 80 percent of all music sales in Russia were counterfeit.

Video piracy was widespread in Russia in the early 1990s. Because of censorship under the Communist regime, there were only 731 video titles available in 1990, but on the black market there were an estimated 10,000 titles. In 1991, in protest over widespread state-condoned video piracy, the MPAA banned future sales of U.S. films to Russia. In 1993 the Russian Federation enacted its Law on Copyright and Neighboring Rights. Significant loopholes in the copyright law remained, notably in regard to protection of preexisting works and sound recordings.

With the collapse of the Soviet system, organized crime made inroads into every part of the market. "The Russian mafia are more formidable than anything the IFPI has ever encountered," says Mike Edwards, director of operations for the IFPI. "To our knowledge, they are the most brutal and ruthless crime group anywhere in the world."

The IFPI set up an office in Moscow during the mid-1990s and hired the former head of enforcement for the Department of the Interior, who was in charge of the fight against organized crime, but he resigned in 1998. Many experts expect Russia to become the largest music pirate at the beginning of the twenty-first century.

The lack of an international body of intellectual property law has played a role in the counterfeiting epidemic. In place of an international body of law, there are conventions where the signatory countries agree to treat member countries as national countries, otherwise referred to as "national treatment." For copyrights: there are the Berne Convention for the Protection of Literary and Artistic Works (the Berne Convention), which was established in 1886 under the leadership of Victor Hugo and which has 130 signatories today; the Universal Copyright Convention (U.C.C.) signed in Geneva in 1952 (the Geneva Convention, 1952). For musical compositions: there are the Convention for the Protection of Producers of Phonograms against the Unauthorized Duplication of their Phonograms (the Geneva Convention, 1971), and the Convention for the Protection of Performers, Producers of Phonograms, and Broadcasting Organizations (the Rome Convention). The international registration of trademarks is governed by the Madrid Agreement, which was signed in the late 1800s (the Madrid Agreement) and today has over 19,000 trademarks. For patents, utility models, designs, trademarks, and trade names, there is the Paris Convention for the Protection of Industrial Property, which was drafted in 1883.

Most Western European countries are signatories to one or more of the conventions previously mentioned, and belong to the European Common Market, which has made post-1992 Western Europe the world's largest market. Nonetheless, each state retains in large part its own national laws and wide differences exist between the states as to the mechanism and effectiveness for dealing with the manufacture, distribution, and sale of counterfeit goods. Successive surveys by the European Association of Industries of Branded Products (AIM), located in Brussels, Belgium and other interested organizations have established that counterfeit goods are widely sold in the Single European Market, as well as the broader European Economic Area. According to AIM, a number of countries in Western Europe are well known as sources of counterfeit goods.

THE THREAT TO THE U.S. BUSINESS COMMUNITY

Since the mid-1970s, when counterfeiting losses started to escalate, the United States has been hit harder than any other industrialized country. Most of these losses have been borne by the United States business community, which is the primary victim of commercial counterfeiting. The losses suffered by U.S. businesses are a natural consequence of America's emergence as the post–World War II industrial leader. Commercial counterfeiting is a business crime. According to the Department of Commerce, 750,000 U.S. jobs have been lost worldwide because of counterfeit products. It is estimated that 62 percent of all counterfeit items produced in the world are sold in the United States.

On March 12, 1987, U.S. Trade Representative (USTR) Clayton Yeutter conducted an investigation into the foreign protection of intellectual property rights and the effect on U.S. industry and trade. Investigation no. 332–245 was conducted by the USTR, acting under the direction of President Reagan, and in accordance with Section 332(g) of the Tariff Act of 1930. The results of the Investigation were compiled by a questionnaire that was sent to 736 U.S. companies, including all of the Fortune 500, appropriate members of the American Business Conference, and smaller firms in concentrated industries known to depend on royalties or sales of goods protected by intellectual property.

A public hearing of the Investigation 332–245 was held on May 5, 1987 at the U.S. International Trade Commission Building. The results of the Investigation were published in January 1988. The aggregate losses by industry groups were: scientific and photographic industry ($5 billion), computers and computer software ($4.1 billion), electronics ($2.3 billion), motor vehicles and parts ($2.2 billion), entertainment ($2.1 billion), pharmaceuticals ($1.9 billion), chemicals ($1.3 billion), and petroleum refining and related products, including plastics ($1.3 billion). Worldwide losses due to intellectual property inadequacies were an estimated $23,845,223.

In the USTR's investigation, piracy of audio and video tapes and computer software was identified as the most easily accomplished large-scale violation of intellectual property. This vulnerability, and its high profit potential, combined to make such piracy the most widespread violation in the world. In the years since the USTR's investigation, the importance of the computer industry and the entertainment industry to the U.S. economy has grown, as has the counterfeiting problem.

The entertainment industries are especially vulnerable to counterfeiting. Piracy in the entertainment industries is largely a problem of unau-

Figure 2.2
Software Piracy Estimates 1995

Region	Piracy Rates	Losses (U.S. $, Million)	Share of Worldwide Total
W. Europe	49%	3,576	27%
E. Europe	83%	674	5%
N. America	27%	3,287	25%
L. America	76%	1,142	9%
Asia/Pacific	64%	3,991	30%
Africa/M. East	78%	521	4%
Total World	46%	13,191	100%

Source: Business Software Alliance (BSA).

thorized copying. Much of the technology is readily available and sold without restriction. Not only are the products easy to duplicate, but much of the success of the entertainment industry rests on a handful of big-name artists. Most counterfeiting in the music industry involves analog cassettes and compact discs (CDs); in the motion picture industry, video cassettes.

The computer industry is one of the great success stories of the U.S. economy. The computer software business is America's third-largest manufacturing industry, paying wages twice the national average.[14] Like many industries protected by copyright, the computer industry is especially vulnerable to commercial counterfeiting. The U.S. computer industry, which holds 75 percent of the world market, lost over $15 billion to piracy in 1995 (see Figure 2.2).

The research and development costs and production and marketing costs to develop a computer program like Windows 95 are in the hundreds of millions of dollars. In seconds, a pirate has deprived the legitimate manufacturer of his creativity and of a return on his investment by illegally copying the program. In many countries, where the rate of computer piracy is over 90 percent, the legitimate U.S. computer companies are being shut out.

In 1995 and 1996, the Software Publishers Association (SPA), a trade group based in Washington, D.C., labeled China and Russia as "one-copy" countries, where piracy is so high, virtually a single legitimate copy of software could satisfy the entire country's demand. In 1995, the U.S. computer industry reported sales in Asia of $797 million—against estimated "losses" of $4.4 billion. By a seeming sleight of hand, the U.S. computer industry is "losing" more than it is earning in revenue. Such huge piracy losses are not losses that will show up on a balance sheet. The losses represent unrealized profit. Within the computer industry and other industries, such massive piracy losses have begun what is called the "disincentive to produce." Ultimately, such losses are weakening the competitive edge. The products are produced slower, because ultimately the manufacturer has to compete against a pirate market for a product that it owns. "The products are still coming out, but at a slower pace," says Kim Willard, a public affairs representative for the BSA.

The American pharmaceutical industry saw its competitive edge weakened during the 1970s due to widespread piracy in Latin America. "We knew they were stealing our know-how, but we lived with it," says Edmund T. Pratt, chief executive officer of Pfizer.[15] Ultimately, many pharmaceutical manufacturers had no choice, but to pull out of Latin America due to widespread piracy and lack of intellectual property laws. The result was loss of profits, higher research and development costs, and ultimately higher costs to the legitimate consumer.

Intellectual property is one of the chief exports of the United States. To protect its intellectual property rights abroad, the Office of the U.S. Trade Representative (USTR) has become the mainstay of U.S. industry. The USTR has been active in protecting U.S. intellectual property on a unilateral and bilateral level during the last quarter of the twentieth century.[16]

On the multilateral level the USTR has been active in seeking greater IP protection through the General Agreement on Tariffs and Trade (GATT), the precursor to the World Trade Organization (WTO). In 1977, as part of the Tokyo Round of multilateral trade negotiations, the United States and the European Communities (EC) proposed an agreement to control international trade in goods bearing counterfeit trademarks. Discussion continued after the Tokyo Round, and the United States and the EC succeeded in establishing an experts group on trade in counterfeit goods in 1984. A negotiating group, the Trade Related Aspects of Intellectual Property (TRIPS), was eventually established and began deliberations in 1987. TRIPS was concluded in 1994, as part of the Uruguay Round agreement, and became part of the GATT. TRIPS broke new ground with commitments to a comprehensive set of rules establishing minimum standards for protection of IP rights and stronger enforcement measures internally and at international borders.

"The idea of TRIPS is to make every country down to the least understand that everybody benefits from protection of IP," says Risher of the AAP. "Even the smallest country is capable of producing IP, and many countries are seeing IP as the way to piggyback their economy. Even if you are not a producer, you can be a licensee."

On the bilateral level, the USTR's authority to investigate trade disputes has been enhanced by the Omnibus Trade and Competitiveness Act of 1988, which amended the Trade Act of 1974. Under Section 301 of the Trade Act of 1974, the USTR is authorized to investigate trade-related complaints submitted by U.S. industries regarding unfair trading practices and to impose trade sanctions, if necessary. Under the Omnibus Trade and Competitiveness Act of 1988, the USTR's authority was broadened to include Section 301 investigations involving intellectual property; because they involve intellectual property, they are referred to as "Special 301" investigations. The USTR has conducted several Special 301 investigations since 1988, including two investigations involving the People's Republic of China.

The United States has also strengthened its domestic intellectual property laws in numerous ways, notably the passage of the 1984 Trademark Counterfeiting Act, which will be covered in a later chapter, and passage of the Anticounterfeiting Consumer Protection Act of 1996.

On March 12, 1996, the House Judiciary Committee unanimously approved the AntiCounterfeiting Consumer Protection Act, HR 2511. The bill was introduced in the House of Representatives by Bob Goodlatte (R-Va.). Speaking before the full Committee, Goodlatte said that HR 2511 takes strong steps toward helping trademark and copyright owners recover meaningful damages suffered from the counterfeiting of their goods. Additionally, he said the bill creates a significant deterrent to counterfeiters by providing for increased jail time, criminal fines, and asset forfeiture.

"Counterfeiters know that although criminal penalties exist on the books, criminal actions are rarely initiated against counterfeiters because of the inadequacy of the criminal penalties and misperceptions about the gravity of the crime. . . . This legislation takes steps to attack this problem," Goodlatte said.

Representative John Conyers, Jr. (D-Mich.), ranking Democratic Member on the House Judiciary Committee and an original cosponsor of the bill, pushed for a favorable Committee report and congratulated lead House sponsor Representative Goodlatte for addressing what he and other lawmakers have deemed "a growing concern for American consumers."

Commenting on the importance of HR 2511, Conyers said that one of the bill's greatest strengths is that it fights organized crime, which is now heavily involved in product counterfeiting. Specifically, the proposed Act makes trademark counterfeiting and copyright piracy predicate acts for purposes of the Racketeer Influenced and Corrupt Organizations Act (RICO) and would give law enforcement the ability to seize the fruits of the counterfeiter's trade.

The Anticounterfeiting Consumer Protection Act was drafted by the IACC member companies in response to the growing tide of product counterfeiting. The Trademark Counterfeiting Act of 1984, which was also drafted by IACC member companies, was proving insufficient. "Current law was not enough," says John Bliss, president of the IACC. "The private sector and law enforcement were outgunned, outmanned, outfunded, and almost out of time. Unless Congress acted, our country would have been awash with substandard and at times, lethal counterfeits."

Bliss knew well the dangers posed by product counterfeits. He was formerly a member of the House Judiciary Committee and had access to reports by industry, government committees, and trade groups telling of the growing threat posed by substandard products. In 1991, with the nation in the midst of a recession and unemployment rising, Bliss decided to leave government for the private sector, and he became the president of the IACC. Although there are many trade groups, organizations, and corporations that have an active anticounterfeiting program, the IACC is one of the few that is devoted full-time to the problem. The IACC was founded in 1978 by the Levi Strauss Company and fifteen other corporations that were concerned about the growing counterfeiting problem.

Located in the IACC's headquarters in Washington, D.C. is a "Hall of Shame" that has samples of counterfeit products donated by IACC member corporations. There are counterfeit auto parts, perfumes, tee shirts, and many other items donated by IACC members. (Other notable collections are the museum of counterfeit goods that is located in the law firm of Tilleke & Gibbons in Thailand, which contains 530 pieces and has been featured on CNN, BBC, Australian and Danish National Television; and the Counterfeit Museum in Paris, France, which has a collection of over 300 counterfeit goods based on famous French product brands.)

Particularly disturbing to Bliss is the upswing in criminal organizations engaged in counterfeiting activities. Industry reports indicated a significant, even frightening, upsurge in criminal activity.

"In three recent raids conducted in Los Angeles, counterfeit Microsoft software and other material with a potential retail value in excess of over $10.5 million was seized," Bliss says. "Implicated in this activity were three Chinese triads—the Wah Ching, Big Circle Boys, and the Four Seas."

According to Bliss, Chinese-organized crime syndicates, commonly known as triads, are turning to trademark counterfeiting to fund other illegal activities. The Irish Republican Army and Loyalist paramilitary groups in Northern Ireland are known to fund their terrorist activities through the sale of counterfeit perfumes, video games, software, and pharmaceuticals. In Russia, after the collapse of the Soviet system, organized criminal activity became rampant. Bliss blames the increase in criminal involvement in trademark counterfeiting on the lack of legislation; criminals who get caught are not going to do significant jail time for engaging in product counterfeiting.

"Do you know how many people are in jail right now for trademark counterfeiting?" Bliss asks. "You can probably count them on one hand!"

In 1994, the prison population in America rose to over one million inmates; yet sadly, the number of inmates convicted and serving jail time for trademark counterfeiting is small. According to Bliss, stronger laws are needed to address the growing numbers of criminals involved in commercial counterfeiting.

One of Bliss's first tasks as president of the IACC was to draft legislation that would update the 1984 Trademark Counterfeiting Act and give law enforcement greater authority. The result would be the Anticounterfeiting Consumer Protection Act of 1996, S 1136, which was introduced into the Senate by Senators Orrin Hatch (R-Utah) of Utah and Patrick Leahy (D-Vt.) of Vermont.

"The 1996 Act is essentially an effort to update the 1984 Act, which was drafted by IACC members," Bliss explained. "Because of the growing sophistication of the counterfeiters, more sophisticated enforcement tools are needed. For example, under the 1996 Act, it is a criminal offense to counterfeit holograms, which are a security device to deter counterfeiters. Ten years ago, holograms were not widely used in product safety."

Some of the provisions of the Anticounterfeiting Consumer Protection Act of 1996 include:

- The trafficking in counterfeit goods or services will be subject to punishment under the Racketeer Influenced and Corrupt Organizations Act (RICO).

- Goods seized by U.S. Customs at port of entry will not be returned to the country of origin. Under current customs law, seized counterfeit goods are returned to their owner. Not surprisingly, the owner will try to get the goods back into the country by shipping into another port of entry.

- All federal officers will be able to conduct ex parte seizures.

- The Act will allow law enforcement to seize vehicles used in transporting counterfeit goods.

- If convicted of trafficking in counterfeit merchandise, each defendant faces a maximum of ten years in federal prison and a $2 million fine.

The Act was signed into law by President Clinton on July 2, 1996. Only two weeks earlier, on June 17, 1996, the United States narrowly averted a trade war with the People's Republic of China by the signing of an agreement regarding greater protection of intellectual property by the Chinese government.

NOTES

1. "Secret Codes to Catch Copycats," in *Financial Times*, April 27, 1995.

2. "Why Counterfeit Goods May Kill," in *Business Week*, September 2, 1996.

3. See "Counterfeiting Reaches New Levels," *National Law Journal*, May 8, 1995, pp. C19–20.

4. Neil Strauss, "Hong Kong Film: Exit the Dragon?" *New York Times*, August 2, 1998, Arts & Leisure section, pp. 1, 22.

5. Clifford J. Levy, "Cyberfakes: The Latest in Knock-offs: Computer-Made Counterfeits," *New York Times*, February 20, 1994, section 9, pp. 1, 8.

6. International Intellectual Property Alliance, *Piracy of U.S. Copyrighted Works in Ten Selected Countries*, August 1985 ("Ten Country Report").

7. International Intellectual Property Alliance. *Trade Losses due to Piracy and Other Market Access Restrictions affecting the U.S. Copyright Industries* (*A Report to the United States Trade Representative on 12 "Problem Countries"*), April 1989 ("Twelve Country Report").

8. Tate Patel, "Operation Noel Aims to Bag Counterfeiters," *Journal of Commerce and Commercial*, December 23, 1994, p. 1A.

9. Willem Hoos, "Bootleg Prince Cassettes Enter Dutch Black Market," *Billboard*, May 21, 1988, p. 65.

10. Stuart Taylor, Jr., "Discount Stores Win 5–4 Ruling in Supreme Court," *New York Times*, June 1, 1989, pp. A1, D6.

11. See "Closeout Sale on Gray Goods" in *Fortune*, April 3, 1995, p. 18.

12. Linda Greenhouse, "High Court 'Gray Market' Legality," *New York Times*, December 9, 1997.

13. Celestine Bohlen, "In Russia's Free Market, Cultural Piracy Thrives," *New York Times*, July 2, 1993, p. A4.

14. Steve Lohr, "Study Ranks Software as No. 3 Industry," *New York Times*, June 3, 1997, p. D2.

15. Earl V. Anderson, "Intellectual Property: Foreign Pirates Worry U.S. Firms," *Chemical and Engineering News*, September 1, 1986, p. 10.

16. See *International Trade and Intellectual Property* (Westview Books, 1994), Chapter 6 by Donald E. deKieffer, "U.S. Trade Policy regarding Intellectual Property Matters."

3

The Trade Dispute with the People's Republic of China

On April 15, 1997, Lee Sands, Assistant U.S. Trade Representative for Japan and China, and Deborah Lehr, Deputy Assistant U.S. Trade Representative for China and Mongolia, resigned from the Office of the United States Trade Representative (USTR).

The unexpected joint resignation brought an informal close to a confrontational stage in U.S. efforts to ensure adequate and effective protection of intellectual property rights in China. Both Sands and Lehr left the government to join their mentor, former USTR Mickey Kantor, as consultants at a Washington, D.C. law firm.

From June 30, 1994 until June 17, 1996, Sands and Lehr were the lead negotiators for the United States in the Special 301 trade investigation initiated by the USTR into the piracy of American-made intellectual property—notably sound recordings, motion pictures and computer software—by the People's Republic of China. The investigation also involved market access for those products and trademark protection.

The investigation, which began on June 30, 1994, ended with the signing of an agreement on February 26, 1995. The failure of the Chinese government to abide by the terms of the 1995 Agreement led to the signing of another agreement on June 17, 1996. The trade dispute riveted national attention on the piracy problem in China, and on the Special 301 trade investigation that nearly led to the imposition of trade sanctions in 1995 and 1996. In both years a trade war between the United States and China was avoided by the signing of an agreement regarding protection of intellectual property.

The trade dispute spotlighted the political power of the USTR to investigate unfair trading practices and to impose trade sanctions. The

USTR is a cabinet-level position established during the Kennedy administration, and most of the USTR's authority to investigate trade disputes is governed by the 1974 Trade Act. Section 182 of the Act, as amended by the Omnibus Trade and Competitiveness Act of 1988, requires the USTR to initiate a Section 301 investigation involving intellectual property—usually referred to as a "Special 301" investigation. Besides infringement, counterfeiting, and other unauthorized usage, the investigation may involve unfair trade-related practices concerning quotas and market access for intellectual property.

Upon identification of a Priority Foreign Country, the USTR has thirty days to decide whether or not to initiate an investigation. After passage of the Omnibus Trade and Competitiveness Act of 1988, the USTR developed a system of classifying countries that failed to provide adequate protection of intellectual property. Countries can be placed on the Watch List, the Priority Watch List, and the Priority Foreign Country List. The process has been referred to as the "good guy–bad guy list," because countries can be upgraded from one designation to a higher designation for bad behavior, and downgraded for good behavior. Much depends upon the industry complaints submitted to the USTR, by the progress of negotiations conducted by the USTR to resolve those complaints, and by the failure to abide by an agreement.

The Special 301 investigation that began in mid-1994 focused on enforcement of copyrights, clarification of how the trademark law would be administered and enforced, and the creation of a system for enforcement of trademarks and copyrights at the border through China's customs service. The USTR conducted a Special 301 investigation and a Section 301 investigation of China in 1991, but unlike the 1991 investigations, the 1994 investigation attracted international attention.

The trade dispute occurred at a time of increasing tension between China and the United States. "The 1995 Special 301 was much more intense than the 1991 Special 301," says Valerie Colbourn, Microsoft corporate attorney working with the BSA's antipiracy unit based in Hong Kong. "The 1995 action was the first attempt to get a bilateral agreement in place, whereas the 1991 action involved only the general issue of copyright protection. Moreover, throughout 1994 to 1996, IP had to be placed in the broader context of U.S.-China relations. There were a number of other issues going on that made the relationship more confrontational."

After the Tiananmen Square massacre in 1989, relations between the United States and China steadily declined. The approach to China pursued by all U.S. Presidents since Richard Nixon had been one of comprehensive engagement, with the goal of bringing China into the world community through a mixture of diplomacy and trade. Critics of the policy argued for containment; China was an aggressor and needed to be dealt with forcefully. The number of congressmen advocating containment began to increase in the 1990s. Every year since passage of the Jackson-Vanik Amendment, the United States has debated revoking China's Most Favored Nation (MFN) privilege, which comes up for congressional approval each June. MFN, now referred to as Normal Trade Relations (NTE), allows China the same tariff-free privileges as the vast majority of U.S. trading partners. In 1992, Congress passed limits on Beijing's trade privileges, but failed to override a veto by President Bush that would have stripped its MFN status.

In 1993, President Clinton "delinked" Beijing's human-rights record from the annual decision regarding MFN. The Clinton administration argued that by reinforcing trade ties the United States would be in a better position to influence China on human rights. The policy of constructive engagement, however, had little influence on China's human-rights record. On the other hand, MFN was instrumental in the growing trade deficit with China. From 1984 through 1994, U.S. yearly exports to China rose from $3 billion to $8.8 billion; during the same period, Chinese exports rose from $3.1 billion to almost $38 billion.

China's emergence as an economic superpower had potentially grave implications for the United States in the early 1990s. In 1992, the United States was in the midst of a recession with over 7 percent unemployment, while China had sustained double-digit increases in its Gross National Product (GNP) for over a decade. China, which was possibly the largest military power in the region, was poised to become an economic leader in Asia. A study released by the World Bank predicted that China would surpass the United States as the world's largest economy by the year 2020.

In 1996, the two countries were poised for military engagement over Taiwan.[1] The People's Republic of China has always viewed the reunification of Taiwan with the mainland as a national goal. In late 1995, Chinese troops conducted amphibious exercises on the Fujian coast facing Taiwan and in March 1996 conducted missile tests in response to Taiwan's first direct presidential ballot in which Lee Teng-hui, Taiwan's assertive chief executive, was expected to be reelected. In response, the United States, assembled the largest task force in the Pacific since the Vietnam War, including two aircraft carriers. A book by Richard Bernstein and Ross Munro, *The Coming Conflict with China*, argued that early in the next century, China would invade Taiwan and bring the United States and China into conflict.

During this period of rising tensions between the two countries, the successful conclusion of the Special 301 investigation did much to assure the United States and the Western powers that China, which was recalcitrant on issues such as human rights and arms sales, could be reasonable. For politicians who advocated containment, the trade dispute offered an arena in which the United States had been forceful and the Chinese conciliatory.

The countdown until the actual imposition of trade sanctions provided real drama. In 1995, the USTR set a deadline in early February for the Chinese to sign an agreement regarding protection of intellectual property, with sanctions to take effect on February 26. In 1996, the USTR announced that the United States would impose trade sanctions unless an agreement regarding enforcement of the 1995 Agreement was reached, with sanctions to take effect on June 17. In both 1995 and 1996, China signed an agreement on the very day the sanctions were to take effect.

Trade sanctions had been in effect for a few hours on February 26, 1995, when Deputy USTR Charlene Barshefsky and Madame Wu Yi, the minister of the Ministry of Foreign Trade and Economic Cooperation (MOFTEC), signed the Action Plan for Effective Protection and Enforcement of Intellectual Property Rights, a thirty-page document of dense text.

The 1995 Agreement went into effect on a provisional basis on February 26. The formal close came two weeks later on March 11, 1995 when USTR Mickey Kantor traveled to China and signed a Letter of Understanding with Madame Wu Yi resolving the Special 301 dispute.

"When Ambassador Kantor went to China to sign the Agreement, everyone—from the President of China [sic] on down—pointed to the Agreement and the negotiations as a model of how negotiations should be conducted between the United States and China," Deborah Lehr recalled in a speech delivered at the IACC's October 1995 semiannual convention. "I'm sure that the Chinese were not referring to the use of trade sanctions—but in the context that this was a cooperative effort where both sides clearly benefit. It's good for China to have this Agreement in place; it protects their domestic industry. It's obviously good for the U.S. and for American companies."

Lehr was part of a panel of government and private-sector experts that addressed the piracy situation in China at the IACC's fall meeting, which was held in Washington, D.C. Many IACC member groups had a serious counterfeiting and piracy problem in China. Lehr and the other speakers discussed the terms of the 1995 Agreement and the effectiveness of the Chinese actions since the signing of the Agreement.

At the center of the trade dispute was a situation that can best be described as product counterfeiting gone wild. In cities throughout China, the latest CDs of well-known Western artists Whitney Houston, Barry Manilow, Billy Joel, and many others sold for less than $2. Motion picture video cassettes of recent releases were available in the market centers of most Chinese cities.

The CDs were compilations with a hundred or more popular software programs that at the time were unlike any product available. The CDs contained numerous software programs from American companies like Microsoft, Novell, and Autodesk, all combined on a single CD that sold for under $10. The actual retail price of all of the software programs ranged from $10,000 to $20,000.

The counterfeiting problem was an aftermath of China's change to a market economy. The official reversal of policy was announced at the Third Plenum of the Eleventh Central Committee of the Communist Party, held in December 1978. In January 1979 Deng Xiaoping traveled to the United States to sign the protocols that normalized diplomatic relations with the United States.

Initially, capitalism began in the rural farmlands, where Deng permitted the provinces to dismantle their communes and collective farms. Economic liberalization spread throughout the country. For nearly two decades, China's national growth averaged 10 percent a year.

Deng's experiment in "special economic zones" brought an economic boom to southern provinces like Guangdong, where most of the illegal CD factories set up business. These CD factories, an estimated thirty in number, would become the focus of the 1996 agreement.

Foreign companies vied to open up businesses in the economic boom. Like the prospectors in the 1849 Gold Rush, some companies reaped rewards, but many floundered due to the difficulty of doing business in China.

Most companies planning to do business in China sought out a joint venture partner, rather than go it alone. In some instances, the joint venture partner was an entity that was formerly the government or the military.

"When you pick a joint venture partner, its alter ego is often the Chinese government or former government—and there is always that type of relationship," says Raymond De Vellis, director of trademarks for Gillette, Inc. "Every region is different in terms of their perspective, and there are many different organizations to deal with. There are many factories that are willing to take orders—including orders for counterfeit goods."

Gillette entered into a joint venture with the Shanghai Razor Blade factory, which produces the Flying Eagle brand razor and the Seagull brand razor. Gillette's trading partner had a diverse manufacturing operation with many factories, each producing a segment of the final product. Although Gillette's razors were not being counterfeited, its trading partner, Shanghai Razor Blade, developed a problem when a former factory went back into business and began counterfeiting the Flying Eagle brand razor. Despite repeated raids, the factory remained in business.

"The counterfeiters were recidivists," says De Vellis. "Usually, the local authorities doing the investigation do not examine books or records, but assess damages on the basis of stock on premises. It is hard for the local Administration for Industry and Commerce (AIC) to be too nasty to a local entity, which is providing jobs and paying taxes. The usual punishment is a few dollars, which goes to the local government, not to the aggrieved party.''

Although its razor products were not being counterfeited, Gillette had a large counterfeiting problem involving its pen and ink products.

Product counterfeiting was a common complaint during the 1980s. Although China had adopted its patent law in 1984, there was no protection for pharmaceutical products. The French firm that manufactures RU-486, the so-called abortion pill, was completely shut out of the China market due to widespread copying. Johnson & Johnson, which had invested early in the China market, faced an ongoing battle with pirates.

Even patent holders, whose intellectual property was protected under Chinese law, found the lack of enforcement frustrating. In 1990 Du Pont set up a plant to produce its Londax herbicide. Sales of Londax, which kills weeds in rice fields, were brisk. Du Pont was planning to open up a $25 million plant in Shanghai, when a state-owned Chinese competitor marketed a cheaper version of Londax. In August 1994, Edgar Woolward, who was chairman of Du Pont until his retirement, traveled to Beijing to lobby for better intellectual property protection for patents. Du Pont was planning to enter into a joint venture in 1995 to manufacture equipment for integrated circuits in Shanghai. Du Pont was planning to invest $16 million, but wanted assurances that the Londax problem would not be repeated.

China adopted its first copyright law in September 1990, and the law became effective on June 1, 1991. Previously, the lack of copyright protection was a disaster for many copyright holders. The American book publishing industry was especially hard hit. Throughout the 1980s, China, with a population of over one billion, was the fifth-largest market for English textbooks. Most of the market was for college textbooks—all pirated versions of U.S. works.

One American newspaper columnist discovered that one of her books was being pirated by accident. The Chinese translator, who was a graduate student in the United States, sent her a copy of one of the books that she had translated into Chinese. The columnist called to thank her, but when she inquired about the royalties, the translator grew silent.

American book publishers conservatively estimated their lost revenues in China at a minimum of $100 million annually throughout the 1980s. The American book publishing industry was hampered because its market was small due to censorship and because most of its business was performed through licensees. Much of the book piracy was being done by offset printing plants that were engaged full-time in churning out pirated editions. Ironically, one of the most widely pirated books was

Collier Macmillan's grammar book *English 900*.[2] The book's popularity was due no doubt to increased contact with the United States. Millions of copies of this book were purchased by the Chinese with hardly any royalties ever paid to the U.S. copyright owner.

By 1984, China had enacted a trademark law and a patent law, but there were many obstacles to getting the courts to review a complaint of infringement or piracy, particularly a foreigner's legal complaint.

"The climate legally and culturally was such that any Chinese lawyer would have told you there's never been such a suit, and would advise against filing a suit," says Stephanie Mitchell, corporate attorney for Autodesk and a member of the BSA's antipiracy unit from 1993 until 1996.

Mitchell, who was formerly with the Commerce Department's China Desk, would file many suits in the Chinese courts during her nearly three years in China. She would head up the BSA's first antipiracy campaign in China. Her arrival was auspicious, because the computer and software piracy problem was growing like flames on a windy day. Her first investigation against the Beijing Juren Computer Company was stalled for months, due to endless delays by the court. Other legal actions during the beginning of the BSA's antipiracy campaign were similarly delayed or were passed up by the judicial system.

"In China, it's not the decision at the end of the case that counts—but getting your case accepted by the court," Mitchell explained. "There is an intake office for each court, and they reach a preliminary conclusion as to whether they want to hear that particular case. It's almost a substantive inquiry—a threshold question as to whether the complaint is valid as a matter of law."

The Association of American Publishers (AAP) filed many suits in China after a copyright law went into effect in June 1991, but found the legal process frustrating. "Either you couldn't get access to the courts, or you were told your power of attorney is no good," says Risher of the AAP. "It was very frustrating and time-consuming."

Obtaining reliable intelligence about counterfeiting activities was a major obstacle in pursuing any legal action. For many years, it was illegal in China to use a private investigator that was not associated with the Chinese government. In most cases, foreign companies hired local investigative agencies. This was often a frustrating experience, because it could take years of working with the Chinese to obtain any reliable information.

"A usual situation is that you pay a Chinese investigator an exorbitant amount of money," John Bliss of the IACC explained. "Months later he tells you that you have a counterfeiting problem—with no information as to which province, what factory, or the names of any of the individuals connected."

According to Bliss, the manufacturers of the Mighty Morphins knew they had a counterfeiting problem in China, but it took years of working with Chinese investigators to confirm that they had a problem in China—even then there was no clue as to where the factory was located.

"The industry groups in this region worked together to obtain and share information," says Valerie Colbourn of the BSA. "The IFPI had much more information than other industry groups in China. They were working and licensing factories for a longer time to make music CDs. The BSA obtained its own information through investigators, hot lines, and informers who called us with tips."

The recording and motion picture industries had solid reliable intelligence, which played a crucial role in preparing the USTR's investigation about the piracy situation in China. During the 1980s, the MPAA and the IFPI had established a network of industry offices in the region over many years for combating piracy in many of the East Asian countries. The IFPI, which had opened several offices in China beginning in 1993, was forced to shut its Guangzhou (formerly Canton) office in 1995 after they learned that a death threat had been issued. The death threat is quite likely to have been issued in retaliation for the IFPI's success in its antipiracy efforts. Only a few months earlier, in September 1994, information supplied by the IFPI led to what was at the time the largest seizure ever of pirated music. Over one million illegal CDs were seized from thirty outlets in a major antipiracy raid in Guangzhou that was carried out by thirty police officers and fifteen IFPI personnel. The seized CDs consisted of works by such Western artists as Elton John, Whitney Houston, Billy Joel, and Michael Jackson. This raid was also the first time the Procurator Office had carried out an investigation and raid of this kind.

After the initiation of the Special 301 investigation in mid-1994, the BSA's antipiracy effort gained considerable momentum. Mitchell conducted the first raids against illegal Chinese software retailers in June 1994. Seized in the raids against the Beijing Juren Computer Company, one of China's largest distributors of computer software, and four other outlets in Beijing were more than 300 software programs, a number of CD-ROM discs, and six computers. As part of the legal suit, the Intellectual Property Tribunal of the Beijing Court ordered the defendants to produce their financial accounts and other records. In October 1995, after many delays, the Intellectual Property Chamber of the Number 1 Beijing People's Court found Beijing Juren Computer Company guilty of the illegal sale of software published by Autodesk Inc., Microsoft Corporation, and WordPerfect Application Group.

In June 1995, the BSA won what was its first large settlement in China against the Beijing Gaoli Computer Company, which was one of the retail outlets that had been raided in June 1994 by Mitchell. Under the terms of the agreement, Beijing Gaoli Computer agreed to make a public apology to the plaintiffs and agreed not to infringe upon copyrights of the plaintiffs in the future. Beijing Gaoli Computer also agreed to pay the plaintiffs substantial compensation and to assume the plaintiffs' court costs, investigation costs, notary costs, and other related expenses. In return the plaintiffs agreed to apply for withdrawal of the lawsuits from the Intellectual Property Chamber of the Beijing Intermediate Court.

THE 1991 SPECIAL 301 AND SECTION 301 INVESTIGATIONS

The USTR conducted a Special 301 investigation of China in May 1991 and threatened to impose $1.5 billion in trade sanctions. The 1991 investigation concerned patent and copyright protection and dealt with trademarks and protection from unfair competition. The investigation focused on enacting modern laws in these areas. The signing of a Memorandum of Understanding (MOU) with the Chinese on January 17, 1992 curtailed the imposition of trade sanctions, only a short time before sanctions would have taken effect. Under the MOU, the Chinese agreed to provide greater protection of intellectual property, including provisions on product patent protection for pharmaceuticals, limits on grants of compulsory licenses for patented products, and requirements to revise the copyright law. China also joined the international copyright and related conventions.

In October 1991 the USTR initiated a Section 301 investigation of China regarding market access for U.S. products. The Section 301 investigation was concluded on October 10, 1992, when the United States and China signed an MOU on market access that committed China to significant liberalization of key aspects of its import administration. The Chinese committed to dismantle almost 80 percent of their nontariff import restrictions over the next five years. In return, the United States agreed to terminate the Section 301 investigation, to work with China on its accession to the GATT (later the WTO), and to liberalize restrictions on Chinese access to technology.

China's implementation of all of the measures to resolve the 1991 investigations were subject to monitoring under Section 306 of the 1974 Trade Act. Section 306 covers all measures taken to resolve a Section 301 or "Special 301" investigation and is an ongoing process. The monitoring of the 1995 Agreement under Section 306 led to a determination that China was not abiding by the terms of the Agreement; this, in turn, led to China's being identified as a Priority Foreign Country in 1996.

The Special 301 investigation and Section 301 investigation undertaken by the USTR in 1991 focused on enacting modern intellectual property laws and on market access. These investigations were in line with

China's goal of becoming an economic power and on joining the GATT. China took significant steps to adopt a legislative body of intellectual property after joining the World Intellectual Property Organization (WIPO)[3] in 1980. In 1982, China passed its trademark law. In 1984, China adopted its patent law. China acceded to the Madrid Agreement for the International Registration of Marks in 1989.

China was an original signatory to the GATT in 1947, but withdrew in 1950. In 1982 China was granted observer status in GATT. In 1986, China officially sought entry, and negotiations have been ongoing. The United States and other GATT members continued to negotiate, until China adhered to an agenda of basic obligations, including uniform application of trade rules, national treatment for goods, and a foreign exchange regime that did not obstruct trade. In 1995 China was granted observer status in the WTO and was entitled to participate as a nonvoting observer at meetings and review WTO documents. China continues to press for full membership in the WTO and negotiations have been ongoing.[4]

After signing the MOU in 1992, China amended its patent law, and greatly improved patent protection. China also revised its trademark law in February 1993, although penalties for infringement remained minimal. China adopted its first, modern copyright law on September 7, 1990, and, in an effort to bring its copyright in line with international standards, China acceded to the Berne Convention and joined the Universal Copyright Convention (U.C.C.) in 1992.

The adoption of a copyright law was a lengthy process by the Chinese government. China passed its first copyright law in 1910, but it was repealed the next year when the Qing Dynasty fell. The Kuomintang government passed a copyright law in 1928, but it was abrogated in 1949 when the People's Republic of China was founded. To complicate matters, China's legal system was effectively dismantled during the Cultural Revolution (1966–1976).

China and the United States entered into their first trade agreement in 1979, the U.S.-China Bilateral Trade Agreement. Among the trade matters covered by the agreement was protection of intellectual property. The text of the 1979 Agreement only required the parties "to seek to ensure patent and trademark protection equal to that accorded by the laws of the other country." The commitment did not encompass copyright, nor did it cover other forms of intellectual property rights such as trade secrets. For the next several years, the United States and China discussed in detail methods for improving China's protection of intellectual property.

A Copyright Study Group was established within the Publisher's Association of China shortly after the signing of the 1979 trade agreement.

Drafting a comprehensive copyright law began in 1985, when the National Copyright Administration was formed in China. After numerous drafts, a copyright law was nearly adopted by the Standing Committee of the National People's Congress in October 1987. Heated discussion over certain provisions, notably the lack of protection of computer programs, delayed adoption. After reviewing a draft of the copyright law, the United States refused to renew a science and technology agreement, but opted to renew the agreement on a temporary basis until protection of computer programs was added into Chinese law.

The U.S. computer industry was understandably upset over the lack of copyright protection in China. Software piracy was already a problem, and the failure to obtain significant protection of its computer works in 1988 cost the U.S. software industry $300 million in that year alone.

China's first domestic copyright law, effective June 1, 1991, was adopted by the Standing Committee of the Seventh National People's Congress on September 7, 1990 in Beijing. In addition to protecting author's rights, there was a provision for "neighboring rights." Computer software could be copyrighted, but protection of computer software was not enacted until later.

Under Chinese law, the National Copyright Administration of China (NCA) and the Press and Publication Administration (PPA) were responsible for copyright enforcement. The local Administrations for Industry and Commerce (AICs) had the power to conduct raids and seizures of infringing products and evidence located at commercial establishments, but were generally ineffective.

China had courts that did render decisions on patents and trademarks; however, prior to the signing of the MOU and the establishment of a special court system to handle such matters, there was no effective legal redress for copyright infringement. Under the MOU China expanded its legal framework for intellectual property rights and set up special courts, which were called Intellectual Property Chambers, and which were added to the Intermediate People's Courts in many large cities like Shanghai, Beijing, and Guangzhou. The first decision handed down in favor of a foreign copyright owner came in 1994, when the Walt Disney Company won an award of $77,000 in Beijing Intermediate Court against several Chinese companies that were producing children's books based on Disney's animated films.

Even after the MOU was signed, foreign industries found it difficult to obtain legal redress. The Chinese had failed to amend their copyright laws to provide criminal penalties for copyright infringement. Moreover, the National Copyright Administration of China (NCA), which was designated as the primary agency of enforcement for copyright affairs under the MOU, remained weak and poorly funded.

CHINA'S EMERGENCE AS AN INTERNATIONAL PIRATE

China was identified as a major pirate in the Twelve Country Report submitted by the IIPA in 1989 to the USTR. After enactment of stronger intellectual property laws, counterfeiting of a wide assortment of consumer goods remained rampant due to lack of enforcement. Piracy of audiovisual works was widespread due to high consumer demand and lack of market access for the legitimate producers.

The 1992 MOU was an essential first step toward creating an environment for effective market access. The motion picture and sound recording industries faced de facto quotas and investment barriers that not only limited the ability of U.S. audiovisual producers to distribute and sell their products, but had the unfortunate consequence of encouraging a pirate market. Demand for Western entertainment in China had been growing throughout the 1980s, but with the legitimate Western producers shut out of the market, a pirate market developed. The pirate market grew enormously during the mid-1990s, after advances in CD replicating were introduced to the region. The pirate market was further complicated by the involvement of state-owned entities. For example, state-owned television outlets often showed pirated versions of U.S. films, while the legitimate U.S. product was barred. Chinese authorities permitted the establishment of minicinemas that showed unlicensed videos for profit in China's major commercial centers. Chinese state-owned bookstores openly sold pirated American copyrighted works.

To control the import of audiovisual works, the Chinese government used a complex assortment of official and unofficial controls that effectively blocked the free importation of U.S. audiovisual works. China's domestic audiovisual industry was a government monopoly that never made public the regulations guiding it. Censorship guidelines as well were unpublished, and apparently arbitrary. Censorship was administered by the Communist Party's propaganda department, which had central and local officials. There was an annual quota of 100 foreign titles for videos and sound recordings, with strict restrictions on the import of international pop music. Annually, the Chinese allowed about sixty foreign films to be imported, with 600 hours annually for foreign television programs. Furthermore, only the China Film Import and Export Corporation was authorized to import films. Obtaining greater market access and control of production would become part of the negotiations with the Chinese as part of Special 301.

Two additional factors had an impact in fostering the piracy situation that led up to the Special 301 investigation in June 1994. One was the huge influx of foreign investment into China, principally from Taiwan. The other was the result of technological advances in CD replicating.

In 1992, USTR Carla Hills identified Taiwan as a Priority Foreign

Country under the Special 301, because of its failure to protect intellectual property rights. In response, Taiwan stiffened its intellectual property laws and cracked down. The results were encouraging. The Software Publishers Association estimated that software piracy losses decreased from $70.9 million in 1993 to $36.4 million in 1994. The USTR subsequently downgraded Taiwan to the Watch List in 1994. The pirates that had been operating in Taiwan moved to mainland China. Taiwan's downgrading by the USTR mirrored an upgrading of China to the Priority Watch List in late 1993 and Priority Foreign Country List in 1994.

The BSA had predicted that there would be an upsurge in CD piracy due to advances in CD replication. Compilation CDs came on the market in 1993. According to Mitchell one infamous compilation that was first seen in Taiwan in 1993 was called "the big subsidy," and contained about 100 of the most popular software programs. The price of the compilation CD was $100 U.S. dollars, and it was circulated among the middle level of counterfeiters in Taiwan. By 1996, Mitchell reports that "the big subsidy" was widely available in the streets of Beijing, Hong Kong, and other localities for $3 to $5 U.S. dollars. The drop in value was largely attributed to advances in CD replication and a glut of CD manufacturing capacity.

On November 29, 1995, Jay Berman, chairman and CEO of the RIAA, testified before the Subcommittee on East Asian and Pacific Affairs on the piracy situation in China. As part of his testimony, Berman explained that the CD plants in China were originally from Taiwan, and had moved to China in 1993 due to U.S. successes in dealing with the piracy problem in Taiwan.

> The growth of Chinese piracy, and of CD piracy in particular, began when Taiwan took action against its own CD plants. This shut down what had been the principal source of pirate CDs for the world market with the Chinese government completely [sic]. Some of these very same CD plants soon relocated to China, and with the Chinese government's complicity, foreign investment in pirate production facilities was encouraged.

Technological advances in CD replicating played a major role in the piracy problem. Until the early 1990s, CD replicators were large and cumbersome. To filter out dust that could mar disc quality, the replicators were sealed in a sterilized "clean room." To operate a plant facility, which cost around $30 million for each replicator, required considerable technical expertise. The price for a CD replicator dropped to about $2.5 million after technical innovations were introduced by Lambert Dielesen, president of ODME International BV, located in Veldhoven, Holland. Not only did the price drop significantly, but the facilities needed to begin CD production became much smaller. By the mid-1990s, ODME was the world's largest producer of replicating machines in the world. Asia accounted for 45 percent of ODME's $120 million in sales in 1996. In 1996, the known CD production plants jumped from 220 in 1995 to 370, leading to a glut in manufacturing capacity. The price for illegal CDs dropped to a few dollars, because of the vast manufacturing capability. In Asia, the IFPI estimated that the number of CD plants increased from 100 in early 1996 to 180 by the end of 1997.

"ODME was by no means the only company selling aggressively," says Mike Edwards of the IFPI. "CD equipment manufacturers were doing a major sales job in South East Asia. Machinery was literally flooding into that territory. It was going to Hong Kong for transshipment into mainland China."

Technological advances in CD replicating caused music piracy to soar in the mid-1990s, with China leading the way. In 1996, the IFPI estimated that music piracy amounted to $5 billion. The IFPI figure represented an unauthorized sale of 1.5 billion cassettes and 350 million CDs. Globally, one in three music carriers produced was a pirate copy in 1996.

THE 1994 SPECIAL 301

As a matter of practice, the USTR requests comment on Special 301 early each year, usually in January or February or within thirty days after notice is published in the *Federal Register* requesting written comment. The USTR identifies Priority Foreign Countries under Special 301 within thirty days after publication of the National Trade Estimate Report on Foreign Trade Barriers (NTE). The NTE, as required under Section 181 of the Trade Act of 1974, is usually published in March and contains an inventory of the most important foreign barriers affecting U.S. exports of goods and services, foreign direct investment by U.S. persons, and protection of intellectual property rights.

The NTE is usually published in March. For those offenders classified as Priority Foreign Country, the USTR has an additional thirty days to decide whether to initiate an investigation. Thus, the Special 301 process generally takes until mid- to late-April before the USTR decides to initiate an investigation of a Priority Foreign Country. The statute provides a number of reasons for not initiating an investigation, but also authorizes the USTR to initiate an investigation whenever a factual basis for an investigation is established. Thus, the statute provides for conducting "out-of-cycle" reviews, or, as in the case of China, delaying initiation for some time to establish the necessary factual basis.

In mid-February 1994 the RIAA submitted its Special 301 filing, outlining the trading problems it was having. The RIAA recommended that China be listed as a Priority Foreign Country and pressed for immediate action in Bulgaria, where the government is part-owner and operator of a CD plant that primarily produces counterfeit CDs of U.S. recording artists. The plant was responsible for a 98 percent piracy rate and had destroyed the legitimate local market in that country and surrounding markets.

The RIAA Special 301 report identified twenty-six CD factories in China that were producing upward of 75 million CDs annually. Even more ominously, the RIAA report pointed out that the local market in China for compact CDs was small, because CD players had only recently been introduced into the country. Hence, the CD plant production capability bore no correlation to the demand for legitimate products in China. The RIAA estimated that the legitimate market in China represented less than five million legitimate CDs in 1993. Nearly all of the yearly production of CDs consisted of pirated CDs of U.S. artists.

"The CDs were going to other countries in the region—Hong Kong, Singapore, and Taiwan and to other regions outside China," says Neil Turkewitz, senior vice president international for the RIAA. "There was a major flow of pirated products in Russia, central and eastern Europe. Pirated product could be found in Paraguay."

According to Turkewitz, the counterfeit and pirated products could be determined in many instances by simply looking at the product. Often there was no insert card inside the CD. The cover art was blurred and otherwise of poor quality.

Another method by which the counterfeit CDs were tracked was the absence of a source identification code (SID). SID is a nearly universally used process of marking the molds used in the CD manufacturing process so that all CDs produced by that factory can be identified. The SID is a series of numbers that are pressed onto the CD's surface at both the mastering and replicating stages. Ironically, the absence of an SID code was a means of tracking the CDs back to China.

The 1994 NTE, published in March 1995, duly noted China's lack of copyright enforcement and rampant piracy. The 1994 NTE mentioned that twenty-six CD and laser disc factories were located in central and south China. Fifteen of the factories were on-line in 1993 and had produced approximately 50 million pirated CDs and laser discs for export to markets in Hong Kong and Southeast Asia.

Evidence of Chinese piracy and counterfeiting was becoming overwhelming. In figures released by U.S. Customs regarding seizures of fake goods for 1994, China led the list in value of goods seized, with a domestic value of $7,983,921. Hong Kong was second, with a domestic value of goods seized of over $7 million (see Figure 3.1). By the end of 1995, China accounted for 19 percent of all seizures of fake goods, or just over $8,745,000. Most of the seizures involved trademarked products.

By the beginning of 1994, China had been moved up the USTR's "bad-

Figure 3.1
Top Ten Offshore Offenders (Counterfeit Goods Seized by Country of Origin, 1994)

Country	No. of Seizures	Domestic Value (U.S. $)
China	178	$7,983,921
Hong Kong	169	$7,154,303
Unknown	521	$6,192,672
Taiwan	115	$3,941,863
Korea	803	$2,935,577
Thailand	62	$1,421,492
India	18	$1,380,869
Pakistan	22	$1,156,898
Indonesia	7	$ 674,400
Bangladesh	2	$ 368,796

Source: U.S. Customs.

guy" 301 list and was only a step away from an investigation by the USTR. On November 30, 1993, the USTR upgraded China to the Priority Watch List from the Watch List. In late April 1994, USTR Mickey Kantor placed thirty-four countries on the Priority Watch or Watch lists under Special 301, but delayed identification of any Priority Foreign Country for sixty days. The RIAA was concerned with the delay, and strongly urged that the statutory deadline be adhered to. The trade group wanted China identified as a Priority Foreign Country so that an investigation into the CD production could begin.

On June 30, 1994 USTR Mickey Kantor identified China as a Priority Foreign Country under the Special 301 for denying adequate protection of intellectual property and market access of U.S. copyright owners. At a press conference, Kantor stated that trade investigations, backed up by the possible use of sanctions, would be launched against China if solutions to U.S. concerns had not been reached within six months. Kantor also confirmed that there were an estimated twenty-six CD plants producing 75 million CDs annually.[5]

The United States requested consultations the same day. Most of the negotiations were held in Beijing, although there were bilateral working groups that met in Washington, D.C. The negotiators for the United States met their counterparts within the Ministry of Foreign Trade and Economic Cooperation (MOFTEC). MOFTEC administers a nationwide system of import licensing requirements and, in addition to negotiating with the United States to resolve the Special 301 concerns, was largely responsible for conducting China's negotiations to become a member of the GATT. The head of MOFTEC throughout the negotiations was Madame Wu Yi.

The first obstacle that U.S. negotiators faced was convincing the Chinese that the piracy problem existed.

"When we started the negotiations, we were dealing from the ground floor where we had to go in and tell the Chinese that there was actually a problem," Lehr told the IACC, in a speech given at the IACC's October 1995 semiannual convention. "They denied that the pirating was even an issue."

This was a shrewd tactic on the part of the Chinese. It gave the American negotiators the difficult task of having to prove to the Chinese that the problem existed before any constructive dialogue could begin as to how to resolve the issue. Meanwhile, the Chinese could look for inconsistencies and continue to deny that a problem existed.

The U.S. negotiators were further hampered by the fact that at the time the negotiations began much of the pirate CD product was for export and not as widespread on the mainland as in other countries. The RIAA's 1994 Special 301 filing had noted this, adding that the average Chinese did not even possess a CD player. The RIAA estimated the domestic market in 1994 at about five million, while the CD plants had an estimated production of seventy-five million units. The CD piracy situation on the mainland would change dramatically by the time the Special 301 was resolved and would eventually become a serious importing problem. By 1998, upward of one million counterfeit optical discs were estimated to be coming into China daily.

To convince the Chinese that the problem was a serious one, Lee Sands and Deborah Lehr, the U.S. negotiators, did shopping trips of their own, purchased counterfeit products, and brought them to the negotiations. They also invited U.S. business representatives that were directly connected with the piracy situation to come to Beijing to meet with the Chinese to discuss the problem. Throughout the negotiations, Sands and Lehr called the various industry representatives by phone or met with them, either in Washington, D.C., or in Hong Kong, to verify information.

"Many of the meetings were informal," says Mitchell, who met numerous times with the U.S. negotiators in Hong Kong. "You might see both Sands and Lehr sitting with one group of industry representatives in the hotel's coffee shop, and other industry groups sitting nearby, awaiting their turn."

Throughout 1994 until her departure from the BSA in 1996, Mitchell made an average of two trips each month to Beijing and, in addition to meetings with Sands, Lehr, and the other negotiators for the United States, had frequent meetings with Chinese prosecutors, judges, members of MOFTEC, and other government administrators. She also received phone calls from the negotiators to verify information at all hours.

The Chinese negotiators countered by claiming that the piracy problem was being overstated and that the demands being made were politically motivated. One minister claimed that no copyright problem existed in China, because when you went into a karaoke bar, people were singing in Chinese, not English. His comments brought a rebuff by the representatives of the American music industry.

Among the industry leaders who traveled to Beijing was John Bliss of the IACC. In January 1995, he received a phone call from Lee Sands, Assistant USTR for Japan and China. Sands wanted to know if Bliss would be available to travel to China as part of a delegation of business leaders that were having a piracy problem in China. Bliss replied that he would make the necessary arrangements right away.

Bliss attended a briefing at the Office of the United States Trade Representative (USTR), which was located not far from the office suite occupied by the IACC. The intellectual property community is a tightly knit group, and he knew everyone present: Jay Berman and Neil Turkewitz of the RIAA, Jack Valenti, the president of the Motion Picture Association of America (MPAA), Robert Holleyman, president of the Business Software Alliance (BSA), and many others.

Mickey Kantor thanked everyone for coming on such short notice. "We intend to negotiate aggressively with the Chinese in the next few weeks," Kantor said. "We're expecting the Chinese to take one of two positions in response."

The first position, Kantor explained, was to insist that the U.S. negotiators' demands were political and represented only the demands of the government—not those of the U.S. industry. The second position that the Chinese might take would be to try to weaken the U.S. negotiating stance by offering trade deals—such as improved market access and business contracts—to individual U.S. companies, if the companies, in turn, would speak up in favor of the Chinese.

The USTR was made aware of this trading tactic by U.S. industries, many of which were hard-pressed to remain neutral. Boeing Airlines was one of the pressured companies. Boeing had been in China since the 1970s and had millions of dollars in contracts pending with the Chinese. In order to keep the pressure up on Boeing, China might have awarded several key contracts to Boeing's European rival during the negotiations.

"It is crucial that you remain behind the government during your trip to China," Kantor said firmly. "You may be approached and offered deals by the Chinese during your stay—in which case it is imperative that we stick together and stand behind the government."

The business leaders made separate travel arrangements and stayed at two hotels. USTR Kantor was not present, but Sands, Lehr, and Christopher Meyer, an attorney with the USPTO, stayed at another hotel. During the briefing, everyone had been warned that their hotel rooms might be "bugged," their telephones tapped, and their mail read. When they arrived at the hotel, everyone noticed that their rooms had been reserved in a columnar format, so that each party occupied a room directly overhead another party that made up the business entourage. One floor was noticeably vacant in the column, and everyone surmised that this room contained the bugging equipment.

All of the hotel staff was extremely well briefed, Bliss recalls. The business leaders agenda was supposed to be secret, but this was not the case. One morning, he and Jay Berman of the RIAA were walking down a corridor, when Berman turned to him and asked where they were supposed to be in the afternoon. They happened to be passing a bellboy, who overheard the conversation and politely informed them of the exact location and time.

None of the business leaders were present during the ongoing trade negotiations. They met in turn with the appropriate governmental agencies that corresponded to their area of intellectual property. They also gave several press conferences.

At the end of the first day, Bliss and the other business leaders attended a large press conference in one of the historic buildings in Beijing. Bliss recalls that outside the building he spotted numerous peddlers selling counterfeit merchandise. One vendor had a sports cap that said "San Diego Bulls" instead of "Chicago Bulls." Inside, the press room was packed with Western and Oriental journalists. In turn, the business leaders each made a brief speech and answered questions.

Along with the others, Bliss had been briefed not to comment on the progress of the negotiations. After Bliss delivered his speech, a Chinese journalist asked if he thought that the Chinese government should not be held responsible for the piracy, which was really a social and cultural phenomenon. Bliss recalled that this was one of the responses that the U.S. negotiators had heard from the Chinese. China had a cultural tradition of emulating the master by reciting line by line and copying the teachings of Confucius. It was an old excuse that had been heard before.

"It may well be a cultural phenomenon," Bliss responded, "which causes the Chinese consumer to purchase counterfeits. But there's nothing cultural about a government that allows this to happen."

The entourage of business leaders was returning to the hotel with press cameras snapping photos all along the way. Just outside the hotel lobby, they spotted a street peddler selling counterfeit motion picture CDs. Valenti, the head of the MPAA, called for the hotel manager and told him firmly, "If you don't want an embroglio on your hands, then you need to remove that vendor from outside the hotel lobby—or this entire delegation is moving out of your hotel, and that will make quite a news story!" The vendor was gone in seconds.

Toward the end of their visit, the business leaders attended a meeting at the Great Hall of the People with Dr. Sung, a member of the Chinese Tribunal. They were seated in a grand hall with a single large table shaped in a half-moon. On one side were the Chinese, the Americans on the other. At the top of the circle sat Dr. Sung and Valenti.

Dr. Sung delivered an introductory speech on behalf of the Chinese in which he thanked everyone for coming and looked forward to more harmonious relations with the United States as the result of the trip, and then he invited the American leaders to speak in turn.

Valenti spoke first, in a diplomatic tone. "We come in friendship and we will leave in friendship. But we have a serious problem: our property is being stolen. We hope that the Chinese government can show some support for us and do something about this situation."

Everyone who spoke used a diplomatic, even deferential tone. Bliss wondered if this was the right course to pursue, and as the last speaker, he chose to speak out more forcefully.

"The IACC is an umbrella organization representing all trademark holders," Bliss began. "While it would be very regrettable for sanctions to be imposed against the Chinese, we would have no hesitation in supporting this, unless we see concrete, tangible discernible results—such as the closing of the factories and imprisoning counterfeiters, not just bringing them to justice."

Midway during Bliss's speech, Dr. Sung, who had otherwise been quietly seated throughout, perked up and began taking notes. At the conclusion of his speech, Bliss wondered if he had done the right thing in speaking more forcefully than the other speakers. To his relief, Dr. Sung thanked him and said, "Mr. Bliss, you are clearly an important person, for you represent all U.S. industry affected by counterfeiting. We would like to invite you back to train our people on how better to implement these laws and enforce these laws, and to train law enforcement to identify the counterfeits."

True to his word, the IACC and many of the industry leaders present would be invited to help assist the Chinese in developing an anticounterfeiting program after the 1995 Agreement had been signed.

On their last night, the business leaders attended a sumptuous multicourse dinner hosted by Madame Wu Yi. Prior to the dinner, Wu Yi held a meeting. Valenti delivered a short speech on behalf of everyone. Wu Yi delivered a stern address, apparently the hard line. She stopped short of saying that the United States was threatening China, and said that the issue of national sovereignty was involved. She concluded by saying that the resolution of the trade dispute could have consequences that would be felt beyond U.S.-Sino trade relations.

By the end of 1994, the Special 301 investigation had attracted international press attention. People in mainland China as well were aware that something momentous was taking place, and were by and large in agreement that intellectual property was a matter that needed to be treated seriously.

"Many of the mainland Chinese that I spoke with said they fully understood the need to protect intellectual property rights," says Valerie Colbourn of the BSA. "This was true of the educated people and people in industry. They understood that it was in their long-term interest. But the basic reaction to the U.S. approach was that you can't expect us to get up to your standards so quickly. You often saw the Chinese saying, 'We're trying, you have to give us some credibility'; and the United States saying, 'We don't see enough effort.' "

The Chinese began to negotiate with an end toward remedying the situation for the mutual benefit of both sides, and the Action Plan became a joint effort. Time was running out. Under the Special 301 process, the USTR is required to impose trade sanctions in six months after initiating an investigation, with the possibility of an additional ninety-day extension.

On December 31, 1994, the six-month deadline for concluding the Special 301 had expired, and Ambassador Mickey Kantor issued a proposed determination that China's intellectual property enforcement practices were unreasonable, and burdened or restricted U.S. commerce. In hopes of reaching an agreement, he gave the Chinese until February 4, 1995 to allow negotiators time to pursue an acceptable settlement.

The U.S. negotiators had identified three major areas that needed to be addressed. The first was that the Chinese needed to take effective enforcement measures; the second was that structural changes had to be made; the third was that market access had to be broadened.

To implement these three areas into an action plan proved to be a major undertaking. The first area, taking effective measures, meant performing raids. The second area, making structural changes, meant empowering the various local and state agencies to take effective measures. For example, the local Administrations for Industry and Commerce (AICs) were in charge of trademark matters and had the authority to control trademark counterfeiting, but had never exercised any of their policing power. The third area, market access, meant reorganizing Chinese customs, which played no role in intellectual property enforcement.

Under the Action Plan, intellectual property rights working conferences would be established in each province. Every enforcement agency, including the local AICs, the National Copyright Administration, and the local prosecutors in each province, would become part of what would become a nationwide conference system to devise a plan for enforcement of intellectual property. The conferences reported to the State Council at the central level, the highest level of national government, which was located in Beijing. Under the conference systems, task forces would be created that had the specific task and authority to investigate, raid, and seize pirated product.

Nine days of negotiations on intellectual property rights enforcement were held in Beijing and concluded on January 28, 1995. Although some progress had been made during the negotiations, the Chinese had failed to make the commitments necessary to allow resolution of the Special 301 investigation. On February 4, 1995, Ambassador Mickey Kantor ordered the imposition of 100 percent tariffs on $1.8 billion of imports of Chinese products into the United States. Earlier that morning, Ambassador Kantor met with Ambassador Li Daoyu of China to inform him of his decision. China retaliated shortly afterward with a list of countersanctions, which included goods such as compact discs and cigarettes.

Between the end of January and February 26, the negotiators would produce three drafts of the agreement. To assist in the negotiating effort, Jay Berman and Neil Turkewitz of the RIAA and other industry leaders made several trips to China during February, and testified before Congress on the progress of the negotiations. With only twenty-four hours to go before sanctions would go into effect, neither Berman nor Turkewitz thought an agreement could be reached. However, the final terms of the Action Plan for Effective Protection and Enforcement of Intellectual Property Rights were agreed to on the last day, and the agreement was concluded.

On March 8, 1995, Jay Berman of the RIAA and other industry leaders appeared before Congress to present their views on the recently concluded agreement. The next day, Berman and other industry leaders left Andrews Air Force Base with USTR Ambassador Kantor for the official signing of the Agreement, which took place in Beijing on March 11, 1995.

SPECIAL ENFORCEMENT

The 1995 Action Plan was a national plan for the protection of intellectual property rights. Under the Action Plan, the Chinese were to establish a national system of enforcement task forces engaging police at all levels under the direction of the National Copyright Administration, the Patent Office, and the State Administration for Industry and Commerce. The Chinese agreed to a detailed set of obligations concerning enforcement, mandatory use of the SID codes, and allowing U.S. industry representatives to review all production or export orders before licenses are issued. Penalties were to be imposed if SID codes were not properly implemented or if entities engaged in production or export without obtaining the proper documentation.

One of the most important aspects of the Action Plan was a six-month period of special enforcement. The six-month period corresponded to the six-month period required under Section 306 of the 1974 Trade Act for the monitoring of an agreement. The Special Enforcement period got off to a slow start, not really living up to the expected potential for some time afterward.

"As far as we in the BSA could see, the Special Enforcement period never seemed to take off," says Stephanie Mitchell. "We would send our representatives to the various localities and often we'd be showing the central government notices about the Special Enforcement period, but the local authorities would claim to have never heard about any of it."

As far as Mitchell and others could see, none of the Special Enforcement units appeared until much later. The delay in implementing the Special Enforcement period and other terms of the 1995 Agreement may have been caused by a number of factors. The haste in which the 1995 Agreement was reached, the lack of communication throughout China about the terms of the Agreement, and the possible resentment by some factions within the Chinese government over the terms of the Agreement could have played a role.

Under the 1995 Action Plan, unregistered famous trademarks were supposed to receive protection under the Paris Convention for the Protection of Industrial Property. In January 1996 IACC representatives visited the director of Trademark and Advertising Administration Department of the State AIC in Xiamen. The IACC representatives were acting on behalf of Caterpillar, Inc., which was pursuing several China-based parts traders that were illegally representing themselves as subsidiaries of Caterpillar, Inc. The IACC was surprised to learn that Mr. Huang did not know that China was a signatory to the Paris Convention for the Protection of Industrial Property. Mr. Huang was also unaware that China is required to protect the Caterpillar trade name, even though it was not registered in China.

The 1995 Action Plan had its critics within the United States, who called the Action Plan little more than a letter of intent that lacked definite timetables. They also noted that in some cases the Plan called for regulations that contradicted China's laws, yet the necessary revisions to China's laws were not part of the Standing Committee of the Chinese Congress's 1995 agenda.

Among the contradictory provisions was a stipulation requiring the Chinese to employ local police in future raids and seizures of counterfeit goods; such actions specifically contradicted a regulation issued by the Ministry of Public Security in 1979. The regulation exclusively authorizes the Public Prosecutor to undertake enforcement offensives pursuant to Article 127 of the Criminal Law. The regulation further authorizes the Public Prosecutor to challenge police authority if this exclusive jurisdiction is violated.

Although the Action Plan was off to a slow start, some important steps for the protection of intellectual property were taken by the Chinese. On July 5, 1995 the Chinese State Council introduced criminal sanctions for copyright offenses, which would greatly assist the enforcement efforts.

Mitchell of the BSA spent much of the summer of 1995 engaged in training Chinese customs and other Chinese authorities to identify counterfeit product and overseeing numerous raids.

A raid against the Chengdu Computer Market was the first of its kind in the Sichuan province. The raid was carried out by the Chengdu Administration for Industry and Commerce (AIC) and the Chengdu Trademark Services against twenty-two shops within two major computer markets in Chengdu. More than 1,000 illegal CDs were seized, along with fourteen personal computers and four hard disks loaded with pirated software. The CDs seized in the raids were compilations of many software programs.

The Chengdu raid was conducted shortly after staff members of the Chengdu AIC had received technical training from Mitchell on basic computer literacy and raid procedures, including methods on how to identify the differences between genuine and fake software. All attending AIC officers were presented with BSA certificates indicating their proficiency at software piracy enforcement. The Chengdu sessions followed similar training sessions in Beijing and Shanghai.

Slowly, an enforcement effort was taking place, although at least initially, it was undertaken mostly by U.S. industry. In some areas such as Chengdu, raids did take place. When raids were carried out, the local authorities sometimes did not allow foreigners to witness or participate in the raids, and samples of the seized product were sent to the legitimate copyright holder. In other instances, the raids were carried out by Westerners and Chinese authorities, and were filmed by Chinese news crews.

THE 1996 AGREEMENT (1996 REPORT ON IMPLEMENTATION BY THE CHINESE)

On December 1, 1995, the Clinton administration announced that it might again impose $1.8 billion in trade sanctions in ninety days for the pirating of U.S. intellectual property. The President issued the warning after testimony was given on November 29, 1995 before the Senate Subcommittee on East Asian and Pacific Affairs regarding the progress of the Chinese Action Plan, particularly the six-month Special Enforcement period. The hearings were part of the monitoring called for under Section 306 of the 1974 Trade Act.

Without exception, all of the witnesses who testified expressed dissatisfaction with the progress made by the Chinese. Acting USTR Charlene Barshefsky said that significant progress had been made with the Chinese to date, but pointed out that twenty-nine CD factories, most located in Guangdong Province, were still producing an estimated 75 million counterfeit CDs a year.

"In particular, we remain deeply concerned that China has not honored its commitment to clean up production of pirated CDs in more than twenty-nine factories throughout China," Barshefsky testified.

"Under the Agreement, China was to have completed investigations of all factories by July 1, 1995 and to have measures to discipline, fine, or punish criminally factories that violated Chinese law and regulations. To our great dismay, China has reregistered—that is, given a clean bill of health—to all but one of the CD factories."

Neil Turkewitz testified before the Senate Subcommitte, as did Jay Berman, CEO of the RIAA, and Robert Holleyman, president of the BSA.

"The major shortcomings by the Chinese relate to the continued production by the CD plants," Turkewitz says. "There were temporary closings at the CD plants, but most have reopened. There were two critical elements of the agreement relating to measures to control the illegal CD production—and neither one was working. One was title verification and the use of a standard verifier imprinted on each disc. This was not taking place. CD production continued without verification. Government officials were not monitoring the situation, as called for in the Agreement."

The other failure, according to Turkewitz, was the failure of the Chinese government to issue regulations on joint ventures. One of the critical features of the Action Plan was to permit American record companies to establish their own operations. This feature was meant to allow Western industries to take a more active hand in the manufacturing process, instead of leaving it to the joint venture partner, which was usually a government agency.

"If we're not allowed in the market, then we're not allowed to fully service the market and to expand the base for legitimate product," Turkewitz explained. He credits the Chinese for creating teams and conducting raids, as called for in the Agreement, but from the standpoint of American industry, the number one issue was the halting of CD production by the CD plants themselves, not just at the retail level.

"Raiding at the retail level proved not to be an effective way of combating CD piracy," Turkewitz explained. "Raiding was important in the area of counterfeit tapes, which continued to be sold widely, and the Chinese made some impressive moves in this area, but this didn't address the industry's piracy concern. The RIAA was completely in line with the USTR that the centerpiece of how China is doing in terms of this Agreement is what is happening with these CD plants. You have this major industry that enjoys the protection of the state, and involves the export trade of pirated products."

As part of the 1995 Agreement, the Chinese had placed copyright monitors in the CD plants to ensure title verification. The monitors reviewed the production orders and in most instances approved the order, because everything seemed authentic, including information pertaining to the copyright owner. In fact, many of the production orders used forged information. The use of a ruse of some kind in the production order is used in the United States and elsewhere by pirates in an effort to get an illicit CD production order filled. For example, a pirate seeking to have an unauthorized recording of the Beatles pressed will send in a production order, using a ruse such as "The Beat Brothers" in place of the legitimate copyright holder. As part of its plant education program, the RIAA visits CD plants in the United States, conducts antipiracy seminars, and informs the plants when it receives a tip of an unauthorized recording.

President Clinton's ninety-day warning was meant to coincide with the anniversary of the February 26 signing of the 1995 Agreement. The Chinese failure to initiate an effective antipiracy campaign, as called for under the Special Enforcement period, was the basis for the President's warning. The President also indicated that the USTR might well impose trade sanctions at any time after the anniversary date for failure to abide by the terms of the 1995 Agreement.

Negotiations renewed between China and the United States to resolve the issues raised during the November 1995 testimony. In their February 1996 submissions to the USTR, all of the U.S. industry trade groups urged USTR Kantor to impose trade sanctions under the Special 301. The 1995 Agreement had done little to halt the widespread piracy of U.S. intellectual property. The BSA and other industry groups noted that the flow of pirated goods had actually increased during 1995. The IIPA estimated that its members lost over $1 billion in 1995, up from $412 million in 1992.

In its February 1996 Special 301 filing with the USTR, the IACC noted:

Nothing of real value has been done to halt piracy by the CD plants since the February 26, 1995 Agreement. In fact, piracy appears to have returned to previous levels with third quarter production levels reaching an estimated 45 million units per year. . . . Despite these problems, in the seven months since the Agreement, there has been only one $6,000 fine imposed against a CD plant, and most of the seven or eight CD plants that were closed in the weeks immediately after the Agreement have since reopened.

In early February, the USTR decided to wait beyond February 26, 1996, the anniversary date of the signing of the 1995 Agreement. "We have no deadline, but we won't wait forever," Kantor told reporters. On February 15, 1996 Lee Sands finished a round of negotiations in Beijing, and resumed after the Chinese New Year. Although progress was being made, the negotiations were proceeding slowly, and the terms of the 1995 Agreement still remained to be implemented. On April 30, 1996, the USTR published its list of Special 301 designations. For 1996, only one country was designated as a Priority Foreign Country—the People's Republic of China. U.S. industry leaders were unanimous in their praise of the USTR's decision.

The USTR designated China as a Priority Foreign Country because of its failure to abide by the 1995 Agreement and gave China thirty days to sign another agreement regarding the implementation of key provisions. Negotiations with the Chinese failed to produce an acceptable agreement. On May 15, 1996, the USTR announced that the United States would impose "prohibitive" tariffs on approximately $3 billion worth of imports from China beginning June 17, 1996, unless an agreement resolving the dispute could be reached. The announcement allowed for a thirty-day comment period and allowed the parties to reach an accommodation before trade sanctions would actually be imposed. The proposed sanctions included about $2 billion in textiles and textile garments, and about $1 billion in consumer electronics and other consumer goods. The final list of sanctions applied to approximately $2 billion worth of imports. The Chinese followed with a retaliatory list of trade sanctions.

Jay Berman and Neil Turkewitz of the RIAA accompanied USTR negotiators to Beijing more than half a dozen times to provide expert assistance. On June 12, China announced a prohibition on the establishment of any new CD plants, and the importation of CD presses for any plants. The Chinese revoked the business licenses and seized the equipment of fifteen CD plants, effectively putting the plants out of business.

These actions by the Chinese and commitments to take further actions were the basis for a report from Chinese officials that paved the way for the June 17, 1996 Agreement. The 1996 Agreement was not a bilateral agreement, but consisted of two documents submitted by Shi Guangscheng, the vice minister of MOFTEC. One of the documents was the "Report on Chinese Enforcement Actions under the 1995 Intellectual Property Rights (IPR) Agreement" and the other document was entitled "Other Measures."

After an exchange of letters, the United States agreed to forgo sanctions and in return, the Chinese made four representations. The first was the closure of fifteen CD plants. The second representation was that the Ministry of Public Security would include intellectual property crimes in a "Campaign against Crime" and that the Ministry of Culture would initiate a national "Concentrated Enforcement Period." The third representation was that China agreed to take stronger measures in the area of customs enforcement. As part of China's customs enforcement, a directive was issued that forbade the import of CD production equipment unless approved by three government agencies (the Press and Publication Administration, the Ministry of Foreign Trade and Economic Cooperation [MOFTEC], and the local Administration of Industry and Commerce). The fourth representation provided for greater market access.

At a press conference held on June 17, 1996 in Beijing, Jay Berman said, "The recent actions on plant closures, seizures of equipment, retail raids, and the strengthening of the legal infrastructure are all very positive signs. In the final analysis, these measures and the level of commitment to enforce them will be the true test."

The Agreement was concluded on June 17, 1996, after a meeting between President Jiang Zemin and Vice Premier Li Lanqing and acting USTR Charlene Barshefsky in Beijing.

THE AFTERMATH—SOUTHEAST ASIA

Anyone who visited China after June 1996 likely found counterfeit products a bit harder to come by on the mainland, particularly in Guangdong Province, where many of the illegal CD factories that were the subject of the trade dispute with the Chinese were located. But elsewhere in China, counterfeit video CDs, known as VCDs, were widely available, despite a significant enforcement effort by the Chinese.

"Although exports of pirated CDs were curtailed, China suffered from an importing problem involving huge quantities of unauthorized optical discs coming in daily from Macau and Hong Kong," says J. C. Giouw, Regional Director, Asia for the IFPI, located in Hong Kong.

In an unusual reversal, China's counterfeiting problem, which before the June 17, 1996 agreement was signed was almost entirely an exporting problem, became an importing problem of serious dimensions. By early 1998, according to Giouw, upward of one million optical discs were coming in daily—CD audio, VCD, CD-ROM, and other optical disc products. The piracy problem in China had been curtailed in the coastal areas like Guangdong Province, and the piracy situation in key major cities like Shanghai and Beijing had improved, but not in the rest of the country, according to Giouw.

"As a result of the U.S. trade actions, the Chinese did take action against the CD plants—and considering the size of the country and the infrastructure problems—the Chinese have taken pretty effective action," Mike Edwards of the IFPI in London explained.

"By the beginning of 1998, there was still a sizable piracy problem in the country. However, there was no export of pirate product, except in northern China, where the CDs were going into Russia. Because there was such strict control of the CD plants in southern China, the market took a nose dive for pirate stock. The problem involved the importing of massive quantities of pirated CDs from surrounding regions."

As required under the 1996 Agreement, the Chinese seized the CD plants. The CD plants that were seized were eventually resold and reopened in China under supervision producing legitimate product to meet demand in mainland China. The plants remained under the control of the Chinese authorities.

In only a few years beginning in the late 1990s, China itself had become a leading market for optical discs (CD audio, VCD, CD-ROM, etc.) and by 1998 was absorbing hundreds of millions of these discs annually. This was a change from previous years, when most of the pirated CDs being manufactured were for export to neighboring Asian countries, Europe, and even the United States.

According to Edwards, the crackdown by the Chinese left a backload of CD replicating equipment in Hong Kong. Nearly all of this merchandise was originally destined for China, but when the shippers realized that the Chinese authorities were waiting to seize their stock, the replicating equipment wound up in Hong Kong and other parts of Southeast Asia. During a three-month period in 1997, CD replicating capacity went from 60 million units to 300 million units per year in Hong Kong.

The largest music piracy raid in history occurred in April 1998 in Hong Kong, when the Internal Commission Against Corruption (ICAC) conducted an investigation, based upon information supplied by the IFPI. The ICAC identified thirty CD plants. In a massive seizure, $120 million worth of machinery was seized, along with twenty-two million optical discs, thirty pressing plants, and three laser beam recorders.

"We estimate that about 25 percent of the CD manufacturing capacity was removed in this one operation," says Edwards. "After this raid, the Hong Kong industry became more regulated and exports of CD replicating machinery into Hong Kong virtually stopped. Instead, the machinery was going into Singapore, Malaysia, Taiwan, and Macau."

Indeed, the rerouting and sale of CD replicating equipment into other countries of Southeast Asia resulted in a flood of pirated VCDs. According to Lowell Strong, antipiracy director for the MPAA, based in Singapore, a tremendous market developed in Asia during the late 1990s for VCDs that was unique to East Asia. The resulting piracy problem was attributed to the huge growth in the market for optical discs, which, in turn, was made possible by technological advances in the formatting of CD-ROMs. Until late 1996, according to Strong, video cassette piracy had almost been eliminated in Singapore, but within a year the country was swamped with VCDs.

In 1984, Singapore was labeled the world capital of piracy. Piracy was largely eliminated after implementation of a self-help program, whereby the copyright holder was allowed to police the marketplace. The program, which had worked favorably in the past, was not working by 1997, when a wave of pirated products began entering the country, according to Strong. On March 19, 1998, Strong had a visit with the American Ambassador concerning the growing piracy problem.

"Our situation in Singapore in the late 1990s was the same as that being experienced throughout Southeast Asia—an explosion of pirated VCDs," says Strong. According to Strong, the MPAA was involved in many big seizures in 1997 and 1998. One of the largest occurred on December 18, 1997, when 600 police officers, two armored personnel carriers, and four helicopters carried out a simultaneous raid in Malaysia. During the December raid, approximately 500,000 VCDs, CD-ROMs, and music CDs were seized and two plants and eighteen distribution centers put out of business.

In May 1997, the MPAA became the first nongovernmental entity to enter into a Memorandum of Understanding (MOU) with China Customs in response to the problem of VCDs. By late 1997, China Customs, virtually dormant until the Special 301 negotiations empowered it, was routinely seizing 500,000 and more optical VCDs a day.

The piracy problem that was largely under control by the early 1990s was widespread once again throughout Asia by the end of the 1990s. Nonetheless, the Special 301 investigation initiated on June 30, 1994 and ending on June 17, 1996 did much to contain the problem.

"To say that the trade dispute has undone the antipiracy work done in the past in Southeast Asia is incorrect," says Edwards. "In fact, the trade dispute has enhanced our position considerably. It has transferred the problem from China into a number of areas, where we have had success in the past in eradicating the piracy problem."

Perhaps the biggest winners in the Special 301 were the Chinese. China's huge trade surplus with the United States would have evaporated overnight had trade sanctions been imposed. In 1994, there were many Chinese leaders who were skeptical of the U.S. claims of widespread piracy, but by 1997 there was no one in the Chinese ministry who would have argued otherwise. The successful resolution of the problem aided U.S.-China diplomacy and would play a central role in furthering China's ambition of becoming a world economic power.

NOTES

1. "Rethinking China," *Business Week*, March 4, 1995, pp. 57–58.

2. Clyde H. Farnsworth, "China Called Top Copyright Pirate," *New York Times*, April 20, 1989, p. D7.

3. The World Intellectual Property Organization (WIPO) is a 120-member specialized agency based in Geneva. WIPO's primary mission is to promote the protection of IP rights and to encourage international trade. WIPO administers

seventeen multilateral treaties including the Paris Convention for the Protection of Industrial Property and the Berne Convention.

4. GATT and its successor trade regime, the World Trade Organization (WTO), are essentially contractual relationships among members. The agreements lay out the terms of the contract among the members and also lay out the protocol for acceding countries. China, as any other accession candidate, must accept the terms of the contract.

5. The number of CD factories producing pirated works would increase to 29, although many more "underground" factories were believed to be in operation.

4

The Knockoff

The modern-day counterfeiting problem began in the years after World War II in the developing countries. Many developing countries had no local industry and turned to commercial counterfeiting to jump-start their industrial development. Other developing countries were formerly colonies; after they gained independence, their local industries turned to commercial counterfeiting.

"The Japanese were the masters of counterfeiting," says Paul Carratu, managing director of Carratu International, a private investigation firm based in London. Founded in 1963, Carratu International is one of the oldest firms engaged in investigating product counterfeiting. According to Carratu, in the years right after the war, the Japanese named different sections of their country after famous brands that were counterfeited. Hence, there was whiskey produced in Scotland and steel produced in Solingen.

Initially, the industrialized countries ignored the problem. Because the counterfeits were often of poor quality and were produced and distributed only to the local market, the counterfeiting posed little economic threat. Also, in the years right after the war, there was little that could be done legally. Most developing countries had few intellectual property laws.

The situation changed dramatically by the late 1960s. Advances in technology and the globalization of the economy made trademark counterfeiting a serious economic threat to any industry that had a portfolio of intangible assets. In the United States, one industry that was particularly hard hit by the counterfeiting losses was the garment industry.

Trademark counterfeiting erupted in the garment industry with the

The genuine Cartier tank watch versus a counterfeit copy of it. *Photo courtesy of Cartier, Inc.*

counterfeiting of designer jeans in the early 1970s. Initially, garment manufacturers and others with a counterfeiting problem had little recourse under federal law. As the counterfeiting losses began to mount, American businesses fought back by lobbying for legislation to address the problem.

Trademark counterfeiting in the garment industry was rarely seen until the introduction of designer label merchandise. The conspicuous display of the label was considered gauche by clothiers until the mid-1950s. In the late 1800s, a few Paris fashion houses stenciled their names on the inside waistbands of their clothes; this irritated their clients, who removed the stencils. Louis Vuitton, the luggage manufacturer, was one of the first to begin using its trade name on the outside of its bags. Other companies followed and began initialing suit buttons and scarves with their distinctive company logos.[1]

In the 1960s clothing with "designer" labels entered the marketplace. The most popular designer labels were for denim jeans.

"Denim jeans were traditionally a working man's clothes, known for their ruggedness," says Mauyr Dave, director of product development for Jenalex Creative Marketing, Inc. and a graduate of the Fashion Institute of Technology (FIT) in New York City. "The 1960s was a decade of liberal politics and the 'hippies.' Jeans, a working man's clothes, became a fashion statement for the antiestablishment. The same baby boomers who wore blue jeans as children, now wore them as young adults."

The virtues of denim jeans were popularized in songs like "Bell Bottom Blues" and extolled in the book *The Greening of America* by Charles A. Reich. The popularity of denim jeans soared.

"Most designer jeans are marketed as if they're something special," says Peter M. Phillipes, who was an assistant general counsel at Levi Strauss for seven years beginning in 1979, when the counterfeiting of jeans began to escalate.

"I'm still convinced that the basic pair of Levi jeans are the best jeans around," says Phillipes. "The technology just hasn't advanced that much. Stone-washed or acid-washed jeans are still no better than your basic pair of Levi 500s."

Designer jeans are a marvel of advertising and brand recognition. What primarily distinguishes one pair of designer jeans from another is the label with its registered trademark.

"The explosion in counterfeiting followed the awareness of designer names," Phillipes explained. "Designer names became very important in the apparel industry during the '60s and '70s. You had people like Calvin Klein and others going into product lines you would never have expected—apparel like tee shirts and jeans. These are simple items that are easy to counterfeit."

In the early 1970s, many manufacturers came out with a type of jeans that were referred to as "designer" jeans. The selling point of the jeans was that they had been preshrunk to fit a svelte figure. In the old West, cowboys would sit in a watering trough to shrink a new pair of jeans. Designer jeans were preshrunk, treated by a process developed by the Sanforized Company. Preshrunk jeans subsequently became known as Sanforized. Even Sanforized jeans would shrink from 2 to 3 percent, or about one inch for every thirty inches in the waist or length.

Designer jeans depended heavily on advertising. Calvin Klein entered the jeans business, but did not go anywhere until August 1980, when he launched a series of commercials created by noted fashion photographer Richard Avedon and featuring fifteen-year-old Brooke Shields. In 1977, Gloria Vanderbilt licensed her name to Murjani International. A line of blouses came first, then jeans. The jeans, which sold for twice the price of a pair of Levi jeans, soared in sales because of the blue-blood Vanderbilt name and advertisements featuring Gloria Vanderbilt herself. Gloria Vanderbilt's licensing income jumped to $1.2 million by 1979.[2]

With the introduction of designer jeans into the marketplace, trademark counterfeiting erupted in the garment industry, swept along by the demand for designer jeans. Jeans came in flair bottoms, bell bottoms, bleached denim, stone-washed, and acid-washed. Jeans were decorated with patches and sequins. In 1971, 75 million pairs of jeans were sold; this was 30 percent of the total of men's pants. Jeans sales peaked in 1981 with 502 million pairs.

In 1982, the International Trade Commission estimated that the American garment industry was losing $700 million a year to counterfeits. The ITC estimated that 131,000 jobs had been lost due to counterfeiting over the past few years. During 1980 and 1981, Phillipes and Peter Jones, general counsel for Levi Strauss, appeared on national news programs to comment on the growing counterfeiting problem.

Although trademark counterfeiting was an ages-old crime, it had erupted in the garment industry and attracted national attention. The absence of any specific laws in the United States addressing the crime encouraged people to jump in and get rich. The designer labels on most designer garments were easy to counterfeit. A counterfeiter could double or triple the price asked for a pair of jeans by stitching a counterfeit label onto a pair of jeans.

Copying in the garment industry is rampant, which added fuel to the growing trade in counterfeits. "The industry thrives on copying," says Phillipes. "It's the nature of the business; at best you expect to have exclusivity for a season."

In the apparel industry, copying another designer's creation is called design piracy. Design piracy is grounded in copyright law. Under copyright law, items of utilitarian use are not subject to copyright protection. Items of utilitarian use include clothing, food, and furniture.

Copying in the apparel industry is nothing new. Virtually every manufacturer in the apparel trade keeps abreast of what the competition is doing and "knocks off" the idea. If someone comes up with a hot style, it is sure to be widely copied. For example, the chanel dress was the creation of the French designer Coco Chanel. Not only was the dress design widely copied, but Coco Chanel even encouraged its being copied, in the belief that the copies added to the famed reputation of her design.

"Most designers knock off from other designers," says Mauyr Dave of Jenalex Creative Marketing, Inc. in New York City. Jenalex manufactures small giveaway items for large department stores. As director of product development, Dave spends a good deal of time knocking off what other designers have created.

Dave was formerly employed by a leading department store and was part of a design team that would accompany the department store's product development staff to Europe for the sole purpose of knocking off apparel items. The European design would be copied and knocked off in the Orient, where labor is cheaper, and shipped to the United States, where the product would sell for a cheaper price than the European design.

Copying in the apparel industry is a serious problem. A photograph taken at a fashion show can be faxed overnight to the Orient or Latin America, and knockoffs made and shipped to stores in advance of the products of the legitimate designer. Moreover, knockoff manufacturers in the 1990s have a greater selection of fabrics and are able to imitate the design more easily. At his fall 1994 fashion show, Italian designer Gianni Versace unveiled a $1,232 rubberized-silk minidress. To the designer's consternation, look-alike vinyl versions were in U.S. stores at a fraction of the cost, before his design hit the stores.[3] So serious a problem is design piracy that Marisa Christina, Inc., a New York sweater manufacturer, offers its employees a $1,000 bounty for each knockoff that they discover.

However, some courts are beginning to award damages, particularly when the copying is considered too close, hence a counterfeit rather than a copy. A French court ruled in favor of Yves Saint Laurent for "counterfeiting and disloyal competition" against Ralph Lauren for copying a black tuxedo dress that was created in 1966. Saint Laurent was awarded $395,090 in 1994. It was a bitter suit for both parties: Ralph Lauren was awarded $87,720 in damages against Pierre Bergé, the chairman of Yves Saint Laurent, for comments published in *Women's Wear Daily*.[4]

The initial wave of counterfeit jeans caught most manufacturers by surprise. Although copying of another manufacturer's design is endemic in the garment industry, trademark counterfeiting was unheard of. It would be just as if someone had knocked off a chanel dress, but tried to sell it as an original design of Coco Chanel by fraudulent means.

Private investigator David Woods remembers the first time he was sent out to investigate counterfeit jeans during the late 1970s. His assignment was to visit a small retail operation that was suspected of selling the same type of jeans as the client, but at a lower price.

Woods purchased several pairs of jeans at the suspect location and sent them to the client for inspection. The jeans were identical to the jeans that the client manufactured and sold insofar as the jeans were made of denim; otherwise the jeans were fraudulent.

"The clients went wild," Woods recalls. "They had never seen anything like this."

The fake jeans were not contoured, which was one of the selling features that made designer jeans such a hot item. The fake jeans were the same ill-fitting type of work jeans that had been around for decades. The illegal manufacturer was trying to "palm off" the jeans as another manufacturer's by counterfeiting the label. Because the trademark on the label was a federally registered trademark, the legitimate manufacturer was able to bring an action in federal court for trademark infringement. Eventually, an injunction was brought against the illegal manufacturer.

Private investigator Robert Holmes of Holmes Hi-Tech, located in New Jersey, got started in investigating trademark counterfeiting in 1981. Previously a New Jersey State Trooper, Holmes was involved in security at the Playboy Hotel Casino, before starting his own investigative service. He received an assignment from his former employer to investigate counterfeit Playboy T-shirts.

When the investigation was completed, the director of security for Playboy asked him how he liked handling trademark cases. "I don't know," Holmes replied. "What's a trademark case?"

Holmes received more assignments from Playboy to investigate counterfeit Playboy T-shirts. His business grew by word of mouth. "It was a brand new field," Holmes says. "When I got started, there were only two or three investigators in the country doing this type of work."

The Levi Strauss Company became one of the first companies to fight trademark counterfeiting. According to Phillipes, Levi's counterfeiting problem, which was much greater abroad than in the United States, was two-fold and consisted of trademark counterfeiting and diversion of the product from unauthorized sources. Diversion occurs when a distributor or manufacturer distributes outside the normal distribution channels.

"The counterfeiting problem was strong in the Philippines, Taiwan, Indonesia, and Thailand," says Phillipes. "Enforcement officials in these source countries did not take the problem seriously, which hampered our efforts."

Most jeans manufacturers subcontract their work, usually to licensees in another country; this is to take advantage of cheaper labor. In the late 1970s, Levi Strauss still manufactured over 90 percent of its jeans in the United States. Nonetheless, diversion became a problem for Levi Strauss when foreign subcontractors began to distribute legitimate Levi Strauss jeans in their own country and other neighboring countries to meet the demand in Asia for jeans.

Although Levi Strauss had security forces in Asia to fight the counterfeiting, the lack of legislation and support from local law enforcement made stopping the production of counterfeit jeans difficult. An estimated two million to five million counterfeit units were being produced yearly.

"We did carry out some large seizures abroad—with seizures involving tens of thousands of jeans. Depending on the law in the host country, the jeans were either destroyed or, after the labels were removed, were given to charity."

In the early 1980s, Levi Strauss introduced a security technology that was developed by Light Signatures, Inc. of Los Angeles to encode its jeans with a micro optical scanning system. The process used a computer-generated light beam that was passed through the label and assigned a number. The security system was used to assist in identifying the manufacturing source and was successful in identifying numerous unauthorized trafficking chains in the United States and abroad. The use of the security system was challenged in the U.S. courts, but its use was upheld.

In the 1990s, Levi Strauss's counterfeiting problem was centered mainly in Europe and Mexico. More than 90 percent of all the Levi's jeans sold in Poland, Hungary, and the Czech Republic during this period were counterfeit and sold for less than half the price of the legitimate product.

THE 1984 TRADEMARK COUNTERFEITING ACT

In 1978, Peter Jones, general counsel for Levi Strauss, decided that an organization should be formed to address the growing problem of commercial counterfeiting. Jones's idea was to form a trade group of companies that were taking losses due to counterfeiting of their intellectual property. When Phillipes joined Levi Strauss in 1979, one of his main tasks was to help organize the newly formed trade group, the International AntiCounterfeiting Coalition (IACC).

The idea behind the IACC was to lobby for stronger legislation, enhance public awareness, and initiate national and international programs to fight the growing counterfeiting problem. Some of the original companies in the IACC were the Walt Disney Company and Cartier, the watch manufacturer. IACC member companies would be instrumental in drafting and lobbying for passage of the 1984 Trademark Counterfeiting Act. This was the first federal law against trademark counterfeiting, and made it a crime punishable by up to five years in prison.

By the time Phillipes left Levi Strauss in 1986, the IACC had grown from fifteen members to over 300 members. The first president of the IACC was the charismatic Jim Bikoff, who was formerly in-house counsel for Cartier. Bikoff was adept at public relations and did much to publicize the growing counterfeiting problem.

"The IACC was instrumental in publicizing the counterfeiting problem and the need for a federal law," says Phillipes. "What really put the IACC on the map was a segment on *60 Minutes* hosted by Mike Wallace. We got Wallace to attend an IACC meeting in San Francisco, and to make a buy of counterfeit products in Asia. After the program aired, Jim Bikoff, myself, Peter Jones, and other IACC members were frequent guests on talk shows and radio programs. We were on *Nightline* and on the *CBS Evening News*, and many other such programs."

Bikoff joined Cartier, the watch manufacturer, in 1972. Within a few years, Bikoff reports that Cartier had a substantial counterfeiting problem. He met Peter Jones in 1978, the year the IACC was formed, and volunteered to become the trade organization's first president.

Bikoff took an active role in fighting the counterfeiters. Bikoff wrote articles, appeared on numerous television programs like *The Today Show* and *The David Horowitz Show*, and other local broadcasts, and did much to publicize the growing threat posed by the counterfeiters. In early 1984, he testified before the Pennsylvania Crime Commission, which was investigating organized crime's involvement in counterfeiting in the garment industry.

On April 12 and 13, 1984, the Pennsylvania Crime Commission conducted public hearings to disclose its findings on the counterfeiting problem in the garment industry. Representatives from several major design houses were present to testify. Entered into the record at the hearings were fifty exhibits of counterfeit shirts, jeans, sweaters, and belts that had been seized by Crime Commission agents. The counterfeit exhibits bore the logos of well-known companies such as Izod, Polo Fashions, Jordache, Calvin Klein, and Gloria Vanderbilt.

"I suspect that much of the profits of the drug money is finding its way into the counterfeit business," said Commission Chairman Dean Roach, who previously had been appointed by President Carter to the National Institute of Justice, where he served two terms as Chairman of the Board of Advisors.

In 1982, the Crime Commission was investigating the Bufalino organized crime family, when an informant revealed that a Bufalino associate was involved in the purchase and sale of counterfeit garments. The Crime Commission subsequently spent much of the next two years investigating the manufacture and distribution of counterfeit apparel. Much of the illegal activity was centered in Lehigh Valley. A Bangor wholesaler was believed to be masterminding a multistate manufacturing and distribution operation.

Private investigator David Woods testified before the Commission and listed eastern Pennsylvania as one of the top five areas in the United States where counterfeits are manufactured. Crime Commission agents had determined that counterfeit clothes were being sold to both Pennsylvania and New York wholesalers, then distributed to 150 stores in thirty-six states.

The Crime Commission's investigation into the Bufalino crime family received a boost in March 1983, when representatives from Polo Fashions, Inc. contacted the Commission and reported that a large quantity of counterfeit Polo shirts had been shipped by a retail store located in Pittsburgh to a garment wholesaler in California. In response, the Crime Commission decided to use its four satellite offices to survey flea markets and retail clothing outlets throughout the state. At least thirty retail outlets in Pennsylvania were discovered selling counterfeit designer clothes. Numerous other individuals were observed selling counterfeit garments from vendor stands at flea markets and farmer's markets.

Agents Paul Jones and Steven Keller testified that since 1982, they had found fifty-seven businesses in Pennsylvania and New Jersey that sold or made counterfeits of Izod, Polo Fashions, Evan Picone, and other designer labels. Several operations under investigation had links to reputed mob boss Russell Bufalino, the agents testified.

The starting point of the distribution network was the Erin O'Neil Co. of Allentown, owned by Herbert Katz. The company had engineered the production of almost 10,000 counterfeit short-sleeve knit shirts bearing the Polo by Ralph Lauren label. The counterfeits were assembled with the aid of Ralph Lauren "kits" that consisted of size tags, labels, buttons, and bags purchased from a Philadelphia garment vendor.

Katz and other individuals believed to be engaged in a multistate counterfeiting operation testified under subpoena. Joseph Sciandrea of West Pittston, Pennsylvania, the owner of West Side Clothing, was believed to have ties to the Bufalino crime family, but he invoked his Fifth Amendment rights upon questioning. "On the advice of counsel, I refuse to answer on the grounds that it might tend to incriminate me," he said, repeatedly.

Crime Commission agents testified that many of the perpetrators who were involved in the counterfeiting operation shared the belief that they would not receive harsh penalties if caught. Several even mentioned that they had read news stories in which garment counterfeiters had been apprehended and received a small fine or a cease-and-desist order.

Among the industry representatives who testified was James Bikoff. Bikoff had just finished testifying in Congress concerning passage of the

Trademark Counterfeiting Act, which would soon be signed into law. He was instrumental as well in passage of California's anticounterfeiting statute, the first state statute in the nation.

In his testimony, Bikoff said that the commercial counterfeiting threat went far beyond the counterfeiting of jeans and other garments. Bikoff said that polio vaccines, heart pumps, and aircraft brakes had been counterfeited, along with many other items. He stressed that more states needed to enact legislation to address the problem of trademark counterfeiting.

"California was the first state to enact legislation addressing the problem," Bikoff testified, referring to the recently enacted California criminal statute, which was passed on January 1, 1984. The California statute expressly authorized the seizure of counterfeit goods, and a monetary award for damages and attorney's fees.

"Commercial counterfeiting and piracy are not a new problem. What is new is the vastly expanded scope of the problem. From consumer and designer items such as apparel, jewelry, sporting goods, and records and tapes, counterfeiting has been extended to a wide range of industrial products, many of which are health-and-safety-related products, such as: computers, agricultural chemicals, automotive parts, electrical components, and aircraft parts."

"We're talking about hundreds and hundreds of millions of dollars worth of underground economy," said Commission Chairman Dean Roach, commenting on the growing trade in counterfeits.

The need for a federal law to combat the growing trade in counterfeits was evident and drafting a model bill was one of the first tasks undertaken by Bikoff and the newly formed IACC. In January 1982, Senator Charles Mathias was speaking at an IACC convention in Keystone, Colorado and invited the trade group to draft legislation aimed at stopping the growing trade in counterfeit products. Mathias, who was Chairman of the Criminal Law Subcommittee of the Senate Judiciary Committee, would subsequently sponsor the bill.

For assistance, the IACC contacted the prestigious firm of Mudge, Rose in New York, where former President Richard Nixon had once been a name partner. Jed Rakoff, a former U.S. district attorney, performed the actual drafting and subsequent revisions of the IACC's model bill. In April, Senator Mathias introduced the bill in the Senate, and shortly afterward the bill was introduced in the House of Representatives by Chairman Peter J. Rodino (D-N.J.). The Trademark Counterfeiting Act of 1984 was eventually signed into law by President Reagan in October 1984.[5]

The Act had three key elements. First, it criminalized trademark counterfeiting, making it a crime punishable by a fine of up to $250,000 and a five-year jail sentence. Second, the bill provided for a mandatory award of treble damages and attorney's fees. The third major reform was authorization of the seizure of counterfeit goods on an ex parte basis from persons who would be likely to attempt to hide or destroy the goods if notified of a pending lawsuit.

When the bill was introduced in the Senate, many industry groups were quick to criticize the bill. In September 1982 the Association of General Merchandise Chains (AGMC) testified that the Act was "strictly inequitable" and "manifestly unfair." The National Mass Retailing Institute testified that the bill was "heavy-handed" and "overreaching."[6]

The AGMC and other groups were wary of the ex parte seizure. The ex parte seizure is a powerful weapon and remains the principal remedy in a suit for trademark counterfeiting to this day in the United States. An ex parte seizure allows for a search and seizure under civil law that is conducted without giving notice to the defendant. The ex parte seizure authorizes the seizure of goods, business documents, and machinery used by the defendant. Usually a bond is posted as security against a wrongful seizure. The plaintiff is also required to sequester all of the materials seized until the defendant lays claim for them or an order for destruction is obtained from the court.

The courts had been granting ex parte seizures for several years before passage of the 1984 Trademark Counterfeiting Act. One of the first to obtain such a seizure was Jim Bikoff, who obtained one as in-house counsel for Cartier. Bikoff, like other attorneys, had relied on Rule 65(b) of the Federal Rules of Civil Procedure, which covers the criteria for obtaining a temporary restraining order. Other attorneys had used Section 36 of the 1946 Trademark Act, otherwise known as the Lanham Act, which empowers a court to order the seizure and impoundment of articles that include infringements of federally registered marks. Other attorneys had obtained ex parte seizures under the general equitable power of the court, which allows the court to fashion remedies at its discretion, and under the All Writs Act.

One of the leading decisions in the use of the ex parte seizure was *In re Vuitton et Fils, S.A.*, 606 F.2d 1 (2nd Cir. 1979). The Court granted the ex parte seizure under Rule 65(b) of the Federal Rules of Civil Procedure. The Court agreed with Vuitton, the plaintiff in the matter, that if notice were given it would only encourage the defendants to flee prosecution, which is contrary to the normal or intended role of notice.

The use of the ex parte seizure was to prevent bad faith counterfeiters from evading the jurisdiction of the court by hiding or destroying their illicit merchandise. Yet, honest retailers, reading early drafts of the provision, argued that it might give trademark owners carte blanche to disrupt their business through unannounced seizures. Such fear was not unwarranted. The ex parte seizure allows for an unannounced seizure of all unauthorized products, records, and receipts, and the instruments used in the manufacturing process. The end result to the business that is the subject of an ex parte seizure is usually devastating, and in the case of a small operation, the company is virtually put out of business.

The strength of the ex parte seizure is that it provides an immediate remedy under civil law to the manufacturer whose marks are being counterfeited. Too often criminal complaints are not acted upon by the District Attorney, because the business entity is too small, or the local authorities are too slow to act or do not act at all. Civil suits for trademark infringement take years to come to trial, by which time the counterfeiter has packed up his business and disappeared, never bothering to show up in court and never answering the complaint. The ex parte seizure, upon a proper showing of evidence, allows the legitimate manufacturer an immediate remedy.

In the final drafting of the Trademark Counterfeiting Act, the concerns of the retailing groups were resolved by requiring that the plaintiff seeking an ex parte seizure show that the defendant, or persons acting in concert with the defendant, would be likely to hide or destroy the goods in question.

The 1984 Trademark Counterfeiting Act makes it illegal for anyone to *intentionally* traffic (or attempt to traffic) in goods or services *knowingly* using a counterfeit mark on or in connection with them. Individuals who violate the Act may be fined up to $250,000 or imprisoned for up to five years, or both. Companies may be fined up to $1 million. The Act was later amended, and individuals who violate the Act may be fined up to $2,000,000 or imprisoned for up to ten years, or both. Companies may be fined up to $5 million.

A "counterfeit mark" is defined as a spurious mark (and spurious designations) (1) used in connection with trafficking in goods or services, (2) identical with, or substantially indistinguishable from, a mark registered for those goods and services on the USPTO's principal register (whether or not the defendant knew the mark was so registered) and in use, and (3) the use of which is likely to deceive, confuse, or cause mistake on the part of the consuming public.

The Act also adds two provisions to the Trademark Act of 1946. The first deals with civil actions by trademark registrants arising from the use of a counterfeit mark. It authorizes courts to order the seizure of goods and counterfeit marks involved in the violation, the means of making the counterfeit marks, and the records documenting the manufacture, sale, or receipt of items involved in the violation.

Trademark registrants may apply to the court for such orders without notifying the adverse party (an ex parte seizure order). However, courts will not grant an application unless (a) security (adequate to cover damages the adverse party may suffer as a result of wrongful seizure or attempted seizure) is provided by the person obtaining the order; and (b) the court finds the facts clearly show that the application is likely to succeed in showing that the person against whom seizure would be ordered used a counterfeit mark; that immediate and irreparable injury to the applicant will occur if seizure is not ordered; that harm to the applicant by denying the application outweighs the harm to the interests of the person against whom seizure would be ordered; that the person against whom seizure would be ordered would destroy, move, hide, or otherwise make the goods in question inaccessible to the court if notified of the proceeding; that the applicant has not publicized the requested seizure; that the items to be seized will be located at a place identified in the application; and that an order other than one based on seizure without notice is not adequate under the circumstances.

The second provision of the Act deals with the damages that may be recovered against users of counterfeit trademarks. It requires a court (unless the court finds extenuating circumstances) to provide treble profits *or* damages, whichever is greater, and reasonable attorney's fees.

Under English law, plaintiffs have a remedy at law that is similar to the ex parte seizure: the Anton Piller order. Under English law, the Anton Piller order allows the plaintiff to conduct a search of the premises and a seizure of counterfeit goods. The Anton Piller order generally does not allow the use of force to gain entry, and varies in its application in jurisdictions like Hong Kong, Malaysia, and Singapore.

Like its counterpart in American law, the Anton Piller is a powerful remedy at civil law. The background for use of the Anton Piller order under English law is grounded in the case *Anton Piller KG v. Manufacturing Process Limited* [1976] (1 All ER 779). Lord Denning, who considered the case in the Court of Appeal, looked to the judgment in *EMI v. Pandit* [1975] (1 All ER 418). In both cases, the court permitted an application, ex parte and in camera, which resulted in an order being granted whereby plaintiff was permitted to enter into the premises of the defendant without warning and to search for and to remove all goods that were named in the action.

Before the court will grant an Anton Piller order, the plaintiff must meet a substantial evidentiary threshold. The plaintiff may make application for a Doorstep Piller or Mukhtar order. This type of order contains provisions that are similar to the Anton Piller order, but does not authorize a search of the defendant's premises. In October 1994 the Trade Marks Act was passed in England, which made trademark counterfeiting a crime punishable by up to ten years in prison.

An Order for Description is used in the French and Italian legal systems. The Order of Description can be obtained by the plaintiff in summary proceedings, and allows for a description of infringing goods by the court bailiff; this provides an effective means of securing documentary evidence of counterfeiting for use in civil proceedings without the risk of a wrongful seizure.

In 1989, Peter Jones died tragically in a horseback riding accident. He lived long enough to see the formation of the IACC and to see the passage of the first federal law addressing the problem of trademark counterfeiting.

Despite passage of the 1984 Trademark Counterfeiting Act and despite passage of numerous state statutes addressing the counterfeiting problem, the counterfeiting problem in the garment industry persists. The most persistent offenders are street peddlers and flea market vendors. Louis Vuitton, the luggage manufacturer, estimates that two million to three million counterfeit pieces are produced every year, or about twice the number of genuine products manufactured. Vuitton spends upward of 5 percent of its revenues fighting off the counterfeiters; this amounts to some 1,500 actions or civil proceedings, including seizures, investigators' and attorneys' fees, court fees, and other fees.

In 1992, New York State passed a tough anticounterfeiting statute, making trademark counterfeiting a felony. Despite passage of the state statute, trademark counterfeiting remains a serious problem. In 1994, private investigator Dempster Leech seized more than 200,000 counterfeit tee shirts in a single raid in New York City. During a fifteen-year period, Leech estimates that most of the $500 million to $1 billion worth of counterfeits he has seized involved counterfeit garments and apparel; most of the illegal goods were seized in New York.

In May 1998 the International Trademark Association (ITA) released the results of a study estimating that apparel and footwear companies lost 22 percent of their sales, or $2.1 billion, due to trademark counterfeiting and infringement activity during a five-year period (1991–1995). The study measured the impact of counterfeiting and infringement on trademark owners in forty countries.

TROUBLE ALONG THE BORDER

To stem the growing counterfeit trade along the Mexico-U.S. border, the IACC, Pica Corporation, an Ohio-based private investigation firm, and approximately thirty-eight major U.S. industries launched the largest private-sector intellectual property program of its kind—Operation AMIGO (American-Mexican Industry and Government Organization) in July 1995.

"Pirates have become more organized and sophisticated," says John Bliss. "In order to stay one step ahead of them we developed Operation AMIGO—a program that provides international and domestic law enforcement training, and that centralizes our information gathering into a database of known counterfeit shipments."

Operation AMIGO was launched in 1995 to coordinate federal and state law enforcement and private enterprise on both sides of the border. Operation AMIGO resulted in numerous seizures in California and along the border area in 1995 and 1996. Most of the seizures were on the U.S. side. The most successful seizure occurred in the town of Nogales, Arizona in August 1995.[7] Bruce Kingsland, executive vice president of Pica Corporation, was working with customs at the time in Tucson, when he received a tip. He canvassed and targeted eight stores that were selling counterfeit garments.

After making buys at each of the eight stores, Kingsland obtained an ex parte seizure order for trademark counterfeiting, and returned with the Chief of Police for Nogales, U.S. Customs, and other law enforcement. A huge coordinated seizure took place. It took nine city dump trucks to cart away all of the seized merchandise. U.S. Customs Service agents estimated that $250,000 worth of counterfeit merchandise was seized. Among the 39,000 seized items were tee shirts, pens, handbags, watches, purses, key chains, and sunglasses. Nearly 8,000 of the seized tee shirts had a picture of music star Selena.

Unfortunately, no raid could be arranged in the sister town of Nogales, Mexico where it was believed the counterfeit merchandise being sold surpassed by tenfold the amount of garments seized in Arizona.

One of the Nogales merchants, who was raided stateside, moved his operation to Mexico. He continued manufacturing garments in the United States, but shipped them as "blanks" to Mexico, where the counterfeit labels were attached. This made apprehending him much more difficult. According to Kingsland, this practice of dividing up the manufacturing operation so that the manufacture of the counterfeit labels is performed separately is an often-used ruse. The garments are manufactured and shipped to a warehouse as garments, or "blanks." When the goods are ready to be sold, the counterfeit labels are attached. The counterfeits can be sold in Mexico or shipped back into the United States through U.S. Customs. Although U.S. Customs does an excellent job of policing the flow of goods into the United States, the sheer volume of traffic moving into the country allows for the inspection of only a small percentage of goods.

Attaching the trademark after the merchandise has been shipped through customs is a frequently used tactic. Rod Kinghorn, director of investigations for GM corporate security, reports that considerable amounts of legitimate after-market product enter the United States without packaging or in a legitimate private label package. The GM trademark is attached only after the product is safely secured within the

United States. This tactic minimizes U.S. Customs' ability to identify the product as suspect when it enters a U.S. port. Most of the counterfeit auto parts are coming from the Asia/Pacific and the Middle East regions.

Importing "blank" watches into the United States is a common ruse in the counterfeiting of watches. The "blanks" are watches that are manufactured in Southeast Asia, bear no trademark or other distinguishing mark, and cost a dollar or two to import. The manufacturer will add a dollar or two to cover freight and profit. The printer usually charges $2 to $3 per watch to remove the crystal, stamp the face, and glue on distinguishing trademarks. By this time, everyone in the chain has made about $2 per watch. Wholesalers then sell the counterfeits to distributors at from $10 to $15 per watch, depending on volume, and then the watches are given to street peddlers who charge $20 to $40 depending on the syle and the trademark. The street peddler may also pay the distributor a certain prearranged base amount.

"The counterfeit trade is impossible to stop," says Kingsland. "The best you can hope to do is put a dent in it. The counterfeiters in the United States and across the border operate as organized crime. These are operations with an organized structure. They use runners and lookouts. In some cases, they use abandoned buildings as warehouses."

Trademark counterfeiting is widespread in the border area that stretches 2,100 miles from the Pacific Ocean to the Gulf of Mexico. This 130-mile wide strip is an economic enterprise zone. The Mexicans call it the *fronterzios*. Approximately 11 million people with an economic output of $150 billion live in this border area that encompasses land in the United States and Mexico.[8]

Economic trade in this border area received an unexpected boost after the North American Free Trade Agreement (NAFTA) was signed in November 1993. Business experts predicted that the economies of the two countries would become integrated. After the peso crashed in December 1994, Mexican wages dropped 40 percent. To take advantage of the cheap wages, the number of businesses moving to the border area swelled.

Despite the surge of businesses to Mexico, the crash of the peso deeply hurt Mexico's economy. Unemployment was high in many parts of the country. At least 2.3 million people lost their jobs as a result of the devaluation; a majority of them joined the informal or nonestablished economy. According to a study by the Mexican City newspaper *El Financiero*, an estimated 21.5 million people work in the informal or nonestablished economy.[9]

In the informal economy, self-employed persons work in the streets selling food, garments, jewelry, books, posters, and contraband. On average, street peddlers make twice the minimum wage of $2.50 a day. Not everyone in the informal economy is a street peddler. Some are working off the books at a full-time or part-time job—as such, they pay no taxes.

According to David Shaw, an intellectual property attorney based in Mexico City, the difference between the established business and the nonestablished business is that one has a permanent address and pays taxes, the other has no permanent address and pays no taxes. In downtown Mexico City, according to Shaw, the nonestablished businesses are so numerous they block the streets. Everything imaginable is for sale: televisions, refrigerators, bicycles, stereo systems, and a wide range of consumer items.

Counterfeit merchandise and stolen merchandise are frequently sold by the nonestablished businesses. Trailer robberies and hijackings are widespread. In 1995, Shaw investigated several trailer hijackings of Levi Strauss jeans, and in 1997, an IBM trailer hijacking. Hijackings and piracy on the high seas are common throughout Latin America. In Guatemala, carriers have to hire armed trucking convoys to escort the cargo from the city to the port. In 1997, after fifteen attacks by sea pirates, Brazil established a special agency to track the pirates and to protect its coasts.[10]

In 1995, Mexico nearly defaulted on $30 billion in foreign debt. The devaluation only exacerbated the problems of corruption and violence. The National Chamber of Commerce estimated that street peddlers in forty-five cities paid about 800 million pesos in bribes in 1993, while evading over $14 million in taxes. Drug trafficking is an estimated $22 billion industry. Although president Carlos Salinas and his predecessor Ernesto Zedillo were untouched by drug scandals, relatives and top officials were not. In late 1994, General Jesus Gutierrez Rebollo, Mexico's drug czar, was indicted on drug-trafficking charges.[11]

The sale of discounted pharmaceuticals is legal and widespread in the border area. There are many small Mexican towns along the border whose main source of revenue is the sale of discounted pharmaceuticals. Advertisements on radio, television, and billboards abound on the U.S. side for the discounted drugs waiting in Mexico. Many of the drugs do not require a prescription, and for those that do, there is often a doctor on the premises who for a price will gladly write a prescription for controlled substances. Popular drugs are birth control pills, steroids, and controlled substances such as sedatives, antianxiety agents, and stimulants. In one study, the most widely purchased drug was Valium.[12]

Although the Food and Drug Administration warns travelers about possible risks from counterfeits and products from anywhere outside the United States, the warning has had little deterrent on the drug sales. U.S. Customs is not likely to stop returning visitors unless they have an unusually large amount of drugs.

The Association of American Publishers (AAP) estimates that 25 percent or more of the textbooks used in the Mexican university system are unauthorized photocopies of Spanish-language translations of U.S. textbooks. Particularly hard hit are books on English as a foreign language and English as a second language, which are regularly photocopied without permission. Medical textbooks are also a major problem in Mexico.

"There is a major medical black market in Mexico," says Carol Risher, vice president of copyrights and new technology for the AAP. "It costs two weeks' salary for a neonatology book, but the usual black market price is one-quarter to one-third the price. The black market is so big that distributors routinely make calls to the hospitals to peddle their wares, just like sales reps in the United States."

In 1995, because of the economic situation, unit sales of books decreased 30 percent. Some of the pirated books were sent back into the United States. According to Risher, one Texas book company reported that a teacher ordered books for a class of fifty students at the University of Brownsville, but none were sold. It is common knowledge among the student body of 8,000 that photocopied books can be found across the border for a fraction of the cost.

Until Mexico sought admission to GATT in the 1980s, there were few domestic laws governing intellectual property. One of the first antipiracy ventures was the formation of the Mexican Association of Phonogram Producers and Videogram Producers (AMPROFON) in 1988 to fight video piracy. AMPROFON was formed by domestic producers to combat a large piracy market for Spanish videos. Leading up to the passage of NAFTA, Mexico began to improve its intellectual property protection. One of the goals of NAFTA was to harmonize the intellectual property laws of all three trading partners by requiring the signatory countries to modify their domestic laws to conform to the IP provisions in a number of international treaties. NAFTA also contains border enforcement provisions, including protection of intellectual property.

Despite the protection of IP provisions contained in NAFTA, copyright losses in Mexico are high. The AAP estimated its book losses in Mexico to be $35 million in 1996. The major problem in Mexico for the copyright industries has been the government's failure to provide effective enforcement to deal with the serious piracy problem. After President Zedillo ordered the government to finish a revised copyright law and penal code, a revised copyright law was adopted in November 1996. Further amendments were added to the revised law in March 1997 to make the law more compatible with NAFTA and TRIPS.

According to Shaw, the two most active companies in Mexico are Levi Strauss and Microsoft; both have well-structured antipiracy programs. Levi Strauss, which has had a particularly widespread counterfeiting problem since the 1990s, has established a network of private investigators and informants.

Shaw frequently sets up roadblocks near flea markets and conducts search and seizures of passing cars. Throughout the mid-1990s, Shaw seized up to 15,000 to 20,000 garments a night—and 80 to 90 percent were Levi's jeans.

Levi's antipiracy efforts have reduced the problem to around 40 percent. Shaw reports that the antipiracy efforts began to pay off beginning in 1998. Enforcement has reduced the level seen in the established stores and flea markets, and today counterfeit merchandise is found mostly at the street level. Shaw concentrates most of his antipiracy efforts to raiding factories. In early 1998, he raided a print shop and seized over three million counterfeit labels. The marks being counterfeited included Levi Strauss, Nike, Guess?, Calvin Klein, and many others. Sixty to seventy machines were seized, and four individuals were arrested.

At the criminal level, Shaw works closely with the Attorney General's office; at the administrative level, with the Mexican Institute of Intellectual Property, which has enforcement powers and can impose sanctions up to the equivalent of $70,000.

In 1996, Levi Strauss began airing television commercials as part of a public education campaign. Levi Strauss used a similar public education in the Philippines that was successful in reducing piracy in that country by 40 percent. Counterfeit products are often inferior in quality, the television advertisements warn, and advise consumers not to be fooled. In late 1997, Levi Strauss and Microsoft formed an alliance to jointly produce public education programs.

The popularity of Latin music and lack of adequate copyright enforcement has made Mexico a leading music pirate. In 1995, an estimated 57 percent of all music sales were of counterfeit product. Mexico ranked fourth behind China (59 percent), Russia (79 percent), and Pakistan (92 percent).

On August 10, 1993 agents from the El Paso FBI Office raided an illegal manufacturing facility that was capable of producing 1.7 million counterfeit music cassettes a year. Hours later in Mexico, Mexican police working with the Mexican office of the IFPI raided the Mercado Juarez Flea Market in Juarez, Mexico. 100,000 counterfeit cassettes were seized from the vendors at the Mexican flea market and 300,000 counterfeit cassette labels were seized in El Paso. This joint seizure marked the first piracy investigation undertaken by the RIAA together with the Mexican office of the IFPI.

The RIAA has conducted numerous seizures in the El Paso/Juarez area. Trade is brisk between El Paso, which has a population of 600,000, and its Mexican twin city of Juarez, with a population of 1 million. Every day for many years starting in the early 1990s, hundreds of Mexicans without documents traveled the twenty-mile stretch of the Rio Grande that separates the two cities in search of low-wage jobs. Often, the Mexicans cut through a nine-mile, chain-link fence between the countries. In

September 1993, the U.S. Border Patrol decided to repair the fence and block El Paso's border with Juarez as part of "Operation Hold the Line" to stem the flow of illegal immigrants.[13] The flow of illegal immigrants is blamed for high crime rates in the stateside border towns, as well as a flood of counterfeit merchandise.

Prior to 1993, there was virtually no music antipiracy campaign in Mexico, but during a two-and-a-half year period ending in 1995, the Protective Association of Intellectual Phonographic Rights, a Mexico-based recording industry trade group, estimates that some 16 million pirated cassettes and 700 copying machines were confiscated.

In 1995, Latin music piracy accounted for more than 60 percent of the RIAA's antipiracy actions. Approximately 80 percent of the products seized involved Latin music. In October 1995, a three-year investigation resulted in the arrest of four individuals and the seizure of 60,000 counterfeit tapes of Latin music artist Selena and one million counterfeit insert cards and other raw materials and equipment in Juarez, Mexico.

An estimated 65 percent of Mexico's more than $200 million trade in counterfeit pirated and counterfeit cassettes occurs in the town of Tepito, which has the greatest concentration of pirate tapes known in the music industry.[14]

In late 1993, on the eve of the ratification of NAFTA, Jay Berman and Neil Turkewitz of the RIAA traveled to Mexico, where they had a productive meeting with then Secretary Ernesto Zedillo, who was Mexico's Minister of Education, concerning the piracy problem. This was the beginning round of several trips by the RIAA. In May 1995, Berman and Turkewitz signed several important agreements to address the piracy situation.

One agreement formalized the role of Mexico's Finance Ministry in fighting piracy by allowing the Ministry to use its authority on tax issues as another means of identifying large-scale pirate manufacturing operations. An estimated $100 million a year in revenue could be generated by cutting piracy by 20 percent.

Another agreement was reached with the Tepito street vendors' organization, Mexico's Attorney General, and the Mexican Association of Phonogram Producers and Videogram Producers (AMPROFON). Under the agreement, Tepito merchants consented to stop trading in counterfeit cassettes and to sell only legitimate products in exchange for various incentives offered by individual record companies. The signing of the agreement was followed by a ceremony in which 2.5 million counterfeit cassettes were destroyed.

This agreement was possibly the first time that legitimate industry reached an agreement with an organization representing the pirate trade. The agreement was notable in that it offered a speculative solution to the unique problem of street peddlers, who as a whole are the most numerous and successful counterfeiters. The agreement was intended to assist the street peddlers into becoming legitimate business entities in their own right.

NOTES

1. See "Fashion that Speaks for Itself," *New York Times*, Styles Section, January 7, 1996, p. 32.

2. Peter Hellman, "Sic Transit Gloria," *New York Magazine*, February 15, 1993.

3. Teri Agins, "Fashion Knockoffs Hit Stores before Originals as Designers Seethe," *Wall Street Journal*, August 8, 1994, pp. A1, A4.

4. Amy M. Spindler, "A Ruling by French Court Finds Copyright in a Design," *New York Times*, May 18, 1994, p. D4.

5. See "Commercial Counterfeiting: The Inadequacy of Existing Remedies" by Jed Rakoff and Ira B. Wolff in *Trademark Reporter*, September/October 1983.

6. See "Trademark Counterfeiting Act of 1984 Becomes Law" in *IACC Bulletin*, August-September/October-November 1984.

7. Angelica Pence, "Customs Seizes $250,000 in Counterfeit Goods at 5 Border Stores," *Arizona Daily Star*, August 26, 1995.

8. See "The Border" in *Business Week*, May 12, 1997.

9. Marisa Taylor, "Black Market Blues," *Mexico Business*, September 1998, p. 8.

10. Michael Fabey, "Domain of Dark Deals," *Traffic World*, May 11, 1998, p. 10.

11. "Clueless in Washington," *Time*, March 3, 1997, p. 30.

12. Michael F. Conlan, "Border Pharmacy," *Drug Topics*, March 17, 1997, p. 44.

13. "They Shall Not Pass," *Economist*, July 9, 1994, p. 23.

14. Dianne Solis, "Pirates Face the Music as Mexico Moves to Curb Booming Counterfeit Business," *Wall Street Journal*, September 25, 1995, p. A9.

5

Street Peddlers and Flea Markets

STREET PEDDLERS

Street peddlers have a long history and are found throughout the world. In Mexico, street peddlers constitute the majority of persons employed in what is called the informal economy. Even though the peddlers in the informal economy sell counterfeit merchandise and contraband, the Mexican authorities are often reluctant to prosecute. After the crash of the peso, millions of people lost their jobs and joined the informal economy as street peddlers.

"Judges in Mexico and other countries have other priorities besides sentencing street peddlers," reports David Shaw, an attorney based in Mexico City. "At least the defendant is not stealing in the eyes of the judge. He's trying to feed his family. Additionally, limited prison space is often a factor in releasing the peddlers with a small fine."

After the breakup of the Soviet Union in 1991, many people in Russia joined the informal economy as street peddlers. Books were in great demand. With the collapse of the Soviet system, people were free to read what they wanted; unfortunately, there was no legitimate book industry. In 1993, Carol Risher of the AAP traveled to Moscow to promote the book publishing industry in Russia. She found the book industry in chaos. No books were for sale in the legitimate market. Visiting a bookstore, Risher discovered that the only books available were in glass shelves, like artifacts in a museum. Books were available only in the informal channel, which had replaced the legitimate industry. In the subways, peddlers set up blankets and stacked up books for sale. The purchaser often had no idea of what he was buying, since the books were wrapped in brown paper. While drivers were waiting in a car for a light to change, street peddlers would come to the window with books for sale. Risher found that the distribution point for many of the Moscow peddlers was a local stadium. Inside the stadium was an informal bazaar, where peddlers were buying books in quantities of three or more. The AAP estimates that its members lost an estimated $45 million in 1996 in the Russian Federation.

In many African countries, the street peddlers serve a useful function by selling medicines and food. The African peddlers also use bicycles to travel to local villages to sell medicines and offer medical advice. In industrialized countries, street peddlers are licensed and sell food, jewelry, newspapers, and other items. In many countries, the street peddlers are newly landed ethnic groups. In Italy, the street peddlers are from Morocco. In England, they are from India or Pakistan.

Street peddlers and flea market vendors are the most prevalent and successful link in the counterfeiting chain. Usually the peddlers and vendors receive their goods from small manufacturing operations. Small manufacturing operations are a principal source of counterfeit goods throughout the world. Most counterfeiting operations in the entertainment industries involve just a handful of individuals and duplicating equipment. The CD plants that were the subject of bilateral trade talks between the United States and China during 1995 and 1996 were small operations; thanks to advances in replicating equipment, the entire CD operation could fit into a good-sized living room.

In the People's Republic of China, small manufacturing operations that have the capacity to engage in producing counterfeit goods are widespread. There is a substructure of brokers who are willing to take manufacturing orders, and another substructure of manufacturing capabilities that can produce a variety of goods, including counterfeit goods. In a short time, the manufacturing operation, which carries no inventory, can produce 5,000 to 50,000 units.

"The structure in China is such that there are many people who appear willing to act as brokers to take orders—including orders for counterfeit goods," says Raymond De Vellis, director of trademarks for Gillette, Inc.

According to De Vellis, the counterfeiting is quite open. The counterfeiters often have the gall to show counterfeit packaging in a sampling room. Yet, when the police are brought in to conduct a raid, the most embarrassing excuse is offered, and usually accepted by the police. The counterfeiters will convince the local authorities that the reason they have the counterfeit products is that they bought them at the local market and just happen to have them on hand. If the police ask the counterfeiters how they intended to obtain more counterfeit products, they answer that they would go back to the local market and try to procure some to fill the order. Not surprisingly, if an undercover investigator is sent in the next day, the counterfeiters will say they can make counterfeits in quantity.

"If someone sees a small need—a niche—and wants to be a small vendor of 50,000 units or less, and he has some seed money, he can go to just about anybody and get anything counterfeited in a variety of places with a quick turnaround," says De Vellis. "It's all ad hoc. The vendor can sell the product in the cities, or distribute it in the hinterlands."

In the stalls and small markets in Taiwan and Hong Kong, counterfeit merchandise is openly sold. The BSA reports that the manufacture of counterfeit software is usually performed by a variety of small manufacturing operations. The BSA in Taiwan targets so-called "screwdrivers," or small-time dealers who assemble software packages with copied discs and counterfeit manuals and packaging. Breaking up a manufacturing operation that consists of many smaller subgroups is painstakingly difficult. The entire network has to be raided on the same day, because as soon as one operator is put out of business, the others go underground.

John Bliss, president of the IACC, reports visiting an otherwise infamous shop located in the Golden Shopping Arcade in Hong Kong. Here, he was shown a manual of popular software programs for sale. He was instructed to make his choice, and then come back in twenty minutes and pick up his custom-made CD, which would have all of his computer programs. "The operation is run like a fast-food restaurant," Bliss said. Throughout 1995, the BSA conducted numerous raids in the Golden Shopping Arcade, wrote to Hong Kong Governor Chris Patten about the piracy problem, and solicited the assistance of the Inland Revenue Department.

Most of the counterfeiting chains in Asia and elsewhere are run on a name basis, with no receipt to record the transaction. Investigating and breaking up such tightly run organizations is difficult. Local law enforcement often lacks the manpower and the financial resources to pursue these smaller criminals. Even worse, local law enforcement usually views pursuing street peddlers and conducting sweeps at flea markets as nuisance work. As a result, much of the fight against these smaller thieves is carried out by the business community, either alone or working in trade groups and coalitions. Not only is the battle expensive and slow, but it is also potentially dangerous for the private investigators and attorneys engaged in apprehending these seemingly petty thieves.

In the United States, street peddlers and flea market vendors are part of an underground or informal economy. Including illegal activities like selling drugs and prostitution, this underground economy produces about $600 billion nationally, a sum equal to 6 percent to 10 percent of the gross domestic product. In New York City, which is a port city, as well as an international city with a high pedestrian traffic, the annual revenue of the underground economy is estimated at $33 billion, or 12 percent of the city's economy.[1] Much of the underground economy is involved in the sale of illegal drugs. In the European Community, street peddlers and flea market vendors are a significant source of counterfeit goods, although beginning in the late 1990s, these sources began to dwindle as part of a trend toward passing off the goods as parallel imports and selling directly to established chains.

New York City, which is home to the garment industry in the United States, has a large trademark counterfeiting problem that results in the loss of $350 million annually in lost tax revenues. Much of the illegal trade involves street peddlers. Because of its high pedestrian traffic and cultural diversity, New York City is an ideal location for the street peddlers. The Senegalese street peddlers are one of the largest counterfeiting ethnic groups in New York City. They sell their goods in small groups on the streets and speak Wolof among themselves. In Senegal, they apply for nonimmigrant visas that are good for ninety days, and purchase a one-way plane trip to New York City. Upon arrival, they soon find other Senegalese, who teach them the trade.

Like many immigrant workers who come to the United States, the Senegalese plan to work for a short time and take money home. How to purchase and sell counterfeit merchandise is easy to learn and lucrative.

Many of the street peddlers sell their counterfeit goods in front of quality stores such as Macy's and Bergdorf Goodman. During the mid-1980s, many business leaders, including Donald Trump, demanded that the police crack down on the illegal street peddlers. Groups such as the Fifth Avenue Association, the Manufacturers Against Counterfeiting (MAC), and other groups, in cooperation with the Consumer Affairs Division and the NYPD's Peddler Task Force, initiated a major crackdown.[2]

In early 1984, the Federal Immigration and Naturalization Service staged a sweep against the Senegalese street peddlers, and seventy-five were deported. The action was expensive, and the Immigration Service balked at performing any other sweeps.

Under pressure, the Koch administration assigned more than 100 officers to conduct sweeps. The police issued summonses and made 13,000 seizures.

Salif Diop, one of the Senegalese street peddlers whose counterfeit merchandise was seized by the police during a sweep, told reporters that he earned $120 on a good twelve-hour day, and nothing on a bad one. The police reported arresting peddlers who were carrying thousands of dollars in cash.

The much publicized operation cost upward of $17,000 a day in overtime, and provided only temporary relief. The Senegalese and other illegal street peddlers returned to the streets once the pressure was relaxed.

The Senegalese obtain their watches from Canal Street in Chinatown, which is notorious as a distribution point for counterfeit merchandise. Counterfeit garments are often purchased locally, and usually manufactured from small, underground silk screening operations. Many small operations that engage in the counterfeiting of garments use silk screens; larger operations may involve sweatshops, which are common in Third World countries and are a major source of counterfeit garments and parallel imports. In Mexico there are 2,300 sweatshops or assembly plants known as *maquiladoras* that employ approximately 700,000 Mexicans in the garment trade.

At the beginning of the twentieth century, sweatshops were common in the United States and were notorious for the employment of children. By the end of the twentieth century, sweatshops had dwindled in number, and were often engaged in producing counterfeit apparel to compete with the cheaper imports produced in Mexico and the Orient. In one raid conducted in July 1996 by Brooklyn District Attorney Charles J. Hynes, two sweatshops in Williamsburg, a section of Brooklyn in New York City, were raided and thousands of counterfeit garments and millions of counterfeit labels seized. The illegal manufacturing operation was producing tee shirts, sweatshirts, jeans, jogging apparel, baseball caps, and watches—all bearing counterfeit trademarks of name brand firms that included Warner Brothers, Tommy Hilfiger, Calvin Klein, and many other companies.

The illegal manufacturing operations, which were supplying counterfeit clothing to more than fifty stores throughout New York City, Pittsburgh, and Washington, were classic sweatshop operations. Two fourteen-year-old boys and nineteen other workers were employed, at an average hourly wage that was far below the minimum wage. Authorities said that temperatures inside the factories approached ninety degrees and that flammable liquids were stored near garments. Five persons were indicted and charged with trademark counterfeiting, a felony under New York State's trademark counterfeiting statute, which can bring a prison term of five to fifteen years.[3]

For many years, the IACC has organized a street peddlers' task force, to assist its members in taking action against street peddlers. The task force maintains a database of known counterfeiters and serves as a clearinghouse for IACC members.

"Many of the street peddlers use spotters," says George Abbott, communications director for the IACC. "Operating out of a multiblock area, the peddlers will use kids as lookouts. If a seizure occurs, someone will use a cell phone to alert everyone. The peddlers will pack up everything and jump into a van by prearranged plan and disappear. To make seizure of their goods more difficult, they will often use decoy vans."

Most street peddlers have developed their own evasion tactics. The Senegalese street peddlers usually operate in small groups, with each peddler selling his wares a few feet from another peddler. This arrangement cuts down on sales, but ensures that when a seizure takes place only one or two peddlers will have his illegal merchandise seized. During a seizure, the other vendors pack up and run.

In the European countries and in the United States, many street peddlers operate in small groups. The peddlers often have only a small stock of merchandise on their person, while a "bagman" waits out of sight with the bulk of the illegal merchandise. This tactic was undoubtedly picked up from the drug trade, which also involves street peddlers. Pub sales are a problem throughout the United Kingdom. Pubs are local gathering places in England, and offer a discreet location for peddlers selling counterfeit merchandise.

Pursuing the street peddlers is potentially dangerous, and every private investigator, attorney, and U.S. Marshal has a war story to tell. David Woods remembers one time when he, several investigators, an attorney for Cartier, and several U.S. Marshals had conducted a seizure of a watch counterfeiting operation in New York's Chinatown. The operation had progressed smoothly, and the Marshals asked if they could leave the premises. Thinking it was safe, Woods and the attorney gave them permission, while they took inventory of the seized material. As soon as the Marshals left, several Orientals, who were on the premises and who were part of the illegal operation, began to make verbal threats. To make matters worse, a crowd of sympathetic Orientals who were aware that a seizure had taken place began to gather outside the building.

With their backup gone, the party was defenseless. Hoping to diffuse the situation, Woods told everyone to remain inside the building and he would try to draw away the crowd. As soon as he got outside, Woods started running up the street. Following close behind was a mob of Orientals, some of whom were armed with clubs. To save himself, Woods ran into Little Italy, an ethnic Italian neighborhood that adjoins Chinatown. He ran into a small restaurant. As he hoped, the Orientals did not follow him into Little Italy. He contacted the other investigators and the attorney by cell phone. They had escaped and soon drove by and rescued Woods.

In another case, an attorney foolishly thought he could tail a street vendor. He followed the street vendor downstairs into the subway. The attorney beat a hasty retreat when the street vendor pulled out a knife.

Another attorney, working on behalf of Rolex, had an arm fractured during a scuffle.

In the mid-1980s, a New York City law firm that was handling anti-counterfeiting activities for Polo Fashions, Inc. devised an interesting idea for handling street peddlers. The law firm would often get calls from in-house counsel for Polo because peddlers were selling counterfeit Polo merchandise right in front of corporate headquarters. The law firm would contact a private investigator and draft a cease-and-desist letter that was addressed to an anonymous person—usually a street peddler at the corner of such-and-such street, which was the address given by in-house counsel for Polo. The firm would dispatch an attorney and a private investigator to the designated location, and the cease-and-desist letter would be served upon the anonymous street vendor. As in all such letters, all kinds of legal mayhem were threatened if the vendor did not cease his activity and surrender his illegal merchandise. In fact the letter was a clever bluff. If the vendor chose not to surrender his goods but to simply walk away, the attorney and the private investigator were powerless. Nonetheless, the tactic worked with varying success, and in nearly every instance was good enough to persuade the street peddler to leave.

Sometimes the street peddlers are linked to larger crime groups. In 1991, Tho Hoang (David) Thai, leader of the notorious street gang Born To Kill (BTK), was arrested. When interviewed on the television program *48 Hours*, Thai said that his most lucrative source of income came from the sale of counterfeit watches. In 1988, which was his best year, Thai made $13 million from the sale of counterfeit watches.

David Thai was apprehended partly as the result of investigations conducted by private investigator Dempster Leech, president and founder of Harper Associates. No stranger to street peddlers, Leech once had his head split open with a baseball bat while conducting an ex parte seizure. For many years Leech was involved in investigating watch counterfeiting on New York's Canal Street, in the heart of Chinatown. Leech knew of Thai because he was in charge of a storefront operation that sold counterfeits, and because Thai had been arrested by the New York police, who had discovered a small cache of counterfeit watches in his apartment.

Harper Associates conducted a series of investigations in Jersey City, New Jersey on watch counterfeiting factories. All of the information that was turned up during the seizures was shared with the Jersey City police, who were able to link the counterfeiters with several murders. After a raid on a factory on Orchard Street in Jersey City, the Jersey City police were able to link the operation to the violent Vietnamese gang BTK.

Thai, who had cornered the market on New York City's Canal Street in the heart of Chinatown on the sale of counterfeit watches, killed his rivals. He was apprehended after his gang members robbed a Vietnamese importer. After the importer identified the gang members who had robbed him, Thai gave orders that the importer should be killed. When Thai was arrested at his home on Long Island, the police found a counterfeit-watch operation in the basement.

Threats of violence are seen in other parts of the world. For example, in 1989, after President Reagan had ordered trade sanctions against Thailand, threats were made against record industry officials by suspected Thai underworld figures. In 1993, Ronald Eckstrom, part of Microsoft's antipiracy unit based in Hong Kong, learned that counterfeiters in Jakarta, Indonesia had threatened to kill him, after he had put a software counterfeiting operation out of business in that country.[4]

The AAP and the BSA were threatened with violence numerous times in Indonesia during the early 1990s. In one instance a lawyer, who was working for both the AAP and the BSA, organized a raid on a huge organized ring of pirates who were selling computer books throughout the world. The AAP and the BSA had shared information and joined forces to conduct the raid. The quantity of seized computer books filled a warehouse. After the raid, the BSA learned that the pirates had hired contract killers to retaliate; they then brought in additional investigators from Hong Kong and other countries to continue the investigation and for added protection.

Risher of the AAP recalls one threat of violence that occurred in Puerto Rico in the mid-1990s. "We were pursuing a book piracy case in that country, when someone told one of our witnesses that if he testified, his family would be killed. We stopped the litigation."

FLEA MARKETS

"I don't like to use the term 'flea market'—because it makes them seem smaller than they really are," says William Nix, who was vice-president of business affairs for NBA Properties for several years in the mid-1990s. "There are tens of thousands of flea markets. Many of the counterfeiters at these flea markets are well organized. They have cellular phones and trucks and work in multistate distribution chains."

Flea markets, which are also called swap meets and garage sales, are very popular in the United States and Mexico. They are a good source for antiques and other hard-to-find collectibles. The average flea market vendor may be a middle-class worker, who works weekends, or he may be an itinerant of dubious background. Some flea markets are located in large urban areas, but most are located in rural areas. They are numerous in the southern areas of the United States, where the climate is more temperate than the northern areas. In California, they are distribution points for wholesale goods. Flea markets are numerous as well in Mexico, where they function more as a type of outdoor market. Not as widespread in Europe, flea markets are called car boot sales. In the United Kingdom and Australia, car boot sales involve people selling artifacts out of the trunk of their car.

"Many of the vendors are of a gypsy mentality," says Robert Holmes of Holmes Hi-Tech. "They don't have jobs and don't declare income. Some have never held a steady job and so have little background to investigate. It's largely a cash business, with few records kept for tax purposes."

Holmes used to conduct regular sweeps of the New Jersey flea markets, when he was a state trooper. Often he would pick up stolen merchandise and collar the thieves. Today, on behalf of many corporate clients, he and his agents canvass the flea markets in New Jersey. The assignment is to make buys of merchandise they suspect is counterfeit. The merchandise is sent to the client for verification. According to Holmes, the absence of a New Jersey state statute governing trademark counterfeiting hampers law enforcement.

"I've never seen anyone prosecuted for this kind of crime," says Holmes. "Under New Jersey law, the flea market vendors are treated under the state statute governing criminal simulation, which is a disorderly person crime. At best you get a small fine. The judge slaps you on the wrist, and the vendor goes back to work the same day."

Holmes recommends that his clients conduct an ex parte seizure under the 1984 Trademark Counterfeiting Act. The judge will grant a "John Doe" ex parte seizure. Holmes, the attorneys for the client, and the U.S. Marshals will return to seize the illegal goods. The vendor is not arrested unless he tries to assault someone.

There are many locations in London where counterfeit merchandise is sold. One notorious location is Camden Lock, a bohemian section, which has a large flea market, where counterfeit merchandise is sold. Another infamous spot is the Blackbush Aerodrome, an old military aerodrome located outside London, where rock concerts are staged. On Sundays the Aerodrome is converted into a huge flea market. Mike Edwards of the IFPI recalls participating in a raid in the late 1980s on the Aerodrome that included the British Phonographic Industry (BPI), volunteers from several record companies, and local police. Truckloads of counterfeit merchandise were seized.

In 1996, the flea market vendor problem was addressed by the U.S. Court of Appeals, Ninth Circuit, which reversed the lower court's decision in the case *Fonovisa, Inc. v. Cherry Auction, Inc.; Richard Pilegard, W.d. Mitchell, Margaret Mitchell*, 847 F.Supp. 1492 (9th Cir. 1996). Fonovisa, a California corporation that owns copyrights and trademarks in Latin and Spanish music recordings, alleged that vendors at the Cherry Auction flea market were selling counterfeit sound recordings. The Ninth Circuit found copyright liability where the flea market owner could supervise the activities of its vendors and where there was a direct financial interest. In addition, liability could also arise if the owner, with knowledge of the infringing sale of counterfeit merchandise, induced, caused, or materially contributed to the infringing conduct of the vendor.

Fonovisa was a landmark decision. The IACC filed an Amicus Brief in the *Fonovisa* case in support of a finding of liability on the part of the flea market owners. "This decision sends a clear message to all flea market owners that they cannot turn a blind eye to the sale of counterfeit merchandise by vendors," said Anthony Keats, a partner with the firm of Baker & Hostetler in Los Angeles and counsel for the IACC. "Copyright and trademark owners will now be able to much more effectively protect the consuming public from the sale of counterfeit merchandise."

To get around the court's decision in *Fonovisa*, many flea markets incorporate the booths, with two booths comprising a corporation. This arrangement limits the flea market owner's liability to the sales produced at a pair of booths.

Stamping out the counterfeit trade at flea markets is difficult. The vendors stay for only a few days and move on. Local law enforcement are often reluctant to travel to the flea markets, which are located outside the city limits.

The Shipshewana flea market, located in Indiana, is a large flea market with over 1,500 booths. For many years, the Shipshewana flea market was a known source for drugs and counterfeit merchandise Despite sweeps by local law enforcement and industry, the counterfeit trade at the flea market continued.

The sale of counterfeits at Shipshewana was lucrative. Robert Ogden, who was formerly a vice president of the consumer products division for the Walt Disney Company, recalls that after one of the first raids conducted at the flea market, the judge set bail at $10,000. All of the flea market vendors who had been arrested had $10,000 in cash in their pockets and were able to make bail on the spot.

In the late 1980s, a large seizure was prepared. Buys of counterfeit merchandise were made at nearly forty different booths by a branch of the investigative agency Pica Corporation. Soon afterward, forty Pica investigators carried out the seizure, in conjunction with local law enforcement, customs inspectors, and industry representatives.

Ogden was present to assist in identifying the merchandise. "We had several buses to transport the seized merchandise," Ogden recalls. "There was one police officer and one private investigator for each vendor, in addition to numerous industry representatives like myself, who were on hand to identify the counterfeit products."

Hundreds of thousands of dollars in counterfeit merchandise was seized. Summonses were issued to more than twenty counterfeiters. At the time, there was no state law governing trademark counterfeiting. The legal issue was brought before the Indiana State Supreme Court. In an unusual twist, the prosecuting attorney had the counterfeiters convicted under the state's forgery statute. Under Indiana State law, a trademark is described as "a writing." The prosecuting attorney construed that to mean that the "uttering" of a counterfeit product constituted a forgery. The counterfeiters were prosecuted and sent to jail.

A few years later, Ogden visited the Shipshewana flea market. One of the vendors, who had been convicted, recognized him. He approached Ogden and complained, "Now that I've been convicted of a felony, I can't carry a gun anymore."

FIGHTING BACK

When street peddlers are present in enough numbers effective action can be taken to conduct a sweep. For example, expecting that there would be a big turnout for the New York Rangers' Stanley Cup victory parade, held on January 17, 1994, NHL Enterprises sought assistance in Manhattan Federal Court the day before. In response, the Court authorized U.S. Marshals to assist in the seizures. The following day the streets were packed with spectators and with street peddlers selling counterfeit items—mostly T-shirts and caps.

The street peddlers were easy to spot, and many seizures took place. While the legitimate products sold for $16.99 for shirts and $19.99 for caps, the counterfeits sold for about one-quarter of the price. An estimated $10,000 in counterfeit items was seized. In addition to having to relinquish their fraudulent merchandise, street peddlers who were apprehended had to surrender their earnings to NHL Enterprises, the licensing operation of the National Hockey League, and pay triple damages for any attorney's fees.

The counterfeiting of sports-related apparel began to increase dramatically beginning in the 1990s, as an aftermath of the explosive growth of sports licensing, which involves the licensing of trademarks and copyrights to manufacturers and other vendors. Between 1981 and 1993, sales of basketball-related properties by NBA, Inc. the wholly owned licensing subsidiary of the National Basketball Association (NBA), rose from $10 million to $1.8 billion. Licensing sales for other sports-related intellectual property are equally impressive. In 1993, the National Football League Properties had sales of $2.4 billion. In 1993, Major League Baseball Properties had sales of $2.5 billion.[5]

Most of the items being produced under licensing agreement are T-shirts, jerseys, shorts, mugs, key rings, and other small items and garments. The rise in revenues in sports licensing is the result of an aggressive marketing campaign by the big leagues both at home and abroad, and by a renewed popularity of major league sporting events. Sports figures like Michael Jordan are so popular that they have crossed over and become entertainment figures.

All of the major league sports enterprises have their own anticounterfeiting operations, but in response to the growing counterfeiting problem, the licensing arm of many major league sports organizations joined forces to found the Coalition to Advance the Protection of Sports Logos (CAPS). CAPS was founded in 1992 by four major league organizations, the Collegiate Licensing Company, and Starter Corporation. CAPS supplies its vendors with an 800 number for reporting counterfeit merchandise in the marketplace (1–800-TEL-CAPS).

In 1993, CAPS confiscated $12 million worth of unauthorized merchandise and manufacturing equipment. In one seizure that took place on November 17, 1993, CAPS seized 20,000 pieces of counterfeit merchandise in Los Angeles. Less than a month later, CAPS undertook what would become the largest seizure of sports-related merchandise. This seizure was conducted in Texas at the end of 1993 and netted over $1 million in counterfeit merchandise.

On December 4, 1993, Wayne Grooms, a North Carolina private investigator, traveled to Dallas on behalf of CAPS and identified numerous locations that were selling unlicensed copies of items marketed through the major leagues. A seizure order was prepared and submitted to U.S. District Court Judge Joe Kendall, who issued a seizure order on December 20.[6]

The subsequent seizure was at the time the largest involving sports-related merchandise. Twenty-two defendants—thirteen in Dallas, nine in Houston—were served with legal process. In northwest Dallas, unlicensed clothing was seized from seven outlets; six in Dallas and one in Houston. In all, 47,000 items with a value of over $1 million were seized. "This was probably the largest single seizure of counterfeit sports apparel," says Nix, who was vice president of business affairs for NBA Properties at the time.

Carratu International has conducted numerous investigations for NBA of Europe in the United Kingdom. One investigation conducted in 1998 involved a Pakistani businessman, who had a licensing agreement to embroider sports logos. Business was slow, and the businessman's customers, who knew that he used computer-controlled embroidery machines, asked if he could make cheaper hats. Carratu investigators got wind of the operation and notified officers from the Easling Council Trading Standards, who conducted a seizure under the British 1994 Trade Marks Act. The businessman, who faced up to ten years in prison, was fined £13,000.[7]

The RIAA has spent hundreds of thousands of dollars over the years battling street peddlers and flea market owners across the country. The problem is particularly troublesome in the South and along the border with Mexico. In this part of the country, the winters are milder, and the flea markets are more like outdoor markets, where people spend the entire day shopping and eating. Many of the flea markets in the southern regions sell wholesale goods, with used goods representing only a fraction of the market's business. One of the largest flea markets in the country is located in San Jose. This flea market is so large that it has a helicopter landing pad.

"For years the RIAA had a problem with the San Jose flea market," says Frank Creighton, vice president of investigations for the RIAA. Creighton remembers one seizure at the San Jose flea market in the mid-1980s, when he was new to fighting music pirates. "We had to bring in all of our investigators from around the country to cover all of the booths in the flea market. If we hit only one or two booths, everyone else would pack up until we left." Creighton estimates that the cost for this one seizure was many thousands of dollars and included costs for hotels, travel, meals, and vehicles.

"We conducted surveys and seizures, and tried to elicit the support of the San Jose flea market owner to self-police," Creighton recalls. "Only after numerous seizures were we finally able to send the message to the illegal vendors in this flea market."

The RIAA was not alone in seizing counterfeit merchandise in the San Jose area. In September 1993 CAPS conducted a major sweep of street peddlers in the area, and seized 15,000 pieces of counterfeit merchandise. According to San Jose police, the counterfeit merchandise came from five separate vendors; two of the defendants had prior convictions for selling counterfeit merchandise and were charged with felonies.

To battle the street vendors and flea market vendors, the RIAA developed two programs in the early 1990s. One is the Civil Ex Parte Seizure Program and the other is the Street Vendor Alert Program.

Under the Civil Ex Parte Seizure Program, RIAA investigators make buys on the street, and the evidence is used to obtain an ex parte seizure order under the 1984 Trademark Counterfeiting Act. Armed with an ex parte seizure order, the RIAA investigators, attorneys, and U.S. Marshals return the next day, serve papers on the vendor, and confiscate the vendor's merchandise.

"At its inception, the Ex Parte Seizure Program was very successful," says Creighton. "We seized hundreds of thousands of counterfeit cassettes. The program was very expensive. It might cost the RIAA $25,000 to get an ex parte seizure order, and in some instances only a few thousand tapes were seized. Of course, there was no way to collect damages from the street peddler, who never showed up in court."

The Street Vendor Alert Program involved the record stores in the fight against the street peddlers. The RIAA set up coalitions across the nation, then sent out representatives to the record stores and instructed the managers of the large record chains, regional sales forces, and independent retail stores on how to make a purchase from the street peddler. After determining that the cassette was counterfeit, the RIAA was contacted, and the RIAA, in turn, instructed the retailer to contact the local police to report the situation, and inform them of which state and local statutes apply. Although the RIAA had lobbied for stronger state statutes, many local enforcement officers were unaware of the statutes or how to use them.

The Street Vendor Alert Program was very successful. It allowed the RIAA to stretch its limited manpower by involving the retailing community in the fight against music piracy.

"If a retail store in the Midwest calls the RIAA on our 1–800-BAD-BEAT number, we may not be able to respond that same day," says Steve D'Onfrio, executive vice president and director of the RIAA's antipiracy operations.

"In order to assist the retailers the RIAA set up coalitions across the country with the purpose of establishing an ongoing relationship. We found that by getting the retailer involved local law enforcement often cooperated enthusiastically. The retailer has a voice in the community, and that has a lot more effect than the record company, which is from out-of-town. The retailer is part of the community and is going to be there continually."

According to D'Onofrio, the Street Vendor Alert Program became a point-of-contact. After making a buy, the RIAA would walk the retailer through the process of determining that the cassette was counterfeit and contacting law enforcement. The RIAA would fax applicable state statutes to the police, who in many instances had never used them before. When needed, supporting affidavits in support of a seizure could be sent by overnight mail.

During a five-year period beginning in 1989, the RIAA investigated almost 600 flea markets and assisted in 150 raids. In 1994, the RIAA introduced the Flea Market Awareness Program. Under the program, flea market owners and operators were contacted in an effort to get them to self-police. By accepting the RIAA's expertise in adopting preventive antipiracy measures to prevent sound recording piracy on their premises, the flea market owners assisted in the piracy battle. In its first six months of operation, the Flea Market Awareness Program resulted in the seizure of 75,000 counterfeit and pirate cassettes and CDs at seventy flea markets.

In the early 1990s, two industry coalitions were formed to combat the counterfeiting problem at flea markets: the Eastern Anti-Counterfeiting Alliance (EAA) and the Western Anti-Counterfeiting Coalition (WAC).

WAC was formed in 1993 by a group of trademark owners. WAC's primary goal is to get flea market owners to self-police their market. The idea for the program came from an Australian organization, which had successfully instituted such a program to combat the sale of counterfeit goods at car boot sales. WAC has forty-two members and has an active antipiracy campaign in several states: Washington, Oregon, Nevada, California, and Hawaii.

"The main purpose of WAC is to try to get the owners of the swap meets to self-police," says Cheryl Dawson, director of WAC. "We work with the California Swap Meet Owners Association, and we've done seminars for swap meet managers and personnel in many locations."

Like its brother organization the EAA, WAC sends private investigators to conduct a sweep of the flea market. A sweep involves a visual inspection of the merchandise being sold at the booths. If the investigator suspects that a vendor is selling counterfeits, he will make a purchase, obtain a receipt, make note of the booth number, and include a short description of the vendor in his report. Determining the counterfeits is not always easy. Many swap meets in California sell used Levi jeans, which are collector's items. Sometimes, the counterfeits are interspersed with the real product.

The investigator will return the next day and serve either a notice or a cease-and-desist letter on the vendor. According to Dawson, WAC uses cease-and-desist letters in four different languages because of the ethnic diversity of the vendors. These letters have a clause demanding voluntary surrender of the counterfeit merchandise, but if the vendor refuses to surrender his goods, no action will be taken.

WAC takes no legal action against the flea market vendors, although any of WAC's member companies whose intellectual property has been counterfeited will be notified. The flea market owner is notified whenever a vendor is served. In many instances, the flea market owner will evict the vendor or take steps to ensure that the vendor does not return.

Some of the counterfeit goods that the WAC has turned up come from Mexico or from China. Often, according to Dawson, the goods are locally silk-screened garments such as T-shirts and sweatshirts. In California, the counterfeit goods are sometimes traced back to Santee Alley in downtown Los Angeles, which is similar to the garment district in New York City.

Over the years, WAC has encountered flea market vendors who use cell phones and work in gangs. At the first hint of trouble, everyone is notified at once, and the counterfeit merchandise is tucked away. Day vendors, who rent a booth for a day and move on, are difficult to apprehend, according to Dawson. Some vendors are repeat violators who will return to the same swap meet the next day and use an alias, usually a brother's or other family member's name.

The EAA was formed in 1994 by twenty-four companies. Robert Ogden, who was formerly with the Walt Disney Company, and Lee Sporn, in-house counsel for the Polo Ralph Lauren Corporation, decided to visit flea markets along the East Coast and talk to flea market owners about the counterfeiting problem. They found that many of the owners were proud of their flea market and wanted to maintain a good operation. A procedure was developed for involving the flea market owners in the fight against the counterfeiters.

The EAA uses three private investigative agencies that conduct sweeps of flea markets along the Eastern seaboard. Before conducting a sweep, the flea market owner is notified. Buys are made of any suspected counterfeits. If any vendor is discovered selling counterfeit products, the private investigator will return and deliver by hand a cease-and-desist letter. A copy of the cease-and-desist letter will be given to the flea market owner. No further action is taken—unless the vendor reappears or is found at another flea market. In this situation, the private investigator will return with a cease-and-desist letter and demand surrender of the counterfeits. The vendor's name will be entered into a database of known violators.

According to Ogden, who is chairman of the EAA, the flea market owners cooperate, and often evict the vendor, even if he is a first-time violator. The program began in Florida, which is a large tourist area and has hundreds of flea markets open year-round. Ogden reports that the EAA program has been very successful in Florida and in Georgia.

"There are a few uncooperative flea market owners," says Ogden. "In this case, we notify them that they can be held liable for any counterfeit merchandise under the *Fonovisa* ruling."

By the end of the 1990s, the industry programs, trade groups, and coalitions had done much to control the problem of street peddlers and flea market vendors, although the problem is widespread in the developing countries.

NOTES

1. Francine Russo, "Untaxed and Free to Roam, Workers Cash In," *New York Daily News*, July 16, 1995, p. 28.

2. Peter Blauner, "Out of Africa," *New York Magazine*, February 16, 1987, p. 3.

3. Lawrence Van Golder, "6 Charged with Violating Clothing-Trademark Laws," *New York Times*, July 18, 1996, p. B4.

4. Paul Jaskunas, "The Wild, Wild East," *CCM*, September 1995, p. 46.

5. John Heylar, "Licensed Sports Gear Takes a Hit from Alienated Fans," *New York Times*, February 23, 1995, pp. B1, B10.

6. Bill Lodge, "$1 Million in Sports Apparel Seized in Dallas, Houston," *Dallas Morning News*, January 8, 1994, p. 35A.

7. Jody Lindbeck, "Designer Cap Scam Costs Businessman £13,000 Fines," *Ealing & Southall Informer*, July 29, 1998.

6

Pursuing the Counterfeiters

David Woods has just finished testifying for the plaintiff about how he scammed the defendant by successfully convincing the alleged trademark counterfeiter to sell to him by posing as a legitimate buyer, thus furnishing the evidence needed. Now, it is the defendant's turn to question Woods. The defendant's attorney would love to rip Wood's testimony apart and so pounces on the only opening he sees available: Woods posed as a buyer and he lied to his client.

Although his client has not been charged with criminal conduct and hence there is no issue of entrapment, the defendant's lawyer will nonetheless try to make an issue of entrapment. If nothing else, he will try to convey to the jury that this private investigator, David Woods, is not a fellow to be trusted. This is a frequently used trial tactic, termed character assassination.

The defense attorney goes over the facts very carefully. He wants the jury to understand that Woods lied to his client and comes right out with it. "You lied to my client, didn't you?"

"Yes, I did," Woods replies.

"Are you in the habit of lying to people?" the attorney asks.

Before Woods can answer, the plaintiff's attorney objects to the line of questioning. The judge nods his head and sustains the objection. The defense counsel becomes livid, since he has been shot down before he has even begun his main line of questioning. Obviously, the judge doesn't see the relevancy, the defense counsel thinks to himself; he asks for permission to approach the bench.

"Your honor, I'm trying to establish that the witness tricked my client—that Woods lied to him."

"Not relevant, counselor. It's the witness's job, as a private investigator, to penetrate an organization on an undercover basis. The need for a false identity is obvious."

After a few questions, the defense attorney retires, unable to cast doubt upon the credibility of David Woods.

The result of Woods's skill as an investigator is that the evidence he produces and the methods he employs for obtaining it are never disputable in court. Private investigation is a nebulous art, and Woods has mastered that field of it in which he specializes—trademark counterfeiting.

Woods founded Associated Investigative Services (AIS) in the early 1980s. AIS is one of perhaps a dozen private investigation agencies in the country that specialize in intellectual property matters. Most AIS investigations involve trademarks. The private investigation field is very competitive. Agencies are founded, flourish, and perish in a short time. Much of an agency's success is based on word-of-mouth reputation and referral. AIS, for instance, does not advertise, is not listed in the phone book, is not listed on the directory in the building in which it has an office, and there is no identification on the door of the office itself. All of AIS's business is by referral. Fortunately, the trademark community is a very tightly knit group and, by one means or another, the corporate clients find out about AIS.

"Utilizing a suitable ruse" is a phrase one reads often in AIS investigative reports and in Woods's signed affidavits. It means that, to obtain information or to obtain evidence, Woods has had to pretend to be someone other than a private investigator (PI). For obvious reasons, a frequently used ruse is that of claiming to be a wholesale buyer looking to make a fast buck.

Utilizing a suitable ruse to obtain information is a basic investigative skill and one that, correctly employed, is legal. The legal parameters for employing a scam are not precisely defined, only that it be done by, or under the supervision of, a licensed private investigator, and that the ruse does not involve the use of threats or the impersonation of a police officer, and that the ruse falls within acceptable boundaries (in other words that the ruse will stand up in court).

Utilizing a false identity to obtain information, however, is an element of private investigation work that the television writers have overblown to oblivion.

Some of the things that PIs do not do are:

- Utilize elaborate and frequent costume changes. They prefer to look and dress like you and me—to blend in.

- Impersonate a building inspector or telephone repairman to gain access to a building or apartment. If caught doing so, the PI could lose his license; moreover, information obtained in this manner would never be admissible in a court of law.

- Fabricate incredible scams to obtain information. One only has to think of the television show *Mission: Impossible* where natural disasters and psychic phenomena were created in an effort to scam information out of a suspect. The scams most frequently utilized by PIs involve the telephone and a scam business card.

- Carry guns. Most PIs prefer not to carry them, because guns cause more problems than they solve. David Woods does not own a gun permit and has never applied for one.

"You've got to know how to lie," Woods tells every new would-be investigator. "There's no other way to put it. This entire business is predicated upon the ability of the investigator to utilize a suitable ruse that fits the scenario. . . . No matter what the ruse, you have to feel comfortable with it, be able to maintain a real poker face."

From time to time, Woods brings in new investigators. On average, they last about two months. Contrary to the glamorous image portrayed on television, the reality of an investigator's working life is very difficult. A typical investigator from AIS handles thirty or more investigations at once and has almost as many cover stories to remember. One slip and the would-be investigator is through. Not only has a client been lost, but just as important, a time may come when the PI's life depends upon his ability to sustain a scam. In Woods's estimation, if the would-be PI has not got the talent for scamming, it is time he or she thought about another line of work.

Typically, Woods finds that most police officers and ex-federal agents do not make good private investigators for cases involving trademark counterfeiting.

"They're too used to displaying their badge and saying, 'Answer my questions,' " Woods explains. "The problem with this is, first, you don't know if the information you are getting is reliable; second, as soon as you leave, the person you have just interrogated is going to get on the phone and call everyone he knows, and of course the investigation is blown."

Woods's primary job when he goes undercover is to obtain information. A client wants to know how big a counterfeiting operation is, who the counterfeiters are, and where the counterfeit merchandise is being stored. Once Woods has ferreted out this information, the client will file a complaint, summons, and ex parte seizure order in federal court. Once these legal documents have been filed, and the judge has signed the ex parte seizure order, Woods will return with deputy U.S. Marshals and conduct an ex parte seizure of the counterfeit goods.

To obtain information, Woods has to penetrate the counterfeiter's organization, which is no easy task. The typical counterfeiter operates behind closed doors and has every reason not to trust any stranger who approaches him with the intent of buying merchandise, especially counterfeit merchandise.

The main hook that Woods uses to bait counterfeiters is greed.

"Your usual counterfeiter is a guy who drives a Chevy and wants to drive a Cadillac," Woods says prosaically.

Early in 1985, Woods received an assignment from counsel for Polo Fashions, Inc. The attorney gave Woods the name and address of a manufacturer who was believed to be counterfeiting Polo goods. The manufacturer was located in Jersey City, New Jersey. Woods's assignment was to investigate the company and, if the company was engaged in counterfeiting, to obtain a sample for verification.

This is a typical assignment. AIS does not initiate investigations; the clients do. The clients get their tips from a hundred sources. For example, a customer writes a letter complaining that his Izod® alligator came off in the wash. A cosmetics salesman is told by a client that the competition down the street is selling the same cosmetics for a cheaper price than he can afford to charge. Documents picked up during an ex parte seizure point out other retailers and jobbers. Each such clue can lead to an investigation.

No investigation is exactly like any other investigation. And this assignment for Polo had its own particular problems for Woods to solve.

When he arrived at the location provided, Woods was dismayed to discover that the counterfeiting operation was housed on the third floor of a decrepit and otherwise abandoned building. The absence of any business neighbors denied Woods the use of his best scam technique for penetrating a business organization to conduct an investigation.

Counterfeiters are naturally reticent, which makes the task of investigating them difficult. Yet, Woods has developed an almost foolproof method for gaining an introduction. No matter how devious a front the counterfeiter portrays, his neighbor in the adjoining office or building always has an inkling that a wholesale or manufacturing operation of some kind is going on at the subject's location.

Typically, Woods will first scam the counterfeiter's neighbor. It does not matter if the neighbor happens to be an accountant or the owner of a furniture store; Woods will invent an appropriate ruse to fit the scenario—almost invariably a variation of pretending to be a retailer or wholesaler looking to make some business contacts. Naturally, the unsuspecting neighbor is delighted at the prospect of doing business with the fast-talking Woods.

To complete the ruse, if necessary, Woods or his agents will return several times and fast-talk business. Since the neighbor is not engaged in anything illegal, he always takes Woods at his word. At an appropriate time, Woods will ask the unsuspecting neighbor for a favor; he will ask if he knows of any local leads that might help him out in his search for business contacts, especially in the general types of goods suspected of being sold by the counterfeiter. The neighbor is usually delighted to help out, and soon Woods is knocking on the counterfeiter's door. When the counterfeiter asks who sent him, Woods replies, "The guy next door, your neighbor, recommended you." From that point on, Woods fast-talks. To complete his image as a businessman, he has his scam business cards. The scam companies Woods uses are all listed on Dun and Bradstreet, in case the counterfeiter gets suspicious and decides to check him out.

Woods may possibly make buys of legitimate goods that the counterfeiter has for sale, while waiting for his main ally—greed—to get the better of his unsuspecting prey. Although the circumstances of each investigation change, human greed always remains the central element.

In this instance, the fact that there were no other "neighbors" in the area was stymieing. Woods had no easy excuse for walking up the stairs and knocking on the door. He had not the slightest idea of who was inside or how many people he would find. All he had to rely on was that they were most likely trademark counterfeiters.

It happened that Woods had several hundred counterfeit watches in the trunk of his car from a collection of samples purchased from counterfeiters years before. Woods got a wild idea; he gathered up the watches and proceeded inside the factory building. He walked up the stairs and knocked on the door. An Hispanic teenager answered the door.

Woods fast-talked. He said that he was a watch salesman. Just happened to be in the neighborhood. Thought he would drop by, since the building was in his territory, and get acquainted.

Incredible! There is not another business for blocks, and Woods tells the kid that this nearly abandoned building is in his sales territory. Woods expected to have the door slammed shut. It was merely his intention to get a quick look inside before that happened. Sure enough, he immediately spots embroidery machines in the next room, and he can see that the familiar polo player symbol is being embroidered onto blank knit shirts.

It turns out that the teenager can hardly speak English. "Si, si," he says and smiles.

Woods holds up the watches and communicates with his limited Spanish and with hand signs. He hands the kid a watch, as a present. Of course he would never try to sell any of the watches. A good defense attorney would pounce on that. Even giving the watches away is risky.

Although the watches were never used as evidence, they were once the property of a watch counterfeiter.

"Gracias," the teenager says. Meanwhile, the other workers, all of whom are immigrants of Hispanic descent, stop work and come by to meet this nice "gringo" who is giving away watches.

Woods hands out watches as a goodwill gesture. At the same time, he takes inventory and notes that there are twelve embroidery machines. He estimates that about two dozen shirts are being knocked off a minute.

Woods continues to fast-talk. He does not want to arouse suspicion, but probes subtly. How many workers are there? What are their shifts? Would they be interested in watches for themselves, friends, or family?

Shortly, Woods leaves. After reporting to the client, he returns to the illegal factory the next day. As before, he distributes more sample watches, to the delight of the workers. When he is certain that he has scammed everyone, he asks just what it is that is being embroidered. "Polo," one of the workers says and hands him a shirt to inspect.

Woods expresses an interest in buying a load of shirts. He explains that he can use them to help out with his watch business. The workers are overjoyed. One of them rushes to find the owner of the company, Mr. P.

Like the workers, Mr. P is Hispanic. He is inherently cautious, but is partially won over by this gringo everyone is talking about. He takes Woods on a tour. He shows him skids of counterfeit Polo shirts ready for delivery. He even takes him behind the building and shows him the trucks.

At this point, Woods fast-talks business with Mr. P. Like many counterfeiters, the prospect of exporting his counterfeit goods is appealing. Woods convinces Mr. P that he has a line on sunglasses. Mr. P is completely scammed and tentatively places an order with Woods, after Woods returns from his car with legitimate Porshe Carrera sunglasses—that he convinces Mr. P are phony!

"These are the best knockoffs around," Woods says, as Mr. P inspects the sunglasses. Woods quotes prices that no one can beat, all the while advising that he may have an export outlet to which he could possibly sell shirts for Mr. P.

But when Woods trys to buy shirts, Mr. P is not interested. Woods asks for a sample, and offers to pay cash. Mr. P will not hear of it; he explains that he is manufacturing on contract and that all of the shirts he has on hand have already been purchased.

Woods was baffled. He knew that he had Mr. P hooked, but could not understand Mr. P's reluctance to sell him counterfeit Polo shirts. Without shirts, even a single sample to take back to the client, he cannot get authorization from a judge to conduct a seizure. The attorneys for Polo could still sue Mr. P in federal court, but civil suits are slow. By the time the case comes to trial, Mr. P will have destroyed all his business documents, liquidated his inventory, and disappeared. A criminal complaint could be filed, but the chances that the district attorney will choose to prosecute someone at Mr. P's level of illegal activity are nil. DAs rarely get involved in trademark counterfeiting unless the manufacturer is really large.

Unable to change Mr. P's mind, Woods was forced to leave without obtaining a sample. Only on the drive home did he figure out why Mr. P did not want to do business. Mr. P did not want to sell to a "gringo."

Woods has several investigators whose ethnic backgrounds are useful in such situations. He called Mr. P the next day and told him that he knew a friend who was interested in purchasing shirts.

Knowing that the ever-present greed factor would take over, Woods introduced Mr. P to one of AIS's Hispanic investigators and allowed the investigator to cut a deal for the shirts on his own. The investigator came away with a dozen samples for verification. The shirts were then sent over to Polo for examination and subsequently an affidavit was signed by the president of Polo attesting to the shirts being counterfeit. His affidavit and Woods's affidavit attesting to substantial counterfeiting activity are the crucial documents needed to obtain an ex parte (without notice) seizure order.

An ex parte seizure order was obtained in short order. Woods returned with the deputy U.S. Marshals and conducted a seizure. Mr. P was stunned when he realized that his worst nightmare was becoming a reality. His entire inventory was seized: counterfeit shirts, embroidery machines, and business documents. Mr. P was eventually sued in Federal Court and his counterfeit shirts were destroyed.

Newly landed immigrants and other would-be entrepreneurs with low financial resources often gravitate to the retail business as street peddlers, flea market vendors, and small retail store owners because of the itinerant nature and low overhead involved in such work. These are the ground-level sources for counterfeit merchandise. Deals are for cash, often with no receipt to record the transaction. Counterfeiting chains are run on a name basis and are usually very difficult to crack. AIS's use of minority investigators is unique in the investigative business. Woods jokingly refers to his investigators as his "personal UN." His staff, which is both male and female, includes Jews, Orientals, and Hispanics.

AIS often receives assignments involving street peddlers, who are the most difficult link in the counterfeiting chain to deal with. Suing them in civil court is practically useless, since the peddlers usually have few assets that could be lost in a lawsuit. The police can arrest peddlers of illegal goods and charge them under local statutes dealing with unlicensed vending or criminal simulation, but this rarely happens. Most police units spend their time going after more important criminals. In

New York City there is a Peddlers Squad, but its small manpower is not enough to keep pace with the street peddlers. The Peddlers Squad also goes after various street hustlers, like three-card-monte dealers and hustlers who work the shell game, and other unlicensed street peddlers. However, after a $50 fine, these petty criminals are on the street again.

The most effective method for dealing with the illegal street peddler is to use what is known as a "Roving John Doe" seizure order. A "Roving John Doe" seizure order empowers an investigator or attorney, working in conjunction with U.S. Marshals or other law enforcement officials, to seize the street peddlers' goods without giving notice. The investigator or attorney has merely to make a buy, inspect the goods to ascertain that they are counterfeit, and then call in the Marshals. The street peddler is not arrested, unless he tries to assault someone.

Woods often conducts sweeps in New York City using the "Roving John Doe" seizure order. Many AIS assignments involve Senegalese watch peddlers, who are one of the primary ethnic counterfeiting groups in New York City. Its members often enter the United States on student visas and live, four or five to a room, in the shadier hotels in New York City. Their main objective is to make fast money working as street peddlers and then return to Senegal, Africa.

The Senegalese watch peddlers are "savvy" and well aware of the danger that the "Roving John Doe" seizure order poses. They have developed their own tactics to prevent the seizure of their watches. Working in small groups, the peddlers purchase counterfeit merchandise and then sell the merchandise side by side. While cutting down on individual sales, this tactic assures that only one or two of them will have his goods seized under the "Roving John Doe" seizure order. During a seizure, the other vendors pack up their goods and run.

In 1984, after pressure from major business concerns, the Koch administration ordered a crackdown of the Senegalese and other street peddlers. The police arrested over a hundred peddlers and charged them with fraud and for not having proper identification. When the arrested peddlers were brought to trial, the public defender offered a defense in which he claimed that the authorities were unfairly discriminating against the Senegalese while allowing other peddlers to run free. He won, and the charges against the Senegalese were dropped. After this court case, the pressure by the Koch administration waned, and the Senegalese returned to the streets.

After the failed effort by the Koch administration to clear the streets of the Senegalese and other street peddlers, Woods decided to concentrate his efforts on targeting the source of the merchandise. He was working for Cartier, the watch manufacturer, at the time.

Woods had noticed that the Senegalese peddlers always stayed together in a cohesive group. The same men who shared a hotel room also bought counterfeit goods together and wound up selling their counterfeit goods within visual sight of each other. This made surveillance of the Senegalese relatively easy. He followed one group into New York's Chinatown and noticed that they periodically visited a restaurant located on Canal Street. One of Woods's female investigators was assigned to take "an extended lunch" at the restaurant.

The investigator noticed the proprietor several times descending into the cellar, returning with bags of what was most likely watches and, in turn, selling them to peddlers. Woods sent his office manager, Yet Mui, who is Chinese, to look around and make a buy. Sure enough, this was a major counterfeiting watch operation.

Woods returned shortly thereafter with deputy U.S. Marshals and conducted a seizure on behalf of Cartier and additional plaintiffs Gucci and Rolex. At the request of the clients, Woods was videotaping the seizure for use as evidence. Suddenly, the owner of the restaurant, an Oriental man in his late forties, came rushing into the cellar. He was cursing and gesticulating wildly, with a meat cleaver in one hand. The Marshals usually have little to do at a seizure. Their job is to ensure that the seizure is conducted peacefully. The instant that the owner appeared with the meat cleaver, the Marshals pounced on him, and in seconds had disarmed the man, handcuffed him, and pinned him against a wall. Woods videotaped the arrest, which would later be used as evidence when the owner was charged with assault.

This successful seizure did little to halt the traffic in counterfeit goods on New York City streets. For many years afterward, Woods and his investigators regularly conducted sweeps under the "Roving John Doe" seizure order against the Senegalese watch peddlers and other unlicensed street peddlers, on behalf of Gucci, Rolex, and long-time client Cartier.

Woods's background is undistinguished. He grew up in the suburbs of Long Island. He was a class cutup who often wound up in the principal's office.

A car accident cut short his college education. Eventually, he became an auto mechanic. His career was short-lived. Only in his early twenties, Woods found that he had reached the end of the line as far as earning a living as an auto mechanic. He had already worked for several dealerships, including GM, AMC, and Rolls Royce, and was a top man on the line, earning the highest salary paid under the union scale. Fortunately, his brother, who was an FBI agent, had some connections: he knew a friend who ran a detective agency and was interested in hiring someone part-time.

Woods went from making $350 a week to making about $30 a week part-time. The investigative agency handled insurance, matrimonial, and other investigative work. Meanwhile, he completed a six-month course

David Woods. *Photo by Jean-Paul Picard, courtesy of Cartier, Inc.*

in investigations, security, and fire prevention given at La Guardia College.

The first time that Woods was sent out to obtain information about a retail operation, the director sent him out without a cover or scam business card. At that time, retail investigation was a new field, and consequently there were no investigative guidelines to go by. Woods got inside the assigned target company and tried to scam a manager. The manager listened for about two minutes and then pushed him out the door.

Woods vowed that he would never be so humiliated again. On his own, he decided to learn all that he could about the retail field. He read books and conducted scams. He had his own business cards printed up and practiced by approaching legitimate retailers. He pretended that he was a new buyer who was anxious to learn. Since the businesses he was scamming were legitimate, he received a valuable education over time. He learned about FOBs, import-export, letters of credit, standard discounting practices, and quantity buying.

This industriousness on Woods's part was to be the foundation of his success as an investigator. He knew about every level of the retail trade, from flea market to haute couture. When he fast-talked business, he was improvising about something he knew intimately. Woods easily allayed a counterfeiter's doubts, because of his detailed knowledge about the retail field.

As trademark counterfeiting increased, so, too, did the number of investigations that Woods headed. Soon, he was promoted to director.

Woods, however, was growing increasingly concerned with the way the investigative agency was conducting business. Eventually, he quit. At the time that he resigned he was conducting several investigations in the south. As a matter of professional courtesy, he called the clients for whom he was conducting the investigations and advised them of his decision to resign. He presumed that the agency would continue the investigations, but the clients would not hear of it. The clients wanted Woods to continue the investigations and conduct their seizures for them. Eventually, Woods founded Associated Investigative Services (AIS).

Soon after he founded AIS, Woods came upon that rarest of all items: the seemingly perfect counterfeit.

Puma had come across a wholesaler on Long Island, New York that was selling a particular Puma brand sneaker at a price that was much less than the price they would or could charge. The management at Puma wanted to know why.

Woods went to the location and purchased a pair of the sneakers. He sent the sneakers to the client. He returned to the wholesaler and, utilizing a suitable ruse, discovered the importer's name. The importer was located in Florida, which is where considerable amounts of counterfeit merchandise enter the United States.

Woods traveled to Florida and introduced himself as Tony, an Italian wholesaler from New York City. He fast-talked business with the owner, an Oriental named Mr. W.

Before Woods set up a deal with the owner, he checked with legal counsel at Puma to see if they were ready to file an affidavit attesting to the sneaker's being counterfeit. He learned that the management at Puma was baffled by the sneakers. Puma's experts had inspected every square inch of the sneakers, and found that they were almost perfect. Even normal factory flaws that one might expect to find were missing. How could they call the sneakers counterfeit if they could not prove that they were counterfeit? Could they have been produced overseas by a legitimate factory?

Most counterfeit merchandise is only an imitation of the real. The factory quality on most good designer clothes is not readily reproduced. Usually, designer goods are the product of a large business that has spent considerable time and money to make their products distinctive.

The only easily observable flaw on the sneaker was the leaping Puma on the back of the sneaker; it was jumping in the wrong direction! But this is the kind of factory flaw that could conceivably come from a legitimate factory.

However, a second and fatal flaw was found.

On the tongue of every genuine Puma sneaker the size is punched and appears as a series of perforations. On the counterfeit sneakers, the size had not been punched, but had been silk screened. From a distance, the size mark looked like perforations; only when they were touched could the fraud be detected.

Woods had managed to stall without problem. He had purchased a small shipment of the sneakers and sent it to what was soon to become his permanent office location in Forest Hills, New York.

Woods set up the deal. He purchased a consignment worth $100,000, with $40,000 to be paid in cash upon inspection of the merchandise and the balance upon delivery.

It had all gone smoothly—too smoothly. Shortly after the deal was set up, the owner called Woods and asked him to fly to Florida. Unknown to Woods, while he was boarding a plane for Florida, the owner was boarding a plane for New York. He had become suspicious and had decided to check out Woods's operation.

The owner arrived at Woods's future office, only to find that it was ramshackle. The room needed paint, and the linoleum floor was yellow with age.

As so often happens in such situations, Woods got lucky. It just so happened that Yet Mui and another investigator were in the office getting ready to clean up. The shipment of sneakers that Woods had ordered was lying on the floor—it had arrived that very day.

"Where's Tony?" Mr. W asked and looked around suspiciously.

"He's not here," Yet Mui replied, instantly recognizing the cover name. "He's in Florida."

"He's in Florida? What's he doing down there? I came up here to meet him."

"Oh, you must be Mr. W. What are you doing here? Tony told me that you asked him to meet you in Florida."

Mr. W nodded. He asked Yet Mui why the room was so run down. Yet Mui told him that they were moving to a better location. She pointed out the window toward a nearly completed office building across the street and said they were moving into the building.

Mr. W was suspicious, but when he saw the shipment of sneakers on the floor, he believed what Yet Mui told him. If he had come only a half-hour earlier, Yet Mui and the other investigator would not have been there to intercept him.

On the day that the deal was to be finalized, counsel for Puma asked Woods for a favor. The attorney asked him to bring along another investigator who was based in Florida. Woods did not want to use the investigator, because it is a prime investigative guideline never to use more investigators on an investigation than are needed; but he agreed, reluctantly.

He introduced the investigator to Mr. W as his cousin Bob. For this investigation, Puma provided Woods with $40,000 to show the counterfeiter, which Bob was carrying with him.

The deal was nearly finalized, when Mr. W began to get jittery. He did not want to show them where the merchandise was located. He insisted that Woods give him the $40,000, and he would then give them the location where the merchandise was being stored.

Woods had come across this hesitancy before. In fact, in most deals, the seller usually got nervous at just about this point. Woods knew, too, that it was just a matter of time before the seller overcame his nervousness and showed them the location where the merchandise was hidden.

Woods told Mr. W that there was no way he was going to hand over the money and receive a location written on a piece of paper. Bob, who misinterpreted what was happening, exploded.

"What the hell are you trying to pull!" Bob roared. He grabbed Mr. W by the shirt. Woods quickly pulled Bob away. He did his best to assuage Mr. W, who was so frightened that his legs were rubbery.

"You'll have to forgive Bob—he's my compadre. You know, he's just looking out for me, that's all."

Woods realized that he would have to separate the two, otherwise the deal might fall through. He told Bob to stay in the hotel lobby and count out the money. He took Mr. W aside and told him that only he would accompany him to the location where the merchandise was being stored. If the merchandise was there, they would come back and Woods would turn the money over to him. Reluctantly, Mr. W agreed.

As they drove away, Woods told Mr. W that he had to make a phone call soon and let his wife know that he was all right and that the deal was nearly finished. Actually, Woods wanted to call the seizure team that he was working with and let them know that he and the defendant would soon be arriving. The seizure team was already waiting at a pre-arranged location for Woods to arrive with Mr. W; then the seizure order could be served on Mr. W and he would be taken into custody. Woods typically plants the idea that he has to make a phone call far in advance, so as not to arouse suspicion when the call is made.

The counterfeit sneakers were being stored in a customs bonded ware-house. Because of their nearly genuine appearance, Mr. W had managed to sneak several hundred thousand pairs of sneakers past customs; all he needed was a buyer and the sneakers would flood the market.

Woods made his phone call and he and Mr. W drove back to the hotel to count out the money. As soon as they drove up, Woods gave the signal and the seizure team surrounded the car. At that point, Mr. W became silent. He realized that he was dealing with investigators and that he had been caught.

As AIS's reputation grew, Woods found himself traveling to Florida more and more often. When possible, he would job out the investigations to local investigators, but he grew increasingly dissatisfied with the quality of the investigative work done on his behalf. In 1986, he set up his own investigative office in Florida.

Not all of AIS's business involves trademark counterfeiting. Many investigations involve the unauthorized usage of registered trade names.

In 1988, AIS got an assignment from counsel for Panasonic. Panasonic® is a registered trade name, as well as a trademark. Panasonic also owns the registered trademark Quasar®.

Woods's assignment was to investigate another business entity that was apparently called "Quasar." He was given a business card. Quasar was an electronics store on Long Island, New York.

Woods traveled to Long Island and introduced himself as a buyer for a scam business. The sales meeting was surreptitious. He was taken into a back room, where a man who did not immediately introduce himself started asking questions.

He answered the questions to the satisfaction of the questioner, who then handed him a business card. This card was identical to the one given to him by the attorney for Panasonic. What made Woods suspicious was not only the manner in which the meeting had been conducted, but also the name on the business card. The person who handed him the business card did not fit the physical description provided by the attorney for Panasonic.

Woods did more investigating. He discovered that Quasar used only one business card for all of its business dealings. This was a coverup; the name on the business cards was fictitious, because the persons connected with the business wanted to remain anonymous. Quasar was a name that the company was using without a licensing agreement from Panasonic. The company was trying to cash in on the recognition of the trademark Quasar® by calling itself Quasar. Quasar was eventually sued for engaging in unfair competition under the Lanham Act. The suit was settled out of court.

Trademarks differ from copyrights and patents in that they never expire. The two requirements for maintaining a trademark are: (1) that the trademark owner use the mark in interstate commerce and meet the filing requirements for affidavits of use and renewal; and (2) that the owner police its trademark, which means that an owner must bring legal suit against infringers and counterfeiters. A trademark owner that does not police its trademark could lose it; this can and does occur when the number of infringements and counterfeits in the marketplace become so great that the trademark loses its distinctiveness. When this occurs, the trademark is said to have become generic: the trademark has lost its distinctiveness and become commonplace.

Many trademark owners own trademarks that are difficult to police. Polo Ralph Lauren Corporation (formerly Polo Fashions, Inc.) has brought numerous suits against companies that use infringements of its registered trademarks. Polo, however, does not have exclusive rights to the word "Polo," which denotes a sport and is therefore descriptive. Similarly, Polo does not have exclusive rights to the depiction of a polo player on a horse, but only to a particular rendition of a polo player on a horse. Consequently, the defendants in infringement suits frequently argue that their usage is generic in nature.

Companies can also lose their trademarks through abandonment. Legally, abandonment means that a company has ceased to market its products and hence its trademark. Often, a company going through a financial bad spell takes a product, with its federally registered trademark, off the market. The company may need to raise some cash, and hopes to be able to put the product back on the marketplace before anyone gets wise; or, a warehouse fire may have destroyed the inventory, and the company is waiting for the insurance settlement. Legally, however, the trademark is abandoned. Other companies can bring legal action to have the trademark declared abandoned by the United States Patent and Trademark Office (USPTO), in Washington, D.C. The consequences of the legal action are to make the trademark available to the first taker. Another consequence is that a company threatened with abandonment proceedings may be willing to sell its trademark at an unusually low price.

Most companies that have to discontinue a product line bearing a registered trademark do so secretly. Usually, a company will maintain a quantity of the product line on the market and fill small orders of the product for specially selected retailers. In this manner, the company hopes to keep the illusion alive that the product is still being marketed. The purpose of this maneuver is not only to fool the competition, but also to satisfy the criteria for filing either a renewal or an affidavit of use with the USPTO.

Trademark owners are required to file an affidavit stating that they are using the trademark in commerce periodically and upon renewal of the mark. Along with the affidavit, the owner is required to send samples of the trademark.

Woods is involved with two types of assignments concerning abandonment of trademark. One is buying trademarks. In this type of assignment, Woods, working on behalf of a client, approaches a trademark owner and offers to purchase its mark. The client does not want the trademark owner to know that it is interested in the trademark and so hires Woods. By using Woods, the client hopes to buy the trademark for a cheaper price than might be charged by the trademark owner if he knew who was really interested. This is legal, although it sounds illegal.

The other kind of assignment is collecting evidence that the trademark owner is not using the trademark in commerce. Typically, this involves scamming. Woods calls and pretends to be a buyer. Typically, he tries to place a big order to see if the company can fill it.

If he is lucky, the sales rep on the other end of the line has no idea of what is going on. The sales rep will say that he thinks the product line has been discontinued—in which case, Woods has just blown the corporate cover. Or, the company, aware of the need to keep the product's discontinuance a secret, will have all calls for the goods screened to a particular sales rep or manager. The company will fill small orders, but be unable to fill large ones.

In such a situation, Woods has the upper hand. The company will either sell the product, or it will not because it is unable to. Sooner or later, the person with whom he is speaking will find himself boxed in; after all, Woods is offering to buy. Sometimes, the person on the other end of the line will accuse him of being an investigator. This is a situation that every investigator finds himself in at one time or another, no matter what his line of investigation. Whatever he does, Woods will never drop his cover line in the midst of an investigation. Most likely, Woods will either continue the scam he started, or chameleon-like, improvise and invent a suitable ruse to fit the circumstances of the investigation.

7

The Entertainment Industries

Historically, the entertainment industries have always battled piracy in one form or another. Book piracy was a huge problem in England during the fifteenth and sixteenth centuries and played a great role in the development of modern copyright law. In the late 1800s, England had a problem at home and in the United States over the pirating of printed sheet music. In the United States, film piracy initially involved film theft. Losses were so great that in 1919 the major film studios formed the Film Theft Committee to fight the pirates. In the years after World War II, with the mass production of the 16-mm motion picture projector, a market for pirated prints developed. The market for pirated prints peaked during the 1960s, with much of the market consisting of film collectors, resorts, hotels, and colleges.

Since the mid-1960s, the piracy problem in the entertainment industries has been largely a problem of unauthorized copying. In the music industry and in the motion picture industry, high-speed duplicators have made copying the entertainment product an easy startup operation. In the publishing industry, photocopiers have made copying a book quick and inexpensive.

The entertainment industries are particularly vulnerable to the theft of intellectual property. By the mere act of purchasing a legitimate product, a pirate has a master that can be used for starting up production. No other industrial sector has such a naked vulnerability.

For the entertainment industries, not only are the products easy to duplicate, but profitability in the music industry and the motion picture industry rests on a few products and a handful of big-name artists. For example, CBS Records was the industry leader in 1987, but derived much of its revenue from two superstars: Bruce Springsteen and Michael Jackson. In only two years, CBS lost considerable market share to Warner Records, which had launched several new acts, notably Madonna. Not surprisingly, the most successful entertainment products are the very ones targeted by the pirates.

Underlying the entertainment industries is the law of copyright—or right to produce copies. Although the copyright holder has the exclusive right of distribution under copyright law, the technology to produce copies is readily available. Government and private industry have issued challenges to the copying technology, and the legal debate has played a great role in the development of free speech rights. The introduction of the printing press into England led to a growing trade in unauthorized books in the fifteenth and sixteenth centuries in England. The English government tried licensing books and issued an exclusive license to print books to members of the Stationers' Company in an effort to halt the unauthorized book trade. In the early 1980s the movie industry brought suit against Sony Corporation, the developers of the Betamax video tape recorder, and sought to charge Sony with contributory liability for copyright infringement. Had the movie industry prevailed against Sony, the video tape recorder (VTR), precursor to the video cassette recorder (VCR), might have been banned from the marketplace. To ensure the free flow of information, these efforts by government and private industry have for the most part failed, and the copying technology is readily available.

Entertainment is one of the chief industries of the United States, with the result that the United States has the strongest copyright laws governing unauthorized duplication for profit. Criminal penalties have been part of the U.S. copyright law since 1897, when a provision was added making it a misdemeanor to engage in "willfull and for profit" unlawful performances and representation of copyrighted dramatic and musical compositions. The 1976 Copyright Act provides criminal penalties with a maximum fine of $10,000, which could be raised to $50,000 under certain circumstances.

In November 1992, the 102d Congress increased the felony penalties for all infringement, not just for infringements of sound recordings and motion pictures. Under the 1992 provisions, an infringement became a felony based on a combination of the number of infringing copies or phonorecords made or distributed and their retail value. A penalty of up to five years' imprisonment or a fine, or both, can be handed down if the offense consists of the reproduction or distribution of at least ten copies or phonorecords of one or more copyrighted works, with a retail value of more than $2,500, during a 180-day period. A second or subsequent offense can result in imprisonment of up to ten years. In other cases that do not reach the threshold value or requisite number within the 180-day period, the period of imprisonment is not more than one year.

The 1992 bill was originally introduced in April 1991 by Senator Orrin Hatch (R-Utah) with the goal of increasing the felony penalties, and adding computer programs to the list of works whose infringement could result in felony penalties. After passage in the Senate, the bill was changed in the House to apply to all copyrighted works. The House substitute was passed by the House on October 3, 1992 and by the Senate on October 8. Public Law 102–561 was signed into law on October 28, 1992.

In this chapter, the antipiracy efforts of five industries will be examined: the book publishing industry, the cable television industry, the video game industry, the music industry, and the motion picture industry. The cable television industry differs from the other industries in that cable television involves the transmission of copyrighted work; hence, the piracy involves the theft of the satellite transmission, otherwise referred to in the cable industry as "signal theft." The cable industry suffers from the same naked vulnerability as the other entertainment industries. Satellite-transmitted television programming is available for anyone to steal, and entire countries have engaged in the unauthorized theft and retransmission of cable programming.

BOOK PIRACY

Book piracy is the oldest form of copyright piracy and played an important role in the evolution of a copyright law. There was no need for a copyright until the 1440s, when Laurens Janzoon Koster and Johan Gutenberg invented a printing press that used movable type. The printing press was an instrument for mass-producing copies.

Printing was introduced into England by William Caxton, who set up the first press at Westminster in 1476. Under the medieval system of patent law, the English Crown was the sole patron of new industries. The right to print was granted as a privilege by the Sovereign to a printer, and the phrase "cum privilegio a rege" became the first copyright—or right to print copies.

Special privileges like the printing privilege were common in Europe in the Middle Ages. For example, in 1467 a privilege was granted for the manufacture and sale of paper in Berne and its jurisdictions. In 1469, an exclusive privilege of printing was granted in Venice for a period of five years.

The sovereign offered protection to the work of authorship through a patent of monopoly, which prohibited anyone from reprinting the work or publishing new works in the reserved field. The issuance of a patent of monopoly was a source of revenue for the English Crown, as well as a means of control over what appeared in print. One of the first patents of monopoly, granted in 1539, was a patent for printing bibles in English. Patents of monopoly were granted for Latin grammars, catechisms, music books, law books, schoolbooks, and other works.

Despite the notice of privilege, book piracy and the sale of unauthorized books thrived in England during the turbulent fifteenth and sixteenth centuries. This was a period of religious strife in English history between Protestants and Catholics. Many of the pirated and unauthorized books were religious books aimed at the warring religious factions.

The government was alternately Catholic and Protestant, and the books that were banned from the public changed with the change in rulership. In 1557, Queen Mary I granted a monopoly over printing and the sale of books to the Stationers' Company. Guild members of the Stationers' Company purchased books from the author and had the exclusive right to publish and sell the work for profit. With a monopoly over the printing and sale of books, the Stationers' Company charged high prices. Daniel Defoe was one of many authors who cried out against the power of the Stationers' Company.

Over a period lasting two centuries, the sheer turmoil of two civil wars took their toll—the printing of unlicensed books became unstoppable. In 1694, the British Parliament allowed the Licensing Act of 1662 to expire. The Stationers' Company monopoly had been extended under various legislation leading up to the Licensing Act of 1662. After 1694, the Stationers' copyright, which was the only copyright in force, had no support in the public law.

In 1710, Parliament enacted the Statute of Queen Anne. The Statute of Queen Anne is the beginning of modern copyright law. It is a short statute of eleven sections. Copyright was granted to the author and ran for a term of fourteen years. After expiration of the copyright, the work existed in the public domain. Works in the public domain could be copied by anyone.

The Statute of Queen Anne began the development in Europe of an approach toward intellectual property that had no counterpart in other countries. Intellectual property protection for authors, inventors, and other creators became a vested right that could be defended against the state. This was the period of Enlightenment, an eighteenth-century philosophy that believed in individual rights. Enlightenment thinkers believed that society as a whole would benefit by providing inventors and other creators of artistic works an incentive to produce their works.

Under modern copyright law, the individual's right to disseminate a creative work is limited to permit certain uses such as scholarship and research as long as the uses do not interfere with the copyright holder's right to exploit the copyright.

Book piracy was common in France before the Revolution. The right to print a particular book was granted as a privilege, and was bestowed only on select guild printers and booksellers, who enjoyed a monopoly. To secure their monopoly, the guild members assisted the police in suppressing unauthorized books, which were usually books that had not been authorized by the government. An active underground printing community was at work printing seditious works and pornography. Many of the printers were located in neighboring Switzerland. As much as 50 percent of the French book market may have been pirate at one time.

In 1789, the revolutionary government in France ended the privilege system. In the spirit of revolution, information was held to be free, and everyone had the right to print whatever he chose. The argument that information is free has been used by proponents of the Internet, who argue that information on the Internet should be free and that copyright will disappear. They would do well to examine the historical period after the printing privilege was revoked in 1789. Without a copyright law in place, the result was chaos. A pirate market for books replaced the legitimate market. In 1793, France adopted its first modern copyright law, which was similar to the Statute of Queen Anne in that it granted the author power over his work.

After the Revolutionary War, the early Americans were notorious for their pirating of English literary works. New York City became the piracy center of the world. The English were powerless, because under the U.S. Copyright Act of 1790 only American nationals were afforded copyright protection.

Book piracy produced revenue and culture for the early Americans. The works of Charles Dickens were freely pirated. After an 1842 visit to America, Dickens returned to England and urged his fellow writers not to sell advance sheets of their forthcoming books to American editors and publishers. Dickens's works were widely pirated in the United States; *A Christmas Carol* sold for as little as six cents, compared with two and one-half pounds in England. Robert Louis Stevenson's book *Dr. Jekyll and Mr. Hyde* was a big hit in the United States, but an estimated three out of four copies sold were pirated editions.

The English lobbied the Americans for copyright protection to little avail, although many Americans were sympathetic and joined in the call for better copyright protection. One such advocate for stronger copyright protection was Noah Webster, the father of American spelling books and dictionaries.

The U.S. Constitution recognized rights in copyright and patent, but made no provision for registration or enforcement. In 1783, the Continental Congress passed a resolution encouraging the states to enact their own copyright laws to deal with copyright registration and other pertinent issues. Webster spent the years preceding the 1790 Copyright Act, which transferred copyright matters to the federal government, traveling from one state legislature to another seeking copyright protection for his spelling books. He was rightly concerned that his spelling books might not be classified as an original work under state law.

In 1837, Henry Clay presented a bill to the Senate that would extend copyright privileges to British and French authors on condition that their works be reprinted and published in the United States within a month of their appearance abroad. The bill attempted to reconcile the rights of authors with the interests of the American book trade. The bill was defeated. Other versions were subsequently introduced. Protection for foreign works on American soil was finally granted in 1891, although a foreign publisher could not obtain a U.S. copyright for his work unless the work was published on U.S. soil. This was a protectionist measure for the U.S. book industry. The manufacturing clause, as it was called, remained in effect until 1986.

After World War II, the United States book industry and its licensees in other countries emerged as the largest market in the publishing industry. Members and licensees of the Association of American Publishers (AAP) have experienced significant book piracy and unauthorized distribution of their copyrighted works. Book piracy is prevalent around the world partly because English has become a universal language; partly due to the large number of foreign exchange students who came to study science and medicine in the United States and then chose to teach from the same textbooks upon their return home; and partly due to advances in technology, notably in photocopying.

In 1996, the IIPA estimated that U.S. copyright industries lost $10.8 billion due to piracy in fifty-five countries. This was a conservative estimate based on a survey of seventy-one countries. The estimated trade losses involving U.S. publishers' works amounted to $684 million.

The AAP is a voluntary membership trade association, whose members publish about 75 percent of all books sold in the United States. As of 1998, the AAP had run enforcement campaigns in Thailand, Malaysia, Indonesia, and Turkey. Book piracy is of three types: commercial offset printing, unauthorized translation, and photocopying.

In Malaysia and Indonesia the piracy is primarily photocopying of complete books. In small "mom-and-pop" stores eight to ten photocopying machines are located in a room and are in use twenty-four hours a day. Professional photocopiers turn the pages with their pinkies and can photocopy a large medical book in two hours. Much of the book piracy is of college textbooks. So brazen are the pirates that during the beginning of the school semester, they will bring photocopy machines right in front of the campus library.

In Thailand, an estimated 30 percent of all college textbooks are illegal photocopies. AAP members also have a problem with unauthorized translations. Although Thailand adopted a new copyright law in March 1995, the AAP estimates that its members lost $32 million in 1996.

In several countries in which there is an enforcement campaign, there are commercial offset printers that are engaged in nothing else but producing pirated editions of American books. Nonetheless, the piracy situation in Asia is much improved from that of the late 1980s. During this time, according to Carol Risher, vice president of copyright and new technology for the AAP, not only were U.S. books being pirated widely throughout Asia, but were being brought back into the United States, in some instances by U.S. medical students to help finance their education. Most of the books being pirated were professional books: computer science, physics, chemistry, and medicine. The quality of the printing was terrible, according to Risher. Medical books that were originally published with four-color photos were pirated in Asia on cheap paper and with poor-reproduction black-and-white photos.

One notable book pirate nation was Taiwan. Sixty years of Japanese occupation had left Taiwan with no Chinese language and a disintegrated economy at the end of World War II. There were no major publishing houses, and the population spoke Taiwanese and Japanese, but could not speak Mandarin or read Chinese characters. During the 1960s and 1970s, translations became popular. With no copyright law, however, foreign publishers did not want to do business in Taiwan. Nearly the entire market was pirate. The pirate trade flourished, because many university professors in Taiwan were educated in the United States, and consequently, preferred to teach from U.S. texts.

In 1986, the AAP began its enforcement campaign in Taiwan. According to Risher, when the AAP began to bring legal actions, legitimate sales went up tenfold. In one notable decision by a Taipei district court in 1988, Taiwan's Tan Ching Book Co. and two senior executives were found guilty of pirating the *Concise Encyclopaedia Britannica*. In 1992, USTR Carla Hills identified Taiwan as a Priority Foreign Country. Under the threat of trade sanctions, Taiwan bolstered its copyright laws. So effective was the response by Taipei that Taiwan was downgraded from the Priority Foreign Country under the Special 301 to the Watch List. Most of America's international professional and scientific publishers have offices in Taipei today. The AAP estimated losses in Taiwan at $5 million in 1996.

Another success story for the AAP and other intellectual property owners has been Singapore, which was labeled the "world capital of piracy" in 1984. The AAP has operated an antipiracy program in Singapore since 1988. In February 1987 Singapore passed a new copyright law and entered into a bilateral copyright agreement with the United States in April 1987. By 1996, the AAP estimated that its members lost $1 million in revenues, down sharply from a decade ago. During the trade dispute with the People's Republic of China (PRC) in 1994 to 1996, AAP regional counsel began to investigate CD-ROM piracy coming from the PRC and entering the Singapore market.

The AAP has had some initial success in South Korea, reducing losses from over $50 million in 1988 to $20 million by 1994. In 1996, however, the AAP reported losses of an estimated $30 million. Under U.S. pressure and a Section 301 action by the USTR, Korea adopted a new copyright law in 1986 and joined the Universal Copyright Convention (U.C.C.) in 1987. South Korea does not provide copyright protection for works and sound recordings preexisting its 1987 U.C.C. membership. However, beginning in the mid-1990s the book piracy situation began to deteriorate. Investigations conducted on behalf of the AAP found that book piracy is carried out by a network of small, independent shops that are apparently small enough to operate without attracting attention. The books being pirated are textbooks, reference books, encyclopedias, and scientific, technical, and medical works.

In the countries in which it has an enforcement campaign, the AAP uses local attorneys and private investigators. As plaintiffs, AAP members sue for either violations of the distribution right or the reproduction right, or both. The AAP works with representatives of its members based in pirate countries and retains local counsel to investigate book piracy. They also work with the IIPA to lobby the government for assistance. In Latin America, one of the biggest book pirates is Bolivia, which hosts a "pirate book fair" each year. In November 1996 raids were carried out by Bolivian officials on behalf of AAP members with more than 500 pirate books found at more than ten locations, and eight people were arrested.

FILM AND VIDEO PIRACY

Operation Copycat began in January 1996 when police from the New York City Police Department's special trademark counterfeit unit learned that videos were being sold from a video store in Harlem. Detectives purchased dozens of pirate tapes from the video store and learned that the store was a distributor for a video tape ring selling counterfeits.[1]

For a price of several thousand dollars, undercover police became distributors for the counterfeit video tape ring that was run by two Israeli families in Brooklyn. The ring was so large that it sold franchises and supplied a string of franchises across the country. The ring provided its clients with master tapes, packaging equipment, and, ironically enough, phony FBI stickers that warn against trafficking in counterfeit tapes.

The ring was able to offer for sale counterfeit videos of movies like Eddie Murphy's *The Nutty Professor* before it premiered in theaters. After a six-month investigation, police arrested the ringleaders and thirty

Figure 7.1
Estimated Piracy Losses to U.S. Motion Picture Industry, 1995

Country	Losses in Millions
Russia	$312
China	$294
United Kingdom	$112
Japan	$108

Source: Motion Picture Association of America (MPAA).

workers. The ring had three small factories set up in Brooklyn where tapes were copied around the clock. In one of the factories, forty-five video cassette recorders (VCRs) cranked out upward of 30,000 to 60,000 tapes a week.

The video piracy ring produced more than $100,000 worth of pirated video tapes a week. The ring, which is believed to have ties to Israeli organized crime, was well organized and sold videos across the country by use of a franchise system.

Manhattan District Attorney Robert Morgenthau indicted the gang under New York State's Organized Crime Act, the first time the statute was used to fight trademark counterfeiting.

So prevalent is the piracy problem in New York City that the Motion Picture Association of America (MPAA) hired a retired lieutenant in the Organized Crime Investigations Division in January 1997 to head up an investigative team consisting of an entire squad of former officers to hunt down video pirates. The squad is financed by the MPAA and conducts surveillance, stakeouts of movie theaters, and the collecting of evidence. The MPAA will pay informants up to $2,500 for a good tip.[2]

Video piracy is possibly the most pervasive form of counterfeiting in the world. Video piracy is largely attributable to the invention of the VCR. In the United States, anywhere from 5 to 15 percent of all videos rented are counterfeit. In many countries, the piracy rate is, or has been, at 100 percent, effectively shutting out U.S. distributors.[3]

According to the MPAA, video piracy adds up to an estimated loss of $1 billion yearly (see Figure 7.1). The MPAA with its international counterpart the Motion Picture Association (MPA) is a trade organization made up of the major film studios.

Domestically, video retailers are a primary source of video piracy. There are well over 40,000 video retailers in the United States. Videos are also sold in toy stores, fast food chains, gas stations, and many other outlets.

For many retailers, copying a popular movie is much cheaper than purchasing authentic video cassettes. After demand for the movie has waned, the retailer may be left with dozens of previewed video cassettes. Usually, the retailer will place the used video cassettes in a bin or rack in the store and try to sell them. In a 1987 survey conducted by the American Video Association, which has a membership of 5,000, 30 percent of the members claimed that they knew dealers who had rented illegal copies. In 1986, there were over 1,200 investigations of video retailers with raids on over 100; 38,000 cassettes were seized.[4]

Rack jobbers are also a source of piracy. The rack jobber services the video retailers with current video cassettes. To stretch the inventory, a rack jobber may resort to substituting counterfeit video cassettes.

Back-to-back copying, which involves making a copy of a legitimate video cassette on a VCR, is one of the most common types of piracy. In large-scale operations, high-speed duplicators in the "slave" position churn out copies twenty-four hours a day. The counterfeits are usually identified by one of the following: poor picture quality, use of a brand name on the blank cassettes (legitimate cassettes have none), the absence of a "heat stamp" or some other distinguishing mark, and inexpensively produced labels and packaging.

Piracy in the film industry is an offshoot of tremendous growth. By the mid-1920s, the film studios were producing upward of 740 films a year and employed as many people as the auto industry. Joe Kennedy, patriarch of the Kennedy family, invested early in the fledgling industry. Kennedy purchased a controlling interest in the Robertson-Cole picture company, which produced fifty films a year. With a picture company in his portfolio, Kennedy was in the market for a theater chain and offered $4.2 million in 1928 for the Keith-Albee-Orpheum Corp., known as KAO. KAO had some 700 movie theaters in the United States and Canada.

In 1919, the major movie companies formed the Film Theft Committee to combat film piracy. Film theft involved either obtaining a master of a film and duplicating it, or, more often, hijacking the prints during shipment to a theater. The early pirates supplied the foreign market, which had little access to American films due to lack of distribution. The Motion Pictures Producers and Distributors Association of America (MPPDA) was created in 1922 in New York. The MPPDA, which was originally created to deal with problems of censorship, was the precursor to the MPAA.

The Film Theft Committee put the damper on film piracy during the 1920s. However, in the years after World War II, with development of the 16-mm projector, film collecting opened up a new market for piracy.

Prior to the development of the 16-mm projector, film collecting was a rich man's hobby. Only someone of wealth could afford an expensive 35-mm projector, a screening room, and the storage space for the heavy 35-mm prints. After World War II, nearly anyone could afford a 16-mm projector. The 16-mm prints were far less bulky than the 35-mm prints, which made distribution easier.

For nearly two decades after the war, film piracy was a small, underground industry. The major studios paid little attention to the piracy problem. The market was primarily bootleg prints—copies of older movies that were no longer in distribution and in many cases were creative works that had not been properly registered with the Register of Copyright. The Hollywood studios themselves paid little attention to the older movies and usually dumped the old prints or sent them to salvage companies that recovered the silver in the emulsions. Not surprisingly, the salvage companies became a prime source of movies for the film collectors.

Most of the legal actions taken by the major studios in the 1950s through the 1970s were against the private collectors, not the suppliers of bootleg prints. Animosity developed between the private collectors and the major studios over the collecting of prints. Many of the private collectors were people in the movie industry—the Bel Air circuit, as it was called—with a professional and a historical interest in preserving the older films. Many of the prints held by the Bel Air circuit were prints that had never been returned to the studios, where they were originally copied and lent out or borrowed for private screenings.

During its early years, the Hollywood studios were notoriously lax in preserving the early movies and maintaining the copyrights. The 1909 Copyright Act allowed a copyright for a period of twenty-eight years, renewable for a period of another twenty-eight years. The 1909 Copyright Act required that two copies of the copyrighted item be sent to the Library of Congress upon registration. The motion picture industry, however, had a special agreement with the Copyright Office under which the film companies were allowed to deposit a single copy of a film, and then immediately borrow it back for distribution. This agreement was intended to ensure that the industry derived as much profit as it could, but unfortunately many copies were never returned to the Copyright Office and so were lost to history. In September 1996, what may be the oldest complete American feature, a 1912 version of *Richard III*, was discovered; it had been stored for thirty years in the basement of a one-time theater projectionist in Portland, Oregon.[5]

By the 1960s, many older movies had fallen into the public domain. The only copies of hundreds of older films were in the hands of film collectors, who now had a legal claim of ownership. By not returning copies of the older movies to the Copyright Office, the film studios had weakened their legal rights. Additionally, under the 1909 Copyright Act the question of ownership of a print of a master film was murky. This was partly resolved in 1912, when copyright protection was extended to include films. However, the 1909 Act had provided for the compulsory license of original musical scores, but not for motion pictures. Consequently, how a copied print of a movie should be treated under copyright law remained unclear.

In 1974, as part of an overall sweep of the Bel Air circuit, the FBI raided actor Roddy McDowall's collection. McDowall had a private collection that consisted of films in which he had acted. The criminal charges against McDowall were vague. On the surface, McDowall was being criminally charged for possessing copies of films in which he had acted; yet, under the 1909 Copyright Act, it was doubtful whether he had committed a crime. Supporters rallied around McDowall, and subsequently, the charges were dropped. The Film and Video Security Office (FVSO) was established shortly after the McDowall raid.

"The FVSO was formed to combat the problem of 16-mm piracy and the unauthorized public performances of movies," says William Nix. "The piracy budget was modest. The pirate market was a limited, self-contained market, much like the market for autographs, and was generally limited to the serious collectors, the colleges, and the armed forces. There is still a collectors' market today for the 16-mm prints."

Nix joined the legal staff of the MPAA in 1976. He held several positions, before being named senior vice-president and worldwide director of the antipiracy program of the MPAA and MPA in January 1983.

In 1976, when Nix joined the MPAA, 85 percent of the antipiracy effort was centered in California under Dick Bloesser, a former FBI agent. Nix was in the New York office, with a part-time person in Paris, a part-time person in Hong Kong, and three persons in London. The antipiracy effort focused on criminal cases—about thirty or forty domestic cases a year.

By the time Nix left the MPAA in July 1991, the antipiracy effort had become a truly international operation. Nix was the chief operating officer (COO) with a staff of 500 employees and representatives functioning in sixty countries. Under Nix the MPAA/MPA member companies were filing hundreds of civil cases each year, in addition to initiating several thousand criminal cases each year around the world.

Video piracy was an offshoot of the explosive growth of the home video market. Ironically, the U.S. film industry had initially tried to bar the Betamax video tape recorder (VTR) from the market. The VTR, developed and manufactured by the Sony Corporation, was the prototype for the video cassette recorder (VCR). Had the film industry succeeded in barring the VTR from the marketplace, the VCR might never have been developed and, in turn, the home video market would never have developed as rapidly.

Universal City Studios filed suit against Sony and claimed that Sony should be found liable for contributory infringement as the manufacturer of the VTR. The Court of Appeals overturned a District Court ruling that held that the noncommercial home use recording of material broadcast over the public airwaves was a fair use of copyrighted works and did not constitute copyright infringement.

In *Sony Corporation of America et al. v. Universal City Studios, Inc., et al.*, 464 US 417 (1984), petitioner Sony Corporation appealed to the Supreme Court to have the judgment of the District Court of Appeals overturned.

The Supreme Court reversed the Court of Appeals ruling. The practice of copying television programming for later viewing, a practice the Court called "time shifting," was held to be noninfringing and enlarged the television audience. The Supreme Court held that the respondents in the case, Universal City Studios and Walt Disney Productions, had been unable to prove that "time shifting" had impaired the commercial value of their copyrights or created any likelihood of future harm.

The *Sony* case was argued before the Supreme Court in January 1983, reargued in October 1983, and decided in January 1984. In the years since the legal action was begun, the VCR had revolutionized the film industry, accounting for more revenue than the revenue being produced by film.

"The *Sony* decision marked the end of a philosophy in the entertainment field," says Nix. "Previously, the philosophy in the movie and television industry was to oppose any new technology for fear that it would cannibalize your marketplace. Today, the philosophy has turned around and the studios are avidly seeking new technology to help keep down costs, expand distribution, and create new products."

The phenomenal growth of the video market ushered in a pirate market. When Nix was promoted to worldwide director, the video problem was minimal—but then exploded! "Video was no longer an ancillary product in the movie industry," Nix explained. "Suddenly, a new direct mass market to consumer was created that accounted for 40 to 50 percent of the studios revenue. The ease of recording commercial-less films off of cable television or from legitimate video cassettes opened up a huge pirate market."

The piracy problem overseas grew at an enormous rate. By 1982, sales of pirate video tape cassettes in Europe was an estimated £100 million, an amount equal to sales of the legitimate industry.

In the United Kingdom, the overall piracy rate was an estimated 60 percent. London was dubbed the "capital of video piracy" because the pirate market had usurped the legitimate market. In Belgium, tape piracy was an estimated 70 to 75 percent of the market. In the Netherlands, 60 percent. In Ireland, 50 percent. In 1983, the movie *E.T.: The Extra Terrestrial*, a Steven Spielberg film and one of the most popular films of all time, was never legitimately released on video cassette in any country outside the United States.[6] The pirate market had shut out the legitimate industry.

Video pirates take advantage of the film industry's release schedule. In order to maximize revenues, the movie studios release a film under a sequential release schedule. Often the chain includes a first exhibition of a film in U.S. movie theaters, then to theaters in the international market. After the film has completed the release schedule, the video cassette will be released. The video cassette release schedule will be followed by a release schedule for cable television, and finally a release schedule for network television.

Video pirates find it easy to interrupt the release schedule by beating out the legitimate distributor. Within days of the motion picture release of *Jurassic Park* in June 1993 pirated versions were on the streets of New York City. The videos, which sold for $10, were of poor quality. Seventy-five percent of the videos had no picture or picture with no sound.[7]

International home video distribution may trail the U.S. release of a film by six months or more. A pirate needs only a single copy to fuel his operation, and if he can acquire a legitimate video in the United States, he can send it by overnight mail to a foreign location.

Many foreign pirates are easily able to beat out the release schedule for a film. The first cassette that the MPAA tracked was *Rocky IV* in 1986. Using a secret code, the MPAA was able to track the counterfeit trail as it went from the United States to Thailand, where copies with local subtitles were sent to Malaysia and Singapore. From there, the cassettes went to Jordan, then to Turkey, where they were resubtitled in Turkish and sent to Turkish workers in Germany.[8]

The James Bond movie *The Living Daylights* was internationally pirated before it was released in a legitimate theater. The movie was first shown in England in June 1987 and was due to have its world theatrical premier in the United States within thirty days. MPAA investigators discovered that copies of the movie in video cassette were being sold in the Middle East at least as early as April 1987. Pirated editions were also appearing in Asia at nearly the same time. Undoubtedly, a pirate got hold of a master of the Bond movie in England before the film had premiered.

In September 1987, the Belgian Anti-piracy Federation, working with the Special Branch of the Belgian National Police, shut down a production and distribution network suspected of dealing in high-quality French-language video cassettes throughout Belgium. The pirates were using advance release dates in nearby countries to gain access to the films prior to their commercial release dates in Belgium.

In 1982, Nix worked on an assignment that would lay the foundation for future antipiracy operations around the world. Nix assisted in the planning and creation of the Federation Against Copyright Theft (FACT) in the United Kingdom. FACT was a joint venture between the MPAA members and local distribution and business resources in the United Kingdom to combat film and cable television pirates.

"FACT was the model for a number of similar organizations around the world," Nix explained. "The MPAA joined forces on a multinational level to form a local entity. This was a British corporation with a local board of directors that included the managing directors of each of the major U.S. film studios and several key law enforcement officials, such as Scotland Yard."

FACT tackled video piracy for both the U.S. and U.K. film distributors, and additionally lobbied for better copyright protection and other business matters affecting the film industry. FACT lobbied for key revisions to the U.K. copyright law. In April 1986 the English Parliament published a white paper that set forth the government's official position regarding the FACT proposals. The white paper proposed that copyright protection should be granted for cable television and that the law against parallel imports should be strengthened.

Similar trade groups based on the FACT model were undertaken in several EEC member states and many countries in Latin America, Asia, and Australasia. One such antipiracy organization was the Federacion Anti-Pirateria (FAP), located in Spain, which in 1990 had one of the world's largest home video markets and a piracy rate of 30 percent.

On October 3, 1986, FAP raided one of the largest counterfeiting operations in Spain. Working with the FAP, police in Madrid seized a pirate lab in a bungalow located forty miles outside Madrid. The raid netted fifty-six VCRs that were in the process of taping the movie *Pale Rider*. Also seized were television sets, sound-mixing equipment, and 200,000 inlays and stickers used for counterfeiting. The dollar amount of the seized material was estimated at $28 million U.S. dollars. Police also arrested an electronics expert known as the "Zombie."

At the time of the Madrid raid, "community video" outlets covered nearly one million Spanish households, or 10 percent of the market for cable television. "Community video" is essentially a Satellite Master Antenna Television (SMATV). SMATVs are a private cable system that can be set up in a commercial establishment, such as a motel, trailer park, or apartment complex. In the United States, SMATV operators purchase cable under a commercial leasing arrangement.

In the community video outlets that the MPAA encountered in Spain and other countries, the SMATV operators were pulling down the satellite signal illegally and distributing it, either for free or sometimes for a monthly fee, in apartment complexes throughout the country. Hundreds of suits were filed by FAP against the community video outlets.

In December 1987, the Madrid police shut down a large community video outlet that had been transmitting films to 1,580 apartments without authorization. When the authorities raided the premises, *Karate Kid II* was being broadcast. By 1993, video piracy in Spain had declined to less than 15 percent from 80 to 90 percent in 1984.

FAP also lobbied for better copyright laws to shut down the community video outlets. In July 1985, a court in Seville ruled that community video was to be treated as regular television programming and subject to the same regulation. After this ruling, other favorable judgments were handed down regarding community video.

"After having several test cases handed down favorable judgments, we went back to the Spanish Parliament to have the broadcast laws revised," Nix says. "Eventually, a Royal Decree was passed to regulate community video by the Spanish Parliament."

Community video was a large problem for the MPAA in Israel. For several years the local antipiracy program had been lobbying the Ministry of Telecommunications, but little was done because there were no laws covering cable television. Finally, in August 1986 Israel enacted legislation to legalize cable television. Local police forces in most areas of Israel were cooperative in conducting raids, but the piracy persisted, because there was no legitimate industry.

"I remember seeing many pictures of warehouses full of wires that had been tagged as evidence for prosecution in Israel," says Nix. "Part of the problem was that the Israeli cable and telecommunications laws prohibited the licensing of any cable retransmission, even for legitimate purposes. As a result, the only providers of cable television was the pirate market, and the pirates were able to exploit high consumer demand."

After a revision of Israeli laws, a legitimate cable industry was established. In September 1986 in the central region of Israel, over fifty-five pirate cable stations were raided simultaneously, and twenty-eight persons were arrested. The cable stations were illegally transmitting programming to apartment houses that had an estimated population of between 300,000 and 400,000.

Unauthorized performance is a widespread problem. Under U.S. copyright law, it is not illegal to invite friends into one's home to watch a film on video cassette; such use falls within the fair use exception. However, it is illegal for a tavern, restaurant, club, prison, lodge, factory, or summer camp to show a film on video cassette to an audience, even if no admission is charged. A public performance in places open to the public or to certain groups of people, even if meeting in private, must receive the permission of the copyright holder.

The MPAA has investigated unauthorized public performances in hotels, bars, restaurants, and other public places throughout Asia, Europe, and Latin America. For many years, unauthorized public performances in hotels, pubs, and video clubs was a problem in Ireland. In the late 1980s the unauthorized public performance of videotaped movies was common in Greece, as was signal theft, with one notable transmission station and antenna setup on Mount Parnassus that was rebroadcasting television programming.

American entertainment is very popular in Taiwan. In the late 1980s, unauthorized performance was a widespread problem. What the MPAA encountered were so-called "MTV parlors." MTV parlors were communal screening rooms, usually located at the back of a small retail store. A customer was given a selection of video cassettes—invariably pirated editions not yet released—to view in the screening room. Some of the parlors had room enough for 100 people. Signal theft was so common in Taiwan that it was referred to as the "Fourth Channel," which was the colloquial name for an estimated 200 to 300 networks that offered pirated programming. The Fourth Channel had an estimated 400,000 cable television subscribers in 1992.

MPAA member companies, alone and with local groups, such as the Taipei Distributors and Exhibitors Association, had made submissions to the government outlining the regulations to control the MTV problem, to little avail. In 1988, the MPAA, working through the Federation for the Protection of Film and Audio Video Works (FVWP) located in Taipei, lobbied the Government Information Office (GIO) in Taiwan to raid such establishments.

Finally, action by the U.S. Trade Representative (USTR) forced the Taiwan government to crack down. In its 1989 Special 301 report to the USTR on unfair trading practices, the MPAA estimated that there were 2,000 video parlors in Taiwan. After being identified as a Priority Foreign Country by the USTR in 1992, the Taiwanese cracked down.

Video piracy was widespread in Japan. Much of the market was controlled by the Yakuza—the Japanese mafia. In 1985, the pirate market in Japan was 80 percent.[9] For help the MPAA turned to the USTR, which in bilateral talks in February 1986 made video piracy an issue. In October 1986, Nix, actress Molly Ringwald, and Jack Valenti, president of the MPAA, flew to Tokyo to dramatize the importance of fighting against video piracy. After the United States threatened to impose tariffs on electronic products, the Japanese authorities finally took action. By 1990, the estimated video piracy rate in Japan had shrunk to 15 percent. By 1998, the piracy rate was under 10 percent.

Another type of piracy that the MPAA has tackled is parallel imports. Parallel importing occurs when a distributor or manufacturer in one foreign country decides to export to another country. The tapes being illegally exported are legitimately licensed for sale or rental in the country of origin, but are sold without a license agreement or other authorization. For U.S. film makers, the parallel import problem has been widespread in areas such as Puerto Rico and geographical areas in the United States with a high Spanish-speaking population. Because of the film studios' release schedule, Spanish-language video tapes are released for sale abroad before being made available in the United States and its territories. A parallel importer in South America can distribute in the United

States in advance of the release schedule of the legitimate U.S. film industry.

Parallel imports were a problem in Europe, especially in Spain. The free trade movement of goods between member countries of the European Economic Community (EEC), as specified under the Treaty of Rome, had the unintended effect of adding to the parallel problem. Parallel imports became a problem in Spain, when United Kingdom and German video cassettes were imported to compete with legitimate imports from the United States. The parallel imports were intended for foreign tourists and were illegally exhibited in resorts, bars, and cafés. The traffic in parallel imports was curbed after the Spanish Parliament passed legislation covering public performance.

Internationally, a total of 10,500 investigations were undertaken in 1988, including complaints about illegal public performances. The countries where the largest number of video cassettes were seized are as follows: Japan: 160,808, Italy: 82,400, West Germany: 48,286, Brazil: 37,410, Taiwan: 22,000, and the Philippines: 21,322.

While Nix was overseeing the international antipiracy effort, domestic piracy was handled principally by the Film and Video Security Office (FVSO) under former FBI agent Dick Bloesser in California. Under Bloesser the FVSO became one of the most successful antipiracy operations in the world. From the beginning of 1985 through mid-1986, the FVSO seized nearly 50,000 illegally duplicated video cassettes. The overall result was to keep the level of piracy in the United States at a 10 to 15 percent level. In 1988, the MPAA reported a total of 3,799 raids against video pirates in the United States, with 612,738 illegal video cassettes seized. This total represents a 17 percent increase in the number of video cassettes seized over 1987. A majority of the 2,644 lawsuits filed in 1988 involved criminal actions.

In the mid-1990s, Nix, who had set up a worldwide matrix of trade groups and film security offices for the MPAA to fight video and cable piracy, joined the NBA Properties. In addition to overseeing the domestic antipiracy effort and other business matters for the NBA, he set up a worldwide matrix of trade groups that was a mirror of the organization that had been constructed for the MPAA.

SIGNAL THEFT

> "Good Evening HBO from Captain Midnight
> $12.95 a month? No way! (Showtime/The Movie Channel Beware.)"
>
>   —Pirate broadcast by Captain Midnight,
>   aired for four or five minutes on April 27, 1986

This surreptitious broadcast was seen by hundreds of thousands of cable subscribers in the East and Midwest during a broadcast of the movie *The Falcon and the Snowman*. Although the sender—John McDougal who lives somewhere in Florida—was eventually caught by HBO, his sentiments regarding the rising cost for premium cable television and signal scrambling are shared by many.

In January 1986 HBO and Cinemax, then owned by Time, Inc., became the first two cable programmers to scramble their satellite signals, thereby preventing satellite dish owners from watching their programming without paying a monthly subscription fee. In May 1986, little more than a week after Captain Midnight's pirate broadcast, Showtime and the Movie Channel scrambled their signals.

Signal scrambling prevents people from viewing premium cable programming without paying for the service. Nonetheless, despite the use of signal scrambling and a significant enforcement effort by the cable industry and the MPAA to apprehend illegal users, signal theft is an enormous problem. According to the National Cable and Television Association (NCTA), approximately one-fourth of all cable viewers in this country do so without paying for the service. In 1992, the NCTA estimated that signal theft amounted to a loss to the cable industry of $4.75 billion.

Signal theft is a problem outside the United States. Entire countries, most notably in the Caribbean basin, engage in the unauthorized retransmission of U.S. satellite-based programs.

There are two types of signal theft: satellite theft and cable theft. Satellite theft involves the unauthorized reception of the transmission sent by programmers such as HBO. Satellite theft involves satellite dish owners, who are also called television receive only (TVRO) users. Cable theft involves either an electronic or a mechanical theft. An electronic theft occurs when a party hooks up an illegal descrambler to the television to unscramble the picture. Mechanical theft generally involves an illegal feed that is run into the cable system. By far, electronic theft is the most prevalent type of signal theft.

Currently, most legitimate cable subscribers and TVRO users use a descrambling device. Cable subscribers rent or lease a set-top converter/descrambler, while TVRO owners purchase a descrambling unit. Both of these descrambling systems will eventually be redesigned to prepare for interactive television.

Interactive television is the result of a merger of the technologies used in several industries: computer, cable, television, and telephone. Interactive television will allow the subscriber to "interact" with the television. The interactive cable subscriber will be able to talk face-to-face with his neighbor or his boss, do shopping and banking from his television, as well as view movie and other television programming.

Most satellite signals being transmitted for interactive television will likely be digitally compressed. Each television channel that is transmitted occupies 6 MHz of bandwidth. Using digital compression, 2, 4, 6, even 10 channels can be transmitted within the same 6 MHz of bandwidth. The headend used by the cable operators has a 550-MHz receiving capacity, and many have gone to 750 MHz. The maximum number of programs that can be received by a cable operator is about 78 to 80 channels. Using digital compression, the receiving capacity will increase as much as ten-fold.

In June 1994 British television viewers got their first introduction to interactive television. Two commercial broadcasters, Carlton Television and London Weekend Television, joined forces with a cable operator to offer an experimental interactive London news channel. The cable operator's 65,000 subscribers can choose from four strands of programming to concentrate on weather, traffic, community and social action reports, or the main news program.

There were several interactive television projects underway in the United States, notably the Orlando project. In late 1994, Time Warner Cable Systems planned to introduce interactive television to some 4,000 homes in Orlando, Florida. The project was originally to cost $5,000 per household. Digital Equipment and General Instrument joined forces to produce the interactive equipment, which included Digital's microprocessor, distribution, and storage technologies and GI's encryption system, which allows financial and other information to be sent confidentially.[10]

Security has become a major concern in the cable industry. The need exists for a security device, such as signal scrambling, that will protect the transmission of digitally compressed satellite signals. In the twenty-first century, a pirate who has the technology to intercept a digitally compressed signal may have access to a person's bank account, ATM number, phone number, and other personal information.

Speaking about interactive technology in an article for *Newsweek*, October 11, 1993, Bill Gates, the chairman of Microsoft Corp., said, "The requirements here for security, privacy, and scale are really incredible."

The starting point for the scrambling that will be used for interactive television is the encryption already being used for digitally transmitted signals. Starting in the mid-1990s, digitally transmitted signals began being used by several programmers, including HBO. Because of the expense, the number of cable operators who have upgraded their equipment to receive digital programming has been increasing slowly—but the pace could accelerate dramatically when interactive television is developed.

Digital technology offers many advantages over analog. The analog signal can be compromised directly by an add-on decoder device. There is intelligence in the analog picture—even when the signal is being scrambled. With digital, there is no picture information, until the digital information is reconstructed into a picture.

Signal theft began with the growth of the home satellite market in the 1980s. Home receiving dishes first became available in 1979, and were a boon to rural residents. At that time, a home satellite cost $10,000. With a dish-shaped antenna aimed at one of several communications satellites circling the globe, the TVRO could pick up television programming.

In just a few years, the cost for satellite dishes dropped to $2,500. Demand for the dishes surged. People in urban areas began to purchase them. Signal theft became a growing concern to programmers. A greater concern was what could the industry do to prevent signal theft? The answer at that time was signal scrambling.

If the signal is scrambled, adjusting the TV receiver will not correct the reception. In order to unscramble the signal, a device called a decoder or a descrambler must be used. It is generally located between the antenna (or cable output) and the television receiver. The descrambler is used in conjunction with a converter. The converter, which adds receiving capacity, can be legally purchased by an individual. Descramblers and converter/descramblers are sold only on a wholesale level to legitimate cable operators. Most devices in use today are a combination converter/descrambler.

Signal scrambling upset consumers and other industries. Sales of satellite dishes, which had reached 70,000 a month, fell to fewer than 15,000 a month. The early types of signal scrambling proved easy to defeat. A black market developed for illegal satellite decoder devices.

As more advanced decoding equipment was developed, the consumer electronic products used in TV sets and VCRs and the electronic equipment used by the cable industry diverged. The Cable Act of 1992 ordered the FCC to improve the interfaces between cable and television electronic products. The Electronic Industries Association (EIA) and the National Cable Television Association (NCTA) were unable to agree on how to accomplish this. The EIA cited signal scrambling as a major source of difficulty, and blamed it for making such television features as picture-in-picture and wireless remote control, and recording one channel while viewing another, virtually useless.

Signal theft became a federal crime under the Cable Communications Policy Act of 1984 (Title 47 USC Section 605). Passed by industry lobbying, the 1984 Act made it illegal for any person to intercept or receive or assist in intercepting or receiving any communications services offered over a cable system without authorization.

The Act is very clear about including the equipment used for signal theft. The 1992 Cable Television Consumer Protection and Competition Act (Title 47 USC Section 553), increased the fines and imprisonment for anyone caught engaging in signal theft: a fine of $50,000 and imprisonment for up to two years, or both, may be handed down. A repeat offender can be fined up to $100,000 and imprisoned for more than five years.

Only a manufacturer or distributor of illegal decoders or other descrambling devices is likely to receive imprisonment under the Cable Acts. A homeowner with no criminal record rarely goes to jail for illegally connecting to the cable system. In fact, in many instances, the homeowner will be offered "amnesty" by the cable company. The cable company will shut the homeowner off and a salesman will call and try to sign him up. If the person is not interested in becoming a subscriber, no legal action will be taken.

"Our department performs many functions," says Robert Astarita, senior vice-president, corporate security for Cablevision, the fifth largest multiple system operator (MSO) in the country.

"One of the most critical functions is what we call a tap audit function. Security technicians literally walk the system and make a determination if anyone is connected improperly or illegally."

In the first instance, according to Astarita, the illegal tap is treated as an unauthorized connection. An unauthorized connection is one in which the receiving party is receiving programming through no fault of his own. For example, someone moves into an apartment and hooks himself up because the prior occupant forgot to contact the cable company and have the service discontinued.

After the programming is cut off and the connection removed, a salesman will call and ask if the party would like to subscribe. If a tap audit discloses that the party is hooked up illegally a second time, it is treated as an illegal theft. The illegal connection is photographed and removed for use as evidence.

"Now you are illegal," says Henry Hack, vice-president, telecommunications services New York metro area, for Cablevision. "You have committed a crime. Theft of services is a Class A misdemeanor in New York State. You will be sent a cease-and-desist letter, and the security department will monitor the situation."

A cease-and-desist letter is a warning to a party to cease its illegal activity or face legal action. No legal action will be taken unless the party hooks up for a second time. After the second offense, Cablevision will initiate either a civil action or a criminal action.

In a criminal action, a police officer will come to the house, determine that the party is hooked up illegally, and issue a desk appearance ticket. In New York State, theft of services is punishable by up to a $1,000 fine or a year in jail. In most instances, if the homeowner has no criminal record, he will be able to plea-bargain to a lesser offense. Most legal actions involve a civil suit. Damage awards start at about $1,500 in a civil suit.

"When I think of a pirate, I think of a seller or a distributor of illegal electronic products, not a homeowner," says Hack. "This is a business entity that advertises openly and is aware of the law."

According to Hack, in order to avoid prosecution under state law, most illegal distributors refrain from selling in the state in which they reside. A typical advertisement will have a notice that states "No sales in Florida"—where Florida is the resident state.

A typical brochure from a mail-order operation will display seemingly top-of-the-line equipment with brand names such as General Instrument, Panasonic, Toshiba, and Scientific Atlantic. Usually, the converter, which can be legally acquired, will be offered for sale, along with the add-on or stand-alone descrambler—also called a starbase, a blackbox, a pancake, or a hotplate in the pirate trade.

In some instances, the equipment was received from a cable operator who is about to upgrade the equipment in his franchise, and has sold his current inventory to a distributor who diverted the equipment to a pirate operation.

"Piracy goes well beyond electronic hobbyists," Astarita said. "We encounter people who are Ph.D.'s and others who have extensive background and degrees in many other disciplines."

Astarita, who is a former FBI agent, heads a staff of former law enforcement professionals. He and his staff conduct buy-and-bust operations and information gathering against pirate operations as part of their daily job. Astarita's budget for antitheft campaigns runs about $2.5 million a year, some of which covers sixty employees.

One of the most serious problems caused by the proliferation of pirate electronic equipment is signal leakage. To hook up an illegal decoder requires some technical expertise and certain tools. When a decoder is improperly connected, there will be signal leakage. Signal leakage occurs when microwaves leak into the atmosphere, where they can pose a threat by interfering with the FAA frequencies being sent from the control tower to the planes.

"We're supposed to be a closed system, and there should be no leakage," said Hack. "The FCC does flyovers and measures the signal leakage; if the amount exceeds the cumulative leakage index (CLI), we will be heavily fined. Most cable operators have CLI teams who canvas in a truck with a mounted antenna."

The technological battle between the cable companies and the pirates has provided some interesting antipiracy devices. In April 1991 American Cablevision of Queens, New York, filed suit against 317 cable pirates who had been caught after firing an "electronic bullet."[11]

Jerrold Communications, a division of General Instrument, learned that its converters were being compromised by an override chip. The black market chips were installed in a basic converter to obtain basic programming for free. Having obtained several of the pirate devices, Jerrold engineers devised a strategy for outwitting the chip. The engineers devised a "bullet" that used the chip's own programs to neutralize it.

"The bullet is designed to blow out a box that has been tampered with," Hack explained. "Our computers talk directly to the decoders that we purchase from the manufacturer and tell it what to authorize. To use the bullet, we send a signal down the line that says, 'Ignore the next message'; and the legitimate boxes will ignore the next message—the next message being: 'Blow yourself up.' There is no frying or electrical charge or 'bullet'—just a deauthorization."

Incredibly, the success of the electronic bullet was due to irate homeowners who called the cable company to complain about the lack of reception. Of course, the homeowners were unaware that a "bullet" had been fired.

Despite the penalties afforded under the 1984 and 1992 Cable Acts, the sale of illegal equipment is rampant. Illegal decoders are offered for sale in electronics stores, through mail-order companies, and are even advertised in national magazines. The sale and advertisement of illegal decoders can be found throughout the country.

The cable industry confronts a piracy problem that is similar to that encountered by the recording industry. Despite the stiff penalties and jail time provided under the Copyright Act of 1976 and the Trademark Counterfeiting Act of 1984, pirate, counterfeit, and bootleg music cassettes are offered for sale in second-hand music stores, record conventions, at flea markets, and are even advertised in leading music magazines. Despite a sizable enforcement effort by the RIAA, music piracy remains a big problem.

William Nix was involved in organizing a nationwide effort to combat signal theft.

According to Nix, at one time during the 1980s about 50 percent of the decoders sold by General Instrument were being compromised by a computer chip called "the three musketeers." A satellite dish owner who paid for one premium channel could receive all of the premium programming available upon inserting the three musketeers into the decoder. Hence, the chip's name: it offered the user "all for one and one for all."

"General Instrument wanted to transfer its in-house antipiracy effort into a larger, national effort," Nix says. "We were able to organize the Office of Cable Signal Theft (OCST) as a joint effort by the Satellite Communications Broadcast Association (SCBA) and the MPAA."

OCST was formed in 1986 and today is part of the National Cable

Television Association (NCTA), located in Washington, D.C., and is funded by both the NCTA and the MPAA. OCST works closely with the Department of Justice, the FBI, U.S. Customs, and state and local prosecutors, as well as with law enforcement agencies throughout the country. Between 1990 and 1993, OCST was involved in the seizure of 400,000 illegal decoders.

Many of the more than 10,000 cable operators are members of OCST and the Coalition Opposing Signal Theft (COST), which is part of the OCST advisory committee. Robert Astarita of Cablevision has served as vice-chairman of COST.

The technological battle against the pirates in the satellite industry led to the development of a generation of VideoCipher modules by General Instrument. The most recent version is the VCRS (VideoCipher Renewable-Security). The VCRS is the result of an industry-wide need for a new encryption standard. The VCRS has the ability to use smart cards to change the encryption in a designated area as soon as a break is detected. Pirating the VCRS requires such an investment of capital that it is considered too expensive an investment in advanced technology by pirates to be feasible.

The State Department placed the VCRS on its list of technologies that could not be exported. The State Department was concerned that the VCRS might be used as an encoder for military intelligence, rather than as a decoder. However, once several features were removed, the technology was approved for export.

Despite the development of the VCRS, satellite theft remains a large problem, according to Dennis Powers, Chief of Signal Security, Legal Department of HBO.

"The main focus of our signal theft efforts is the commercial misapplication of our satellite signal," said Powers. "We're not necessarily talking about boxes or modules that have been compromised or pirated, but multiple dwelling units like trailer parks, apartment complexes, and recreational vehicle parks that have set up their own cable system under the guise of a TVRO system. The pirate is paying a user fee, but is bringing down our signal and redistributing it throughout the complex and charging a fee to each subscriber."

According to Powers, the illegal user is acting as an illegal distributor or illegal franchise by selling the programming to other users who may, or may not, realize that he is doing so without authorization.

Essentially, the pirate is setting up a satellite master antenna television (SMATV). SMATVs are cloned from cable systems and in most instances operate like them. The principal difference is that SMATV systems operate on private property—apartment buildings, condominium complexes, or private housing developments. Instead of getting a franchise to bury wire along city streets and rights of way, SMATV operators sign contracts with property owners allowing them to bring in cable television.

Other types of satellite theft involve sports bars that pick up sporting events not usually available on broadcast channels or cable networks. Receptions of unedited events are called "back hauls" or "clean feeds" and are essentially transmissions without commercials that are picked up outside the stadium before they even get into the studio.

Satellite theft is difficult to trace. Leads for enforcement come in through many avenues. Agents who work for the major leagues or private investigators visit sports bars throughout the country to monitor what is being shown. In many instances, sports bars will advertise an upcoming fight, which will attract the attention of the MPAA or the cable programmers, both of which keep track of establishments authorized to show the program.

In 1994, NFL Enterprises, Inc. filed civil suits against dozens of bars across the country for buying residential subscriptions to its NFL Sunday Ticket package. Residential subscriptions cost $139 for the football season, while commercial establishments pay from $600 to $2,000, depending on their size. To catch suspected signal pirates, NFL Enterprises sent out teams of investigators to sports bars. During stops in play, the league caused all VideoCipher modules to display their identification numbers on the TV screen so that its investigators could note them and compare them against its subscription database.

The illegal activities of cable technicians and cable operators comprise much of the underground market in signal theft.

"When I first moved to Manhattan, the cable technician who hooked me up asked if I wanted to do this the legal way or the illegal way," says Matthew Sappern, manager of corporate affairs for HBO.

For some cash, the cable technician was offering to hook up the premium channels for Sappern, who would thereafter receive them for free. Sappern's experience is by no means an isolated one. Moreover, the largest source of illegal decoding devices on the black market today are cable operators themselves. Most cable operators who upgrade their franchise try to unload their existing inventory of descramblers. Too often the cable operator knowingly or unknowingly sells his descrambler to a pirate organization, which in turn advertises them for sale.

"We at Cablevision are very aware that a great deal of the illegal product comes from within," Astarita explained. "Cablevision monitors what happens to its old cable boxes, and in some instances, we destroy the boxes if we cannot sell them to a reputable source."

Cablevision prides itself on being a leader in the area of addressing theft. It conducts due diligence inquiries of all contractors and vendors that it does business with. It will sell old cable products only to a distributor who can document the inventory's destination or to a licensed franchise cable operator.

The MPAA has repeatedly cited the Caribbean area as a hotbed of piracy involving signal theft and pirated video cassettes. However, MPAA members do not authorize cable programmers to distribute their services outside the United States. If people in the Caribbean countries want cable services, they have no choice but to engage in signal theft.

"Technically, the footprint of the satellite signal is there," said Sappern. "HBO doesn't have the right to legally distribute and market its services outside the U.S. based on the covenants we have with the Hollywood studios."

According to Powers, the Caribbean Cable Association began lobbying the MPAA and its members in Hollywood in 1994 to allow the programmers to distribute outside the United States. The MPAA membership has thus far not granted distribution rights because of its release schedule for new movies. The release schedule is a marketing umbrella whereby new movies are released first to the U.S. theaters, then to the foreign theater market, before being released for video cassette distribution, cable television, and network television. The release schedule is designed to prevent a movie from appearing in two markets at the same time.

The Caribbean countries are not the only ones engaging in signal theft. For many years, Canada has been engaging in signal theft. This action was addressed after passage of NAFTA, which provided IP protection for encrypted satellite signals. Iran, which has no diplomatic ties to the United States, is another noted pirate; the television show *Baywatch* brings in top ticket price at illegal satellite-dish screenings.

In June 1996 an offshore banker and eight others were indicted in the biggest cable piracy case in history. The FBI investigation, dubbed "Operation Cabletrap," originated from a Kenilworth, New Jersey–based undercover operation that distributed cable television converter boxes ("black boxes") around the country.

Operation Cabletrap resulted in a ninety-two-count federal indictment and involved the alleged bribery of a cable industry security agent who was employed by a major manufacturer of cable television converters and whose responsibilities included investigating cable piracy. The security agent reported the bribe to the FBI and wound up working undercover. In return for $10,000 a month, the security expert was to help shield the operation and assist in obtaining unmodified converter boxes.

By 1992, the bribes amounted to $140,000 and included a $40,000 Porsche Carrera II. In order to hide the bribe payments, one of the defendants traveled to the Cayman Islands and established a money-laundering operation with the chairman of the Guardian Bank and Trust

(Cayman) Limited ("Guardian Bank"). A sham corporation was established and a gold VISA card was issued to the security expert, allowing him to access bribe money without revealing the existence of the offshore account.

The indictment involved the theft of more than 16,000 cable television converter boxes, including the July 1994 theft of approximately 3,500 boxes that were being held as evidence by the Los Angeles Police Department. FBI Special Agents executed arrest warrants in Florida, Texas, California, and Hawaii as part of Operation Cabletrap.

PIRATED VIDEO GAMES

The first video arcade games came out in the late 1970s. One of the most popular games at that time was "Pong." Installed in local bars, Pong was so popular that several of the games had to be closed down because they were taking in too many quarters.

The 1980s saw an explosion in video arcade game popularity. In the United States, the five largest video arcade manufacturers are SEGA Enterprises, Inc. (USA), Williams Bally/Midway, CAPCOM (USA), Namco of America, and Konami of America. Williams is based in Chicago; the other four companies are subsidiaries of Japanese companies.

During the 1980s, the American Amusement Machine Association (AAMA), a trade association of about 120 manufacturers and distributors of coin-operated amusement games, developed a serious counterfeiting problem. Most of the popular video games produced during the 1980s— from Pac Man to Mortal Kombat—were pirated.

The pirates were located in Asia, notably Korea and Taiwan. Nearly all of the counterfeiting was done by manufacturers of printed circuit boards. The printed circuit boards powering the video games were smuggled overseas to compete with the legitimate game. The typical counterfeiting enterprise was a small to midsized computer company. The counterfeiting was divided up among several locations by the parent company, with each location producing a small number of counterfeit circuit boards. This production arrangement made detection difficult. The smuggling pipeline was clandestine; deals were by word-of-mouth. The counterfeit boards were mailed overseas after a sale.

At one time, an estimated 20 percent of all video arcade games in the United States were pirate, and upwards of 90 percent of the games in Mexico and Latin America were pirate. Successful enforcement action by the AAMA, working in conjunction with the Japanese Amusement Machine Manufacturers Association (JAMMA), virtually eliminated the problem by the mid-1990s.

The enforcement effort by the video arcade industry began in 1984, when Bob Lloyd, president of Data East USA, a subsidiary of a Japanese

Company, made a telephone call to a college friend in Atlanta, Georgia. The college friend was Bob Fay, the FBI agent in charge of the white-collar crime squad in Atlanta.

During their conversation, Lloyd said that Data East USA had three hit video games: Karate Champ, Kung Fu Master, and Commando. Lloyd estimated that the company was losing $5 million a year to counterfeits.

Fay told him that this was the first time in nineteen years that someone he knew had called him for assistance. He told his college friend that if his company was losing that kind of money, that qualified as a significant white-collar crime.

Later, Fay called the U.S. Attorney's office in Atlanta. Eventually, several FBI agents, who were already working undercover on financial crimes, initiated a sting operation. The operation resulted in five criminal convictions—two in New York State, one in Tennessee, one in Kentucky, and one in Georgia.

The FBI discovered that the legitimate boards were being reverse-engineered in Korea and shipped through Toronto, Canada, which was the shipping point for the United States. Subsequent investigations turned up a significant pirate market. Many large U.S. distributors were importing the boards and selling them to end users throughout the country.

"When a game flops, the operator can arrange to trade it in for another game, or he can covert the game," says Marc Haim, president of R. H. Belam, a large wholesaler of coin-operated video games in Hempstead, Long Island. "The counterfeiting occurs either when the distributor or wholesaler converts the game by changing the software, graphics, and player control, or when he trades the game in and buys another game."

According to Haim, R. H. Belam discovers counterfeits from time to time in the United States, but the games are several years old. "Counterfeiting in the United States peaked in the late 1980s," says Haim. "Today, the problem is under control."

At one time, R. H. Belam had a significant counterfeiting problem in Latin America. Exporting accounts for about 75 percent of R. H. Belam's business, half of which involves Latin America. According to Haim, his customers often complained of being underpriced by distributors in the Latin American countries.

"The Korean and Taiwanese businessmen are very aggressive," says Haim. "Usually, what we found is a brother-in-law, cousin, or sister who moved from the country in the Orient where the counterfeits originate to Latin America. The Orientals establish a business and not only import counterfeit boards, but assemble cabinets and import monitors from Taiwan."

According to Haim, the most popular counterfeits in Latin America are Double Dragon, Champion Streetfighter, and other games in the Streetfighter series.

Video arcade games cost upward of $15,000; this includes the cabinet, harness, graphics, monitor, printed circuit board, and computer game system. The printed circuit boards inside most video games cost from $1,000 to $1,500. The pirated boards cost only a few hundred dollars to manufacture, and retail for $500 to $600. The pirated boards are sold to wholesalers and distributors, and substituted when converting a game.

Most video arcade games have a basic cabinet that houses the video monitor. The graphics on the side and on the marquee directly above the video monitor can be changed during a conversion. The player control can also be changed, when converting a game. Inside the cabinet is the video game system. The game systems have progressed: 8-bit, 16-bit, 32-bit, and 64-bit systems are on the market. The SEGA Saturn game system, which was put on the U.S. market in mid-1995, uses a double-speed CD-ROM drive for storing digital data, and two 32-bit central processing units (CPUs). The Saturn uses individual processors designed to handle specific visual and aural tasks.

Pirating video arcade games involves computer piracy. The individual games are stored in the printed circuit boards; these are changed to produce a new game. About 90 percent of the circuit board is generic or identical to other circuit boards. What makes the game unique is contained in several ROM chips. Once the pirate has managed to duplicate the information on these large chips, he can produce pirated versions of the game.

Computer piracy is illegal in most countries, but detecting the counterfeit arcade games is difficult. Most arcades and business establishments using coin-operated games are small and have only a few machines. Additionally, policing the diverse market where the games are played is difficult. Coin-operated games are found in bowling alleys, video arcades, gas stations, supermarkets, movie theaters, bars and restaurants, and other small business establishments.

Most of the AAMA's enforcement effort is concentrated at the customs level. Richard Trindle, former director of investigations for the AAMA, trained customs inspectors worldwide on how to detect the counterfeits. Nearly all of the counterfeits can be identified by visual inspection.

"The absence of the manufacturer's trademark name, model number, and country of origin on the printed circuit board is a good sign of a counterfeit," Trindle explained. "The counterfeits either lack the game manufacturer's name or the labeling will be of poor quality.

"The pirate ROM chips usually do not have the manufacturer's name or the name of the game on them. Most ROM chips also contain a series of numbers, whereas the counterfeits do not. Oftentimes, the pirates will use a variety of computer chips from several countries of origin. Legitimate boards contain chips from a limited number of parts suppliers. The legitimate manufacturer will also use its own custom security chips that clearly identify the manufacturer."

Other telltale signs of a pirated board are: (1) the board will usually have chips soldered directly onto the board, whereas the legitimate boards utilize socket holders to protect the chips; (2) the underside of a legitimate board will have a clean, quality solderwave pattern, as opposed to counterfeit boards that often display a lack of workmanship in their solder patterns; (3) the edge connectors, which facilitate a board's electrical connection to the game, are of poor quality.

In addition to a visual test, customs inspectors can send the boards to a lab, where they will be powered up and inspected. There are several tests that will determine if the game is authentic. One sure tipoff is that on most legitimate boards manufactured after January 1, 1989 the warning "Winners don't use drugs" and the FBI seal will be displayed.

American and subsidiary companies that are members of the AAMA are all enrolled in the AAMA Protect Sticker Program. Most of the protect stickers are placed on the printed circuit (pc) boards prior to export from Japan, but in some instances the stickers are affixed after entry into the United States. The AAMA Protect Sticker Program resulted in thousands of pirated printed circuit boards being confiscated as a result of voluntary compliance and search warrants.

Fay joined the AAMA in late 1986 as director of industry affairs and enforcement. His job was to set up an anticounterfeiting program from scratch. He worked closely with U.S. Customs, and set up a customs training program. Most of the pirated boards with the chips in place were being sent via UPS and Federal Express. Customs uncovered numerous counterfeit boards at UPS hubs in Louisville and Anchorage.

Fay also worked with the Royal Canadian Mounted Police (RCMP). In 1988, Canada enacted a new Copyright Act that increased the fines on copyright violations to $1,000,000 and carried a maximum penalty of one year in jail. With stronger copyright laws in place, the RCMP put more manpower onto the video game counterfeiting situation. There were between nine and eleven foreign distributors in Toronto shipping counterfeits into the United States. The distributors, who were nearly all Korean, were put out of business. The counterfeiting pipeline led back to Korea, and the AAMA performed its first criminal raid in Seoul in 1988, when a large factory was raided. This raid led to the first criminal copyright case ever brought to trial in Korea.

By the end of 1988, the situation was seemingly under control, but by 1991, after CAPCOM developed its Streetfighter series, counterfeits began to reappear. To foil the counterfeiters, legitimate manufacturers installed security chips and new hardware and software for each game, which made reverse-engineering difficult.

As the AAMA began to open more export markets, Fay discovered that the counterfeiters had given up the markets in Canada, Japan, and the United States, and were concentrating on South America and Mexico. In early 1992, Fay suggested to JAMMA that it set up an international organization to combat the counterfeiters.

In 1993, the Anticounterfeiting Advisory Group (AAG) was organized, with funding by JAMMA. Fay was the administrator of the AAG, and he hired several other agents to target eight countries: Italy, Spain, Chile, Argentina, Brazil, Mexico, Korea, and Taiwan.

The AAG used local investigators and local attorneys in the target countries. Vince Gambino, a former IRS agent, was based in Rome and handled Italy and Spain. A company in Spain had developed a technology whereby they could extract the data out from the game without breaking the code. With the security chip neutralized, the game information could be extracted. The Spanish company had a connection with a company in Milan, Italy that incorporated the data into ROM chips. The ROM chips were sold in bulk to companies in Korea and Taiwan, which shipped the counterfeit circuit boards to Mexico and South America. Some of the ROM chips even turned up in the United States. In 1991, a New Jersey company, which was a subsidiary of a Taiwan company, was prosecuted for selling pirated pc boards. The company manufactured the boards, but was smuggling in the ROM chips.

Gambino developed a shrewd maneuver that would wipe out the pirate operation in Spain and Italy. He wrote to the Italian government and showed them that they were losing taxes at the border. The Italian tax authorities swooped in and conducted several raids. The same strategy was used in Spain.

In 1992, Fay met a local attorney in Mexico City named David Shaw. Shaw was doing anticounterfeiting activity for Levi Strauss. Fay secured Shaw's services. Subsequently, the AAMA became the first organization to obtain copyright convictions in Mexico. Shaw had some excellent contacts in the government, and the AAMA hit the pirates at all levels—customs, operations, and illegal distribution.

The Asian pirate organizations were flying the illegal boards into Mexico in an effort to avoid U.S. Customs, which was too well trained for the pirates to get through. Since only a few flights came into Mexico each week, the AAMA could target those flights for inspection.

"The high rate of piracy in Mexico was significantly reduced after passage of the North American Free Trade Agreement (NAFTA)," says Trindle. "NAFTA requires a good faith effort by all the countries involved—Canada, Mexico, and the United States—in enforcing intellectual property rights."

In the United States, persons importing pirated video games may be prosecuted under Title 18 of the U.S. Code for conspiracy, false statement on entries, undervaluation, copyright infringement, and trafficking in counterfeit goods.

"The New York Police Department has made many successful seizures in New York City as the result of raids into gambling operations run by organized crime," says Trindle. "New York has one of the toughest state statutes on the books regarding commercial counterfeiting. Possession of a pirated video game can be prosecuted as a Class E felony."

According to Trindle, the percentage of pirate video games in the United States has dropped to nearly zero percent. "There haven't been any real hot games lately—like NBA Jam, Streetfighter, and Mortal Kombat," Trindle says. "This has slowed the counterfeit market. The more popular the game, the greater the likelihood of its being counterfeited. Additionally, our enforcement effort, which has been going stronger each year, has sent the message that the manufacturers will not tolerate a single counterfeit."

MUSIC PIRACY

The International Federation of the Phonographic Industry (IFPI) is the umbrella group for the national industry recording associations around the world. IFPI was founded in 1933 and is incorporated in Switzerland, with its registered office in Zurich. The IFPI Secretariat, located in London, is responsible for central coordination and research. In January 1999, Jay Berman, former chairman and CEO of the Recording Industry Association of America (RIAA), assumed the position of Chairman and Chief Executive of the IFPI.

Like the RIAA, which is a member organization, the IFPI's goal is to ensure that the producers of sound recordings and music videos have control over the use of their product. IFPI monitors the enforcement and the development of music performance rights around the world. The IFPI conducts investigations and accompanies local authorities in the search and seizure of counterfeit and pirated products around the world. During the trade dispute with the People's Republic of China, the IFPI provided invaluable intelligence about the piracy situation in that country.

Music piracy in the United States is combated chiefly by the RIAA, whose member companies are responsible for the sale and distribution of about 90 percent of the legitimate music sold in the United States. The RIAA has its headquarters in Washington, with regional offices throughout the United States. The U.S. music industry lost about $300 million in sales in 1997. The worldwide loss figure for music piracy in 1995 was estimated at $5 billion, according to the IFPI (see Figure 7.2).

The music industry distinguishes three types of sound recording piracy. *Pirate recordings*, which are the unauthorized duplication of only

Figure 7.2
Worldwide Music Piracy, 1995

Region	Legal Sales (U.S. $ million)	Pirate Sales (U.S. $ million)	Pirated Percentage of Total Unit Sale	Share of Worldwide Total
Europe	13,397	945	24%	44%
Middle East	346	106	31%	5%
Asia	9,620	434	28%	20%
Africa	271	55	38%	3%
Australasia	791	6	3%	0%
Latin Am.	2,050	298	46%	14%
N. Am.	13,215	304	3%	14%

Source: International Federation of the Phonographic Industry.

the sounds of one or more legitimate recordings. *Counterfeit recordings*, which are the unauthorized duplication of original artwork, label, trademark, and trade dress in addition to the sounds. *Bootleg recordings*, which are the unauthorized recording of a music broadcast on radio or television or a live concert. Bootlegs, sometimes called boots, are also acquired through a "studio leak" or "outtake" tape.

Music piracy in the United States began in the late 1940s and 1950s with pirate recordings of vinyl records. At the time, the illegal market was difficult to stop because sound recordings were not covered by copyright until 1972. In 1961, the American Record Manufacturers and Distributors Association (ARMADA) estimated the trade in counterfeit labels at $20 million annually. ARMADA lobbied Congress for stronger legislation and in 1962 the counterfeiting of record labels became a federal misdemeanor (18 U.S.C. Section 2318).

Starting in the late 1960s and early 1970s, prerecorded music on analog cassettes provided a new medium for recorded music. In an analog cassette, separate tracks for the left and right stereo channels are recorded simultaneously along the length of the tape. When the first side is recorded, the cassette is flipped to record a second set of stereo tracks on the remaining width of the tape. The cassette offers many advantages over vinyl records. The cassette is compact and suffers no diminishment in sound quality due to the weather or scratching, both of which are problems associated with vinyl records.

Growth in the market for prerecorded music cassettes was astounding. By 1971, just a few years after the introduction of prerecorded cassettes, the market for prerecorded cassettes accounted for 28 percent of total music revenues, or $428 million.

Prerecorded music cassettes also opened up a pirate market. The ease in duplicating the cassettes and the absence of copyright protection for sound recordings in the United States and other countries fueled the pirate market. The cost to buy duplicating equipment and cassettes to fund a small operation was as little as $3,000.

According to the IFPI, between 1972 and 1981 world audio piracy doubled from an estimated $500 million to over $1 billion. In 1973, an estimated 15 percent of the world market involved pirate or counterfeit sounds. In the United Kingdom, the piracy market for 1973 was estimated at 20 million pounds. During the 1970s, the piracy levels in many non-Western countries was well over 50 percent. In Singapore, Thailand, Pakistan, and Korea, the piracy level was an estimated 80 percent. In Indonesia, nearly the entire market was pirate.

In the United States, copyright protection for sound recordings was delayed because of the Supreme Court's decision in *White-Smith Publishing Co. v. Apollo Co.*, 209 U.S. 1 (1908). The case involved player pianos, and the legal issue was whether a piano roll reproduction of the plaintiff's musical composition was an infringement. The Supreme Court held that the piano roll (and, by extension, any sound recording) was not a "copy" of the musical composition.

White-Smith was decided in 1908, and led to the drafting and passage of the Copyright Act of 1909. The 1909 Act clearly did not confer a right of copyright in a sound recording per se, but only in the musical composition that was the subject of the recording. The recordings themselves were uncopyrightable. The 1909 Act made provisions for a compulsory or mechanical license. Once an artist had made a sound recording, anyone could make a sound recording of the same composition upon payment of a royalty. Royalties can be paid directly to the original artist, but are usually paid through a compulsory rights agency, like the Harry Fox Agency in New York City.

The mechanical license was part of the Berne Convention revision that took place in Berlin in 1908, and was adopted by all signatories. The United States was not a signatory to Berne, but enacted legislation in the 1909 Act to cover compulsory licensing. The compulsory license is not a license to duplicate, which would amount to using the compulsory license to pirate the original recording, upon payment of the mechanical royalty. Such a scheme has been tried, and the court found the defendants liable for copyright infringement.

The compulsory license allows an artist to render his own rendition of the underlying musical composition, after the musical composition has been released as a sound recording and upon payment of the mechanical royalty. The compulsory license has added great variety to modern music. There are many popular songs that were recorded in one style of music, and subsequently recorded by another artist in a different music style. One example is the song "All along the Watchtower," which was originally composed and recorded by Bob Dylan, and released as a musical recording several years later by Jimi Hendrix, who added his own interpretation.

In the United States, the lack of copyright protection for sound recordings hindered the music industry and law enforcement, which for the most part was limited to making seizures and arrests of organizations that were engaging in interstate commerce or were part of a network engaged in illegal activity. Despite these limitations, many large seizures of pirated product were carried out. In 1969, two illegal operations were raided that sold about $100 million in copied tapes, accounting for one-quarter of all the counterfeit tapes sold for the year. In 1970, U.S. Marshals raided what proved to be a major pirate operation in an industrial park in Phoenix and confiscated thirty tons of duplicating and packaging equipment. The illicit operation had 100 employees, who were turning out 80,000 tapes a week and selling them in gas stations located throughout the state of Kansas. Many pirates were open about the nature of their operation. One company, Music City Distributing, Inc., located in Houston, offered music cassettes of popular music recordings for $2.75 each through mail order; the company's sales letter was signed "Your friendly bootlegger."

The major music companies had remedies at civil law, and many filed suit for unfair competition and for copyright infringement of the underlying musical composition. The civil suits did little to slow the trade in pirate recordings. States had begun granting common law principles of rights in sound records, but by the late 1960s, the legitimate industry was lobbying for copyright protection at the federal level.

By 1970, piracy accounted for 5 percent of all music sales in the United States, or about $60 million. In 1971, hearings were held to amend the 1909 Copyright Act to grant copyright protection to sound recordings. At the hearings, Stanley M. Gortikov, former president of Capital Records and director of the RIAA, testified as to the growing piracy problem.

> We have spent hundreds of thousands of dollars and have brought scores of cases to trial in state courts; and there have been no unfavorable decisions. Only one of these cases went as far as appeal, and it, too, was won by the record industry. Yet, the problem persists and, indeed, it's growing. What is needed is the creation of a federal copyright with broadened remedies to meet the problem on a national basis.

In a memorandum submitted by the RIAA in support of the Sound Recording Amendment, the costs borne by the pirates were compared to the legitimate costs borne by Atlantic Recording Corporation to record and distribute a typical album for the well-known recording artists

Crosby, Stills, and Nash. Atlantic had paid approximately $80,000 to record the band's last album, and another $20,000 to advertise and promote the album. The cost to manufacture the prerecorded tapes was in the neighborhood of $600,000. A pirate, on the other hand, needed as little as a few hundred dollars for duplicating equipment and blank tapes for a small operation. Moreover, the pirate had the further advantage of piggybacking on the album's popularity.

Copyright protection for sound recordings was enacted in 1971 by amending the 1909 Copyright Act and was effective for sound recordings first fixed on or after February 15, 1972. Sounds fixed prior to February 15, 1972 were covered by state law. Federal copyright protection for the sounds on some older recordings could be obtained if they were multi-track sources by remixing the original sound tracks and creating a new mix.

The 1976 Copyright Act guarantees copyright protection to sound recordings, and even protects unpublished recordings provided they are copyrighted.

The RIAA's antipiracy program was established in 1970. From 1981 until 1999 Steven D'Onofrio was executive vice-president and director of the antipiracy program. D'Onofrio joined the RIAA as an intern in 1980. Frank Creighton, vice-president of investigations, succeeded D'Onofrio as director of the antipiracy program. Under Creighton and D'Onofrio, the RIAA's antipiracy program has grown into a formidable operation that is well known for its aggressive pursuit of music pirates.

Music piracy today generally is found in the secondary market. The primary market is where legitimate manufacturers market current releases, usually record stores. The secondary market is used record stores, collectors' conventions, and specialty mail order. The secondary market is for serious collectors. The other market in which pirated music is found is through street peddlers and flea markets.

Piracy in the primary market was practically eliminated after several executives of the Sam Goody chain were indicted for the interstate transportation and sale of counterfeit sound recordings. See *U.S. v. Sam Goody, Inc., et al.*, 506 F. Supp. 380 (E.D.N.Y. 1981). In the sixteen-count indictment filed February 28, 1980 the government charged Sam Goody, Inc., the president, and vice-president in charge of procurement with various offenses arising from the corporation's business of buying and selling musical phonograph records, eight-track tapes, and cassette tapes. The indictment charged that the defendants knowingly defrauded the public, various sound recording companies, and various recording artists and musicians by dealing in unauthorized recordings of copyrighted works. The recording artist Billy Joel testified at trial. The FBI had established and maintained a retail record store to serve as a front for undercover operations directed against suspected criminal activity in the music recording industry. Using surreptitious recordings obtained with a concealed body recorder, the FBI obtained enough information to put together a case charging that the president and vice-president in charge of procurement for Sam Goody were involved in the interstate transportation of counterfeit sound recordings. The defendants had been in the interstate commerce between Maspeth, New York and Minneapolis, Minnesota, dealing in counterfeit tapes valued in excess of $5,000.

The RIAA's antipiracy operations virtually eliminated sound recording piracy during the early to mid-1980s in the Southeast part of the United States, particularly in the Carolinas, and in California. After repeated seizures in these areas, music piracy shifted to the Northeast. Just prior to 1990, music piracy was rare in the Northeast, but by the end of 1992, many of the seizures conducted by the RIAA occurred in the New York City area (see Figure 7.3).

The antipiracy effort was assisted greatly by passage of the Trademark Counterfeiting Act of 1984, which allowed an ex parte seizure of the counterfeit goods. "Trademarks, under the 1984 Act, cut across the labels," D'Onofrio explained. "You can seize the pirate's entire inventory covered by the counterfeit trademarks."

Starting in the late 1960s, the IFPI began to take an active role in the music piracy battle. The first place that IFPI set up an office that reported to the London Secretariat was in Hong Kong, which was the center of music piracy, both vinyl and cassettes.

"It took about ten years to get the problem in Hong Kong under control," says Mike Edwards, director of operations for the IFPI. "Stronger legislation was enacted, and a special division was set up in Hong Kong for intellectual property enforcement. By the end of the 1970s, the piracy rate had been reduced to 5 percent from over 90 percent."

According to Edwards, the domestic music industry in Hong Kong came into its own after music piracy had been eliminated, and Cantonese pop ("Canto-pop") became a huge success across Southeast Asia.

For a period of twenty years, the IFPI was engaged in a piracy battle that came to resemble trench warfare. After setting up an office in Hong Kong and eradicating the piracy situation, the focus shifted to Singapore, then to Indonesia, and then to Malaysia. In each case, once the situation in a particular country had been brought under control, the piracy problem shifted to a neighboring country, and in each case, the IFPI responded by setting up a regional office in the country to battle the pirates.

"Singapore became the pirate source for the world after the situation in Hong Kong had been put in order, with an estimated seven million cassettes a year," says Edwards. The counterfeit pipeline from Singapore stretched through Asia and into the Middle East, Africa, and Latin America. After setting up an office in Singapore, the IFPI was carrying out

Figure 7.3
U.S. Antipiracy Statistics

Counterfeit/Pirate Seizures	1992	1993	1994	1995	1996
Counterfeit/pirate cassettes	2,548	2,307,917	1,212,110	1,505,326	1,076,155
Counterfeit/pirate CDs	690	17,845	14,845	25,652	208,797*
Counterfeit/plant LPs	NA	83,445	13,675	0	7,245
Counterfeit/pirate cassettes (in-process)	165,610	370,600	158,630	155,385	9,536
Counterfeit cassette labels	32,377,125	34,449,500	23,126,036	28,477,450	20,070,650
Bootleg Seizures	**1992**	**1993**	**1994**	**1995**	**1996**
Vinyl	2,667	NA	175	155	34,620
Cassettes	4,719	2,100	7,381	3,310	529
CDs	16,213	965	3,000	84,965	1,261,961
Video (music related)	4,458	10,754	8,450	3,417	2,720
Actions Taken	**1992**	**1993**	**1994**	**1995**	**1996**
Search Warrants/ Consent Searches	116	101	69	82	96
Arrest/ Indictments	224	275	329	441	225
Sight Seizures (without the necessity of a search warrant)	1,423	839	742	605	134
Guilty Pleas/ Convictions	128	144	191	234	80
Civil Suits Filed	3	5	2	2	2
Judgments/ Settlements	6	6	3	3	4

*Approximately 95 percent pirate CDs.

more than one thousand raids a year—with minimal impact on the piracy production.

"It took two years to eradicate the problem in Singapore," says Edwards. "What finally settled things came after the United States threatened to rescind GSP benefits. After that, the Singapore government realized that the U.S. was serious about the piracy problem, and piracy was eliminated in about six months."

Next came Indonesia, which was listed as one of the four worst intellectual property offenders in the IIPA's 1985 Ten Country Report. From mid-1985 to the end of 1987, extensive bilateral talks by the USTR took place in seven of the ten countries that the IIPA targeted in its 1985 report, including Singapore and Indonesia.

In the early 1980s the RIAA's antipiracy operation received a tip that an employee of the Indonesian embassy in New York City was using the diplomatic pouch to ship counterfeit music cassettes past customs into the country. Through the assistance of an informant, Kenneth Giel, a former FBI agent, was brought in to act as a legitimate U.S. businessman interested in purchasing counterfeit music products. In his undercover capacity, Giel was introduced to Anthony Dharmawan, who was sneaking in counterfeit cassettes of recordings such as Madonna's *Like a Virgin* and the benefit concert *We Are the World*. Giel offered to invest several hundred thousand dollars, and a deal was arranged. Dharmawan was arrested outside the Indonesian embassy consulate only moments before he was to receive the sum of money Giel had used as bait. A few years later, Giel was put in charge of the RIAA's Flea Market Awareness Program.

In 1986, the IIPA petitioned to deny GSP benefits to Indonesia unless copyright protections were undertaken. That same year, Indonesia nearly lost its trading status within the EEC, which accepted a petition by the IFPI to declare Indonesia in breach of its trade agreements with the member countries because of the seriousness of the audio piracy situation. In 1987, Indonesia enacted a new copyright law, enabling it to stay in the GSP program. Within one week from the time an EEC-Indonesia agreement became effective on June 1, 1988, audio piracy in the country was eliminated.

In May 1988, Nick Garnett, who was head of the IFPI's Singapore office, was attending a meeting in Jakarta, Indonesia, with the local pirates with the goal of reaching an agreement to end music piracy in the country. This meeting occurred little more than a week before the June EEC agreement was signed. During the meeting, someone knocked on the door. In an excited voice the messenger said something, and immediately everyone left the room. Puzzled, Garnett asked someone to translate what the messenger had said. The message was that President Suharto had declared piracy was over and would no longer be tolerated within seven days. The pirates had scrambled out of the room to unload their stock as quickly as possible. Within one week of the signing of the agreement with the EEC, the rate of piracy in Indonesia went from 95 percent to 0 percent.

By the early 1990s, the IFPI declared that music piracy in East Asia had virtually been eliminated. Only three years later, the People's Republic of China would emerge as an international pirate. Thanks to advances in CD replicating, the Chinese would emerge as the largest pirate encountered by the legitimate music market in East Asia.

In the early 1990s, the RIAA launched two programs to battle the problem of illegal street peddlers and flea market vendors: the Street Vendor Alert Program and the Civil Ex Parte Seizure Program.

In August 1990 the Civil Ex Parte Seizure Program was launched. The ex parte program involves an application for an ex parte seizure under civil law. After a federal judge has issued the ex parte seizure order, U.S. Marshals accompanied by RIAA antipiracy representatives can seize counterfeit product. Between August 1990 and April 1992 nearly 290,000 counterfeit cassettes were seized under the program or in subsequent criminal seizures evolving from the program. Among the cities targeted in the ex parte program were Baltimore, Dallas/Fort Worth, Hartford/New Haven, Houston, Miami/Fort Lauderdale, New York, and Philadelphia, as well as Puerto Rico.

In January 1991 the Street Vendor Alert Program was launched. The program encouraged retailers to work with the RIAA legal staff to battle illegal street peddlers and flea market vendors. The RIAA set up coalitions as part of a nationwide outreach program. The results were impressive. Nearly 85 percent of all illicit products seized at the retail level in 1992 took place in regions in which coalitions were formed. From January 1991 to April 1992 the program resulted in the seizure of 102,890 counterfeit cassettes and more than fifty-four arrests. The program was especially active in Alabama, Arkansas, Delaware, Georgia, Illinois, Louisiana, Maryland, Nebraska, New Jersey, New York, Ohio, Oklahoma, Tennessee, Washington, D.C., and Wisconsin.

In addition to lobbying for stronger intellectual property protection at the federal level, the RIAA has lobbied for stronger state legislation. The three most commonly used state laws are: (1) true name and address statute, which mandates that the actual name and address of the manufacturer of a sound recording be displayed on the package; (2) unauthorized duplication statute, which is directed at pirate and counterfeit sound recordings "fixed" prior to February 15, 1972; (3) antibootleg statute, which makes it a crime to manufacture the sounds of a live performance of an artist and to distribute these reproductions.

The typical illegal manufacturing operation involves duplicating equipment set up in lines of machinery. The duplicating equipment for a typical line in the early 1990s cost about $11,000. A legitimate recording is used as a master. The blank tapes are custom-timed. It takes about one minute to produce a copy on both sides. Twenty tapes are recorded in a minute from each line of machinery. A large-sized manufacturer will have about four to eight lines of machinery. With a staff working twenty-four hours a day in two or three shifts, 10,000 to 25,000 tapes can be duplicated in a single day. Insert cards and shrink wrapping complete the illegal manufacturing operation. Many operations manufacture their own insert cards. In a record-setting raid in August 1992 the RIAA raided a counterfeit cassette manufacturing operation in Los Angeles and confiscated 17 million counterfeit insert cards.

The finished product is shipped to warehouses or picked up for immediate distribution. Most distribution is on a small scale: "mom-and-pop" stores, street peddlers, flea markets, and record conventions.

"I've seen street peddlers lined up, as if they were waiting to get inside a movie," D'Onofrio says of an illegal operation that was located in upper Manhattan. "The distribution point was a storefront disguised as something else. The peddlers picked up their merchandise on the second floor in the back."

The custom-timed cassettes are ordered through a tape loader, who may or may not be aware of its illegal use. Lack of actual involvement in the counterfeiting was usually used as a defense by the tape suppliers. In March 1996 the RIAA won a $7 million monetary settlement against a supplier of timed blank cassettes. At the time, this was the largest settlement ever won by the RIAA. The court came to its findings based on the raw materials confiscated, even though there was no evidence that the defendant engaged in the actual recording of counterfeit merchandise.[12]

As a preventive measure against the growing problem of CD piracy, the RIAA initiated a CD Plant Education Program. The focus of the program was to emphasize the methods that pirates use to submit illegal recordings for manufacture. Although plants are expected to scrutinize all digital audio tape copies of recordings that are submitted to the plant to be duplicated in CD format, pirates often present falsified copyright papers attempting to dupe the CD manufacturer into believing the pirate owns the rights to the recordings. If an illicit order is received, the CD plant may choose to either refuse the order or assist the RIAA and law enforcement in a sting operation. The latter course involves the plant actually manufacturing part of the order and delivering it under the control of law enforcement.

The plant education program has played an important role in keeping the problem of domestic CD piracy at a minimum. The on-site seminars are held with the CD plants' manufacturing, marketing, and sales personnel. CD piracy seizures decreased by 56 percent in 1992, due to the success of the CD Plant Education Program.

"There is a finite number of CD plants in the United States," says Creighton. "The CD plants in this country do not want to be held liable for pressing pirated material. For our mutual benefit, the RIAA decided that the best way to tackle domestic piracy would be to work with these plants. We visit the plants and give what we call a 'dog and pony,' where we sit down with the plant personnel and profile the potential pirate and describe the ruses used."

When a hot tip comes in, Creighton and the other members of the antipiracy staff immediately notify all of the CD plants in the country. Several years ago, the antipiracy staff received a tip that someone had managed to get hold of a copy of U2's *Achtung Baby* album, which had yet to be released. All of the CD plants in the country were immediately notified, while the antipiracy staff scoured the streets and flea markets for bootleg "rehearsal tapes" of the upcoming album.

In 1996, CD seizures overtook the seizure of counterfeit cassettes. The CD seizures were primarily bootlegs and Latin music piracy. From January through June 1996, the RIAA assisted law enforcement in confiscating 896,594 illegal CDs and 449,733 cassettes. According to the RIAA, bootlegs constituted the bulk of the seized CDs, accounting for 745,081, compared to less than 19,000 bootlegs confiscated in the first half of 1995.

The majority of seized CDs came from two record-breaking raids. In April 1996 in Los Angeles, more than 200,000 alleged bootleg, pirate, and counterfeit CDs were seized in a case initiated by the RIAA in conjunction with the IFPI's Asia Pacific Regional Office. The bootleg CDs were being manufactured by a Taiwanese CD plant and brought into the United States by a California CD broker.

In another raid, on June 26, 1996, 425,000 alleged bootleg CDs and 2.3 million bootleg insert cards were confiscated in Nassau County, New York; at the time, this was the largest bootleg seizure in RIAA history. The seizures were the direct result of an ongoing investigation that culminated in the arrest of Charles LaRocco. The arrest was precipitated by numerous alleged infringing shipments of CDs coming through U.S. Customs en route to LaRocco. The Fraud Division of the U.S. Customs Service and the Asset Forfeiture Bureau of the Nassau County Police Department, New York, assisted by the RIAA, executed several search warrants in connection with the investigation. The first search warrant, executed at a warehouse owned by the defendant, uncovered approximately 25,000 bootleg CDs and 25,000 bootleg vinyl sound recordings. Another search warrant was executed at the defendant's house, and the third was executed at a warehouse that was suspected of functioning as a headquarters. Among the seized recordings were bootlegs of Hootie and the Blowfish, the Dave Matthews Band, Phish, Bob Dylan, the Beatles, and many other major artists.

LaRocco, who ran a one-man operation, was referred to as "Mr. Big" in the bootlegging underground. Between 1990 and his June 1996 arrest,

LaRocco earned an estimated $15 million. He was arrested again in May 1997 for selling bootleg CDs. While on bail and awaiting sentencing, LaRocco was caught for an unprecedented third time in January 1999 by U.S. Customs for selling bootlegs on an Internet auction site.

Bootlegs, or boots, are found only in the music industry. Boots are usually live recordings and unreleased songs. As such, they usually contain material that was not previously released, and hence are not covered under copyright law. Under the copyright laws of some countries, notably Italy and Germany, live recordings are considered part of the public domain. Boots are usually issued in the CD format.

The record that most influenced the rise of the bootleg record industry on long-playing (LP) albums was *The Great White Wonder* by Bob Dylan in 1969. The bootleg became a collector's item and sold more than 50,000 copies.

The *Basement Tapes* were originally a series of bootlegs, and in 1975 became a legitimately released two-record set by Bob Dylan and a band originally known as the Hawks. In the summer of 1966, after a serious motorcycle accident, Dylan left the commercial arena and retired with a small group of disciples called the Hawks, later called the Band.

The main sources worldwide for bootlegs were Germany and Italy, where bootlegs were legal. Italy has one of the most serious music piracy problems in Europe, with total pirate sales estimated to be at least 20 percent of the market in 1998 (an estimated $85 million). Organized crime is known to control much of the pirate production.

In a major action against one of Italy's most notorious crime gangs, the Camorras, the Guardia di Finanza and the antimafia police raided an illegal music cassette plant located in Naples. The raid took place in 1998 and involved more than fifty policemen and a helicopter.

One of the most widely bootlegged bands is the Beatles. The bootleg CD boom began in 1988 with the appearance of the *Ultra Rare Trax* series, which included alternate versions and outtakes of songs by the Beatles.[13] In 1995, the Beatles released *Free as a Bird*, which was their first single since 1970. The 1977 demo tape that was used as a master was widely available on bootleg cassette for many years.[14]

Bootleggers steal music by taping radio and TV broadcasts, and by surreptitiously tapping into studio mixing boards. Most bootleg CDs are made in Germany, Italy, Asia, and Eastern Europe. The illicit CDs are then smuggled into the United States and other countries. In October 1993, rock star Phil Collins scored a rare victory against the bootlegging of a concert he gave in California in 1983. *Live and Alive* was a bootleg CD pressed in Germany and distributed throughout Europe. The European Court of Justice in Luxembourg ruled that Collins had to be given the same protection as German artists, including the right to stop sales in Germany of a recording he had not authorized. The ruling allowed

Collins to go back to the German courts to get an injunction barring sales of the CD.[15]

Many recording artists started to come out with their own bootlegged albums. Frank Zappa came out with a "Beat the Boots!" campaign and released a ten-album *Bootleg Box*, which featured his own music that had been bootlegged. In 1991, Bob Dylan released *The Bootleg Series, Vols. 1–3*, which featured unreleased tracks. In June 1991, Paul McCartney authorized a limited release of *Paul McCartney Unplugged, the Bootleg*.[16]

When President Clinton signed the General Agreement on Tariffs and Trade (GATT) in December 1994, a federal antibootleg statute was created. Until then, only state statutes had been available to law enforcement.

On July 26, 1995, the Fraud Division of New York City's Customs Office, assisted by representatives of the RIAA, executed the first seizure under the new federal antibootleg statute. Approximately 2,900 alleged bootleg CDs en route from Luxembourg were intercepted by customs agents at JFK airport. A controlled delivery, under the auspices of customs, was then made to Zapp Records, Inc., in Greenwich Village. At that location an additional 5,500 alleged unauthorized CDs, primarily in bootleg form, were confiscated. The CDs, which contained performances by the Doors, Phish, Madonna, Prince, Led Zeppelin, 10,000 Maniacs, R.E.M., the Beatles, Nirvana, Pearl Jam, Bruce Springsteen, Nine Inch Nails, and the Rolling Stones, among others, were seized. The seized goods had a value in excess of $10,000.

Operation Goldmine, which was the largest seizure of bootleg CDs in history, occurred on March 27, 1997, after a year-long undercover operation by the U.S. Customs and Assistant U.S. Attorney A. B. Phillips of the Orlando Division of the U.S. Attorney's Office. The bootleggers were operating in twelve foreign countries, as well as in the United States. Thirteen individuals, many of them bearing European citizenship, were indicted, and approximately 800,000 bootleg CDs were confiscated. Many of the thirteen individuals indicted were among the most notorious international bootleg manufacturers and distributors known; each faced a maximum prison term of five to thirty-five years.

"The bootleggers had been lured to the United States," says Edwards. "After ratification of the GATT, Germany and Italy changed their laws. Some of the bootleggers moved temporarily to Luxembourg, until IFPI got the laws changed in July 1997. All the major bootleggers were trying to unload their stock in the United States, when they were caught."

In addition to China, the IFPI focused its antipiracy effort in the former Communist countries, particularly Bulgaria, during the mid-1990s. Bulgaria, with a CD-manufacturing capacity of 80 million units, was a major supplier of pirate CDs entering Russia and other countries.

Bulgaria was first identified by the RIAA in its 1994 Special 301 filing.

The biggest pirate CD producer in Bulgaria was the DZU-DMON plant at Stara Zagora, which was a military computer research center during the Soviet era.

"Bulgarian product was found in the UK, Germany, France, and Russia," says Edwards of the IFPI. "The antipiracy campaign started in 1994. We set up an office there and hired local enforcement to do intelligence gathering. IFPI did seizures in Holland, Finland, UK, Latvia, Germany, Italy, Greece, and Turkey."

Bulgaria's proximity to Russia and Western Europe made it an ideal location for music pirates. In 1995, just hours before the USTR's announcement on Special 301, a U.S./Bulgaria agreement was reached. Bulgaria subsequently joined the Geneva Convention, 1971, and the Rome Convention, amended its copyright law to provide criminal penalties, and established a task force that would tackle the copyright violations. Bulgaria also agreed to license CD plants and to use SID codes. To assist the Bulgarians, the IFPI financed a firm of engineers from Oxford to travel to Bulgaria to assist with the implementation of the SID code into the manufacturing and replicating process.

Despite the 1995 agreement with the Bulgarians, piracy continued unabated. Without effective enforcement in place, the tougher copyright legislation did little. As in Russia, there is a very powerful crime element in Bulgaria and widespread corruption. In 1998, under continued pressure from the United States and the European Union, the government got involved and transferred authority from the Cultural Ministry to the Department of the Interior, which had control over the police. At one point, every CD plant in the country was sealed, and for one month, no CDs were made. The plants were relicensed with a twenty-four-hour police guard.

"If the Bulgarian plants weren't financed by Russian organized crime, they were certainly the main customers, directly or indirectly," says Edwards. "Significant quantities of product were going into Russia from Bulgaria. With the music situation in Bulgaria under control, the IFPI began to concentrate on Russia, where we believed that plants had been set up in the Ukraine and Moldavia. The IFPI is also concentrating on building up the legitimate market in Russia. The legitimate music market has quadrupled between 1996 and 1998."

Many expect Russia to become the top music pirate in the twenty-first century. With an estimated rate of music piracy of 70 percent in 1998, Russia became the largest pirate market in the world, accounting for an estimated loss of $350 million. The industry's monitoring of movements of CD production equipment, raw materials, and criminal networks indicated that Russia and the Commonwealth of the Independent States (CIS) were the targets for CD pirates who previously had been operating in other parts of Eastern Europe and the Far East. Russia's first official destruction of pirate CDs took place in early 1998, following the conclusion of a major criminal case conducted by the Ministry of the Interior. A total of 300,000 pirate CDs were confiscated, and 8,724 were eventually destroyed. This seizure was followed by a visit by the IFPI's European Executive Committee, which visited Moscow in April 1998 to raise the recording industry's concerns that Russia and the CIS may become the next world center of pirate CD production unless enforcement is stepped up.

NOTES

1. Barbara Ross and Corky S. Siemaszko, "100-a-Week Video Pirate Ring Busted," *New York Daily News*, June 25, 1996, p. 3.

2. David B. Halbfinger, "Stalking the Video Pirates," *New York Times*, Metro Section, March 10, 1998, p. B1.

3. "A Scourge of Video Pirates," *Newsweek*, July 27, 1987, pp. 40–41.

4. David Bollier, "Video Dragnet," *Video*, March 1988, p. 51.

5. Bernard Weinraub, "Movie History Emerges from a Basement," *New York Times*, p. A1.

6. David Bollier, "At War with the Pirates," *Channels*, March 1987, p. 31.

7. Audrey Farolino, "Fake Dinos Hit Street," *New York Post*, June 22, 1993, p. 29.

8. Aljean Harmetz, "Film Industry Escalates War against Pirates," *New York Times*, June 23, 1986.

9. Faye Rice, "How Copycats Steal Billions," *Fortune*, April 22, 1991, p. 162.

10. "Video-on-demand Deal," *USA Today*, July 12, 1994.

11. Ken Foley, "Cable TV's Infamous Bullet," *Radio-Electronics*, January 1992, p. 33.

12. "Record $7 Million Judgment Made in Counterfeit Case," *Billboard*, April 20, 1996, p. 8.

13. "If You Can't Beat 'Em . . . ," *Time*, July 8, 1991, p. 44.

14. "Free as a Beatle," *Time*, December 4, 1995, p. 80.

15. "Collins Cuts Off a Bootleg" (Reuters), *New York Post*, October 21, 1993, p. 37.

16. Michael Konik, "Hot Tracks," *Crimebeat*, November 1991, p. 47.

8

The Pill Pirates

In April 1995, a major epidemic of meningitis struck the country of Niger. A drought added to the woes of this country of 8.4 million people. Niger authorities requested international assistance, after an estimated 2,500 had died and 26,700 people became sick. International aid delivered nearly five and one-half million doses of vaccine. Pharmacists Without Borders (Pharmaciens sans Frontières), a French-based relief organization, undertook a large-scale vaccination campaign.

To assist in the crisis, the government of Nigeria offered 68,000 doses of vaccine. The vaccines, which were allegedly manufactured by Rhone-Poulenc affiliate Pasteur Merieux and SmithKline Beecham, were offered with great publicity by the regime of General Sani Abacha, the unofficial president of Nigeria, in an effort to bolster the country's dismal human-rights image. Unfortunately, the vaccines that Nigeria donated were counterfeit. An additional 3,000 people died because of the counterfeit vaccine, sparking an international incident.

"The counterfeit drugs were illegally manufactured by someone with a high technological and professional competence," said Dennis Fontaine of ReMeD (Réseau Médicaments & Développement), a French relief agency. "The individual or group responsible for the deed has never been identified."

Pasteur Merieux alerted the French authorities and filed a formal complaint. The Nigerian government formally denied the French charges of having supplied copies of the original vaccine to Niger. Judge Courroye of Lyon, France, who was handling the case, launched an inquiry concerning the counterfeits through Interpol.[1] The counterfeit vaccines were rumored to have come from Spain, but discerning a motive for the outrageous act was difficult, since the vaccines were donated.

The Niger incident brought international attention to the painful, but largely ignored problem of counterfeit pharmaceuticals. Much of the trade involves the Third World countries or industrialized countries where the central government has become unstable—countries like Russia, since the demise of the Soviet Union, and South Africa.

Counterfeit and substandard pharmaceuticals represent a markedly different problem from that involving the counterfeiting of designer clothing, recorded music, and computer programs, which are products of affluence. For many people in Africa and other Third World countries, there are no drugstores or hospitals. The only doctors are itinerant vendors or other semiprofessionals with limited medical background, who travel by foot or bicycle to the villages. In Morocco and Algiers, the vendors sell drugs and medications that are displayed on blankets in the crowded marketplaces; or they travel by bicycle from village to village, where they give medical consultations and sell drugs. In Nigeria, the vendors travel from village to village on foot. Their medicine bag is a bowl balanced atop their head; inside the bowl are cough syrups, vitamins, and medications. The situation is desperate in parts of war-torn Africa, where peddlers fear to travel and international relief brings medical supplies to the civilians at great risk.

Health authorities recognize many types of irregularities concerning the drugs that are sold in the marketplace. *Misbranded and unbranded drugs* are drugs that contain false or misleading labeling. *Contaminated drugs* are drugs that may contain impurities or traces of another drug. *Substitutes* are drugs that are different than the drugs being prescribed. *Adulterated drugs* are drugs that may include a substance that is not part of the chemical compound. *Pirated compounds* use stolen formulas or trade secrets or chemical compositions protected by patent. *Imitations* are drugs that are manufactured to resemble another company's product, and differ from *counterfeit drugs*, which are exact copies of a legitimate product, including brand name. *Counterfeit drugs* are always considered to be misbranded, and their compounds may be a pirated composition, or have compounds that are adulterated or contaminated.

The pharmaceutical drugs that are used in Africa and other Third World countries vary considerably in effectiveness, come from many sources, and may fit any of the categories previously listed. The problem varies from country to country. In some countries, the situation is caused by a lack of pharmaceuticals, but in other countries, an overabundance is the cause. Usually poor economic conditions play a role, but rich countries like Nigeria and South Africa are havens for counterfeit drugs. Poor storage conditions and distribution procedures, as well as poorly trained doctors and technicians, exacerbate the situation.

Although the problem varies from country to country, the absence of a strong regulatory authority such as the Food and Drug Administration (FDA) or a strong health ministry is almost always the primary reason for the poor quality of drugs found in many Third World countries.

The United States has the strongest regulatory agency in the industrialized world. Every person in the United States ultimately comes under the regulatory power of the FDA, which is authorized to regulate food, cigarettes, medical devices, medicines, drugs, and cosmetics. The FDA conducts inspections and has the authority to seize improperly manufactured medicines, cosmetics, and foods. The FDA also approves drugs for use in the marketplace and inspects foreign drug supplies that are used in the manufacturing process.

"Drug regulatory authorities have been established in all industrialized countries," says Dr. Martin ten Ham, chief of the drug safety unit for the World Health Organization (WHO). "Their principal duty is to safeguard the consumer from medicinal products or drugs that have an unacceptable profile of safety and efficacy. In situations where improper manufacturing has occurred, the diminished bioavailability of the active ingredients may result in a failure of the therapy. Depending on the disease and the patient, death can result."

The WHO drug safety unit is responsible for maintaining a worldwide program on drug safety monitoring, and works with the appropriate governmental agency, usually a health ministry or national center, in some fifty countries. The unit completed a three-year project on counterfeit medicines in 1997, and has been collecting information on cases of counterfeit drugs and adverse drug reactions, as reported in the published literature and as the result of questionnaires sent to drug regulatory agencies in the industrialized nations. To date, the drug safety unit has cataloged almost two million reports of adverse drug reactions.

According to ten Ham, every time a new drug is introduced its scientific background is scrutinized, and after a detailed evaluation a judgment is rendered as to the drug's safety. By definition, a fake drug has not gone through such a process of review by the governmental drug regulatory authorities and consequently there is no guarantee that the drug meets the standard of quality. Drugs of unsatisfactory quality pose a potential health risk of grave consequences.

The situation found in many Third World countries today—where there are few trained doctors and medicines are of spurious origin—was the normal situation throughout the world until the beginning of the twentieth century. Many remedies were home, folk, or traditional remedies invented by trial and error, and passed down by word of mouth. Many of these traditional remedies became the foundation for modern medicine and are used today. For example, the Incas used cinchona bark, which contains quinine, to reduce fever. On the other hand, many medical practices were harmful. Bleeding was a common medical treatment. Bleeding was supposed to release the foul elements inside the body. In fact it did little good, and an unknown number of patients died needlessly. One victim of bleeding was George Washington, the first president of the United States, who is believed to have died as a result of the treatment.

Counterfeit ointments and salves developed at nearly the same time that mankind began to use home remedies to relieve pain and illness. The Greek term *Pharmakon* means both medicine and poison. Frankincense and myrrh, widely used as ointments in biblical times, were imitated. Nero's surgeon Dioscorides wrote *De Materia Medica* to thwart peddlers of spurious drugs. Illustrated herbals were introduced in the Middle Ages primarily to help physicians and patients differentiate between plants with proven medicinal value and look-alike species of no worth.

From biblical times until modern times, alcohol was a common cure. Wine was a common medicinal; it was used as an anesthetic and a disinfectant, and also as a solvent and a coolant. Many tonics sold during the Middle Ages up until the time of the U.S. Civil War contained alcohol as the main active ingredient, although it was not often labeled as such. During the Civil War, the drug of choice for wounded soldiers was whiskey. Often, the opium, chloroform, and paregoric that were in the surgeon's field kits were adulterated and of little practical use.

The use of patented medicines arose in England during the 1600s. The inventor of a medicine could patent it as a useful invention. A medicine that was patented seemingly had more authenticity than other home remedies. Yet, in fact, a patented medicine meant only that its ingredients were registered with the government.

Many reputable English drug manufacturers chose not to patent their medicines and preferred to keep their ingredients secret. This was a useful way of foiling imitators and counterfeiters, who could manufacture the drug themselves once they had access to the ingredients. The counterfeiter might be the local pharmacist. At the time of the Revolutionary War, it was a common practice for someone who had purchased a bottle of a popular remedy to bring the bottle back to the pharmacist for a refill. The pharmacist, in turn, often refilled the bottle by mixing up a batch from what knowledge he possessed of the remedy. This practice of refilling the drug continues to this day, only the dispensing of drugs and refill are done under prescription in the industrialized countries.

Until modern times, patented and unpatented medicines were sold side-by-side on the shelf in most apothecaries. Patents date back to the Middle Ages in Europe. In England, patents were a form of inventor's privilege, protected by the Crown. The British Statute of Monopolies, passed in 1623, granted an inventor a time-limited monopoly for use of his invention. In France, patent rights were first recognized by law on January 7, 1791. Under a reform law passed on July 5, 1844 on France, patents were granted for a duration of twenty years.

The discovery of synthetic drugs and antibiotics ushered in an era of unprecedented growth in the pharmaceutical industry. The modern counterfeit market is the result of growing competition among the international drug suppliers to supply the world market. The globalization of the economy has allowed small drug manufacturers in countries like Southeast Asia to compete against the more established drug companies for trade in countries such as Africa and South America. Pill pirates are able to undercut the established companies, which are hampered by the growing research costs to develop the drugs. High birth rates and war conditions have increased the demand for cut-rate drugs.

Although largely confined to the developing countries, drug counterfeiting occurs in the industrialized countries as well. In March 1987 the Prescription Drug Marketing Act was signed into law in the United States. The 1987 Prescription Drug Marketing Act bans the reimportation of drugs produced in the United States by anyone other than the person or company who manufactured the drug. The law is designed to disrupt illicit drug manufacturing chains. In a typical chain a manufacturer will produce a compound in one country and ship it to another party in another country, where the drug will be adulterated, packaged, and shipped back to another party or parties in another country for distribution. The Act was passed after widespread counterfeiting of Ovulen-21 birth control pills.

In November 1984, G. D. Searle and Company of Skokie, Illinois initiated a recall of two suspected drug lots of its popular Ovulen-21 birth control pills.[2] The recall, which cost over a million dollars, came after several reports concerning irregularities. A pharmacist in Racine, Wisconsin noticed that the brand name was misspelled. Other complaints said that the pills caused breakthrough bleeding. The FDA was alerted and an investigation was undertaken. In 1985 and 1986 Interpol and the U.S. Customs Service assisted in the investigation, which had extended to foreign countries. Eventually, two conspiracies were uncovered. One began in 1981 and involved imported drugs from Spain. The second began in 1984 and involved drugs smuggled from Guatemala. A total of 1.5 million Ovulen-21 tablets were seized. In February 1987 six defendants were charged in a twenty-nine-count indictment in the U.S. District Court for the Southern District of Florida; two of the defendants received twenty-four-year prison sentences. A seventh defendant was eventually charged and sentenced to eleven years in prison.

The largely unregulated market found in many developing countries is complicated in that there are three sources of drugs. First, there is the private sector, which operates much like it does in any industrialized country, and includes private hospitals and organized health care. Second, there is the public sector, which includes public health centers and community doctors. Finally, there are the street peddlers, who make up the illicit market. The illicit market sells drugs of unknown origin; in many countries, it is the largest branch of the pharmaceutical trade.

The illicit drug market exists in the industrialized countries as well, although the trade usually involves contraband and narcotics. According to a World Drug Report conducted by the United Nations in 1997, the international business of illicit drugs generates an estimated $400 billion a year in revenues.[3] An estimated thirteen million people use cocaine; eight million people use heroin; and thirty million use amphetamine-type stimulants. Much of the illicit drugs that are sold in the industrialized nations are sold through street peddlers and involve distribution chains stretching around the globe and in underground labs.

In the developing countries, the illicit street peddlers obtain the drugs from many sources and networks. The illicit drug trade is an easy start-up business. The development of the drug is where most of the cost is involved, including animal and human testing. After approval and the granting of a patent, the active ingredients are easy to acquire, and the manufacturing process, including pill presses, is inexpensive. Demand is strong, because health care is a necessity.

"Most people think that counterfeit drugs will kill you, but this is rarely the case," says Paul Carratu, managing director of Carratu International. "The counterfeiters are infringing on someone's patent, and in most cases are producing a pirated compound that closely resembles the legitimate in chemical composition."

With headquarters in London, Carratu International is an international private investigation agency that specializes in intellectual property, especially products protected by patent: perfumes and pharmaceuticals. In November 1993, Carratu International agents raided the largest perfume counterfeiting operation in history and seized 32 million pounds (16,000 tons) of stock. The operation was based in England and funded by the Genovese crime family from the United States. The ingredients and packaging came from eleven different countries. The packaging was from Croatia; bottle caps from Korea; essence from France; bottles from Holland.

Carratu International was founded in 1963 and has been investigating counterfeit pharmaceuticals for over three decades. Carratu International performs investigations for fifteen of the top twenty pharmaceutical firms, and maintains a private database of the investigations undertaken over the years.

According to Carratu, there are three areas in which the counterfeiters can operate. First, there is the manufacture of the active ingredient, which is protected by patent. Second, there is the formulation into tablet form, which is protected by patent. And third, there is the finished product, which is protected by patent and trademark.

Carratu International tries to intervene at the first level, the manufacturing level. This is no easy task, because manufacturers operate clandestinely and sell only to select drug wholesalers and distributors. Over the decades, Carratu International has established cover companies around the world that pose as legitimate drug distributors and buyers. The dummy companies receive samples daily, and all are analyzed. When irregularities are discovered, Carratu International notifies its client. If the client provides funding, an investigation will be initiated.

Carratu International is unique in the investigation field. Most agencies receive their assignments from the client; Carratu initiates its own investigations by monitoring the pharmaceutical products worldwide, an expensive undertaking that is funded entirely by the agency. Over 80 percent of Carratu investigations occur outside of London, where the main office is located. Most pharmaceutical investigations involve pirated compounds.

Usually, the counterfeiters will offer to sell to one of Carratu's dummy companies. In some situations, Carratu agents will infiltrate the counterfeiter's organization by becoming employees or gang members. The work is extremely dangerous and sometimes involves undercover work that can last for years. Carratu investigators undergo years of training before they enter the field.

Not surprisingly, many counterfeiters operate in countries where there is weak patent legislation. In such situations, obtaining evidence is almost useless, because there are no intellectual property laws to prosecute the crime. In such situations, Carratu agents have the manufacturer ship a large consignment to a country where the intellectual property laws are strong and the product can be seized. The seizure usually has the intended effect: either the manufacturer is forced into bankruptcy, or is hit hard enough to permanently disrupt the organization.

European drug imports are the main source of pharmaceuticals for many developing countries, especially in Africa and the Soviet Union. Drug legislation in the European Union (EU) requires pharmaceutical exporters to obtain a license and participate in the WHO Certification Program on the Quality of Pharmaceutical Products Moving in International Commerce, which requires that all bans, suspensions, and withdrawals relating to a drug at the national level have to be declared to the WHO, which, in turn, will distribute the information. The EU has also compiled a list of drugs banned in Europe. Many countries have enacted additional export restrictions applying to drugs without a license and drugs withdrawn from the market for public health reasons.

Although the EU drug legislation is explicit, studies have shown that it is sometimes ignored. In a study conducted in October 1996, the efficacy of drug export legislation in seventeen European countries and the regulatory aspects controlling the pharmaceutical markets were evaluated. The study was entitled "All We Need Is Transparency" (the trade in medicinal drugs between Europe and the developing countries). It was prepared by ReMeD, in coordination with Wemos, a Dutch nonprofit organization working for a better world health situation, and PIMED (Pour une Information Médicale Ethique et le Développement), a French association that aims to provide useful information on drugs and therapeutics.

The loopholes found in the October 1996 study were divided into deficiencies involving manufacturing quality, therapeutic quality, and quality of product information. Problems involving manufacturing quality included the absence of WHO-type certificates, which was found in all countries except Belgium and the Netherlands, and insufficiently controlled free trade zones, which was found in Germany. Problems involving therapeutic quality included no monitoring of the quality, safety, and efficacy of unlicensed products in the exporting country; this problem was found in eleven European countries. Problems of therapeutic quality also included the absence of export restrictions on drugs withdrawn from the market, a problem found in ten European countries. Problems involving quality of product information uncovered deficiencies in regard to the labeling language, a problem found in all countries except Finland.

According to many experts, stronger enforcement of the drug legislation would likely be insufficient to stop the problem of counterfeit and spurious drugs. "You only need a license when you sell the formulated product," Paul Carratu explained, adding that most counterfeiters easily circumvent the import/export regulations by shipping the raw ingredients.

Cut-rate suppliers in countries such as India and China, where patent legislation is weak, have made inroads into the lucrative pharmaceutical market. One source of concern is the generic market. After a patent has expired, the formula falls into the public domain and any country can manufacture the drug. In the United States 70 to 80 percent of the ingredients in the generic market and about 60 percent of brand-name drug ingredients come from overseas. Despite vigorous inspection by the FDA, foreign chemical ingredients of unsatisfactory condition do get into the marketplace. In the late 1980s, at least fifteen Americans had epileptic seizures and two died after taking a generic product intended to prevent seizures. The FDA traced the problem to a Colorado company that had gone out of business, and discovered that the company had purchased subpotent ingredients from Italy.

ReMeD is located in Paris, France and has done numerous studies on the quality of drugs and the rational use of drugs for the French Ministry of Cooperation and for the WHO. ReMeD has no field programs, but provides support for other organizations, and works with governmental organizations and nongovernmental organizations such as Pharmacists without Borders.

Carrine Bruneton of ReMeD has performed numerous studies involving drug samples purchased from the street vendors throughout francophile Africa. ReMeD has also performed many studies of counterfeit drugs, drugs of spurious origin, and contraband for sale in the developing countries. ReMeD has documented the widespread use of counterfeit drugs in over fifty articles and studies and videotape cassette studies. Because the results are often acquired at random and anonymously, Bruneton warns that drawing a scientifically accurate conclusion as to the actual percentage of counterfeit and spurious drugs in the market of most countries is not possible.

In one study prepared for WHO, ReMeD evaluated the quality assurance system in several states in Africa. The study involved an assessment of the quality of 519 samples coming from Cameroon, Madagascar, and Chad. The study was carried out in the three pharmaceutical sectors (private, public, and illicit). The study showed that the overall quality of the drugs was poor; and that substandard drugs were to be found in all three sectors, private, public, and illicit. The study's conclusion suggests that the drugs sold on the street by peddlers are of the same poor quality as the drugs administered in the private hospitals. Other studies involving the overall drug quality in the developing countries have drawn the same conclusion: that the overall drug quality at the private, public, and illicit sectors is poor.

A study involving quality assurance was conducted by WHO in 1995 in Vietnam and Myanmar (formerly Burma). Out of 212 samples tested in Myanmar, only a handful were direct counterfeits, but the overall quality of drugs at all levels of distribution was found to be unsatisfactory (thirty-four were found to be substandard, but genuine; six were found to be mislabeled, but passed laboratory testing; one sample contained the wrong ingredients).

In a large, comprehensive study completed by ReMeD in 1997, the overall drug quality in Cambodia was found to be poor.[4] Like most developing countries, there are three sources for medicines in Cambodia. One is the public center, which includes the Central Medical Store, a central location for the storage and distribution of drugs that is managed by the Minister of Health. The second is the private sector, which is composed of 600 private pharmacies, of which only 150 are recognized and licensed by the government. The third is the illicit sector, which consists almost entirely of drugs of unknown origin.

ReMeD's 1997 study on the quality of drugs in Cambodia was undertaken in coordination with Pharmacists without Borders and the French

Ministry of Cooperation. Drug samples were taken anonymously throughout the entire country and from all three sectors. For each sample gathered, besides general information, the conditions of storage, state of location, and the sale price were noted and taken into account. Particular attention was paid to those regions where contraband medicines are sold, notably on the frontiers with Vietnam and Thailand.

The results of the Cambodia study demonstrated that overall the medications were of poor quality in all three of the pharmaceutical sectors. The study confirmed the need to improve the overall procedure to permit circulation of good-quality medicines in the pharmaceutical market. The study also noted that Cambodia had recently opened up its first national laboratory of quality control, with modern equipment and research facilities.

The results of ReMeD's studies in Africa and Cambodia, along with WHO's results in Asia, were presented at the International Workshop on Counterfeit Drugs, which was sponsored by WHO and held in Geneva in November 1997. The implications of these studies are grave. In many developing countries, rich and poor alike have no access to safe medications. There is little difference between the drugs sold in the street and the drugs administered in the private hospitals.

"Cost is the driving factor for the counterfeit market," says Paul Carratu. "At the private and public level in many developing countries, you find legitimate products that are coming to the end of their life span. Drugs of this kind are cheaper. Many countries are happy to get drugs and see no need to set up a national health ministry that would impede the flow."

For someone who is ill, a drug of whatever quality is seemingly better than no drug at all. The market in counterfeit and substandard pharmaceuticals is inestimable. The harm that is done is equally inestimable. In many developing countries, death rates are calculated on reported deaths and examinations in the hospitals, and do not take into account persons who pass away and are buried or cremated in the rural areas. The multinational pharmaceutical companies, while not engaged in large-scale research into the development of new drugs for the developing countries, assist by way of drug donations to the developing countries and by keeping track of the underground trade. In the mid-1990s, twenty of the largest drug companies banded together to form the Pharmaceutical Security Institute (PSI), which tracks the trade in counterfeit and substandard drugs.

THE FOOD AND DRUG ADMINISTRATION (FDA)

The Revolutionary War ended England's dominance in the drug trade in the United States and ushered in a wave of imitations and counterfeits.

Prior to the Revolution, nearly all of the doctors in the Colonies were trained in Europe. In their place, came a generation of healers, who traveled from town to town by wagon hawking elixirs and "snake oil."

Although more than 100 bills had been proposed between 1879 and 1906 concerning the enactment of food and drug laws to protect the public's health, most died on the House or Senate floor, due in large part to industry lobbying. Publication of *The Jungle* in 1906 exposed a condition so egregious that public outrage forced Congress into action.

Unsafe conditions in the meatpacking industry, fictionalized in the book *The Jungle*, led to the founding of the FDA. Written by Upton Sinclair, *The Jungle* was published in 1906 by Doubleday, Page & Company and is a fictional account of the food-processing business in Chicago.

The depictions of rotten meat, rats, and filthy conditions in *The Jungle* caused a public uproar. The publishers anticipated such a reaction. In concern over possible litigation, an attorney was dispatched to view firsthand the conditions in the meat houses. The attorney reported that the conditions were as bad as Sinclair had characterized, and subsequently wrote an article based on the inspection that was published in *The World's Work*, a Doubleday, Page & Company publication. Prior to publication, galley proofs of the book were sent to President Theodore Roosevelt. Very much taken with the work, President Roosevelt appointed a commission to make a thorough investigation of the meatpackinghouses. The commission's findings would greatly assist in the passage of the Food and Drugs Act and a Meat Inspection Act, which was passed in June 1906.

The Bureau of Chemistry, located in the Department of Agriculture, was charged with administration of the 1906 Act. In 1927, a separate law-enforcement agency was established that in 1931 would be renamed the Food and Drug Administration. An early counterfeiting case was *Edwards v. United States*, 249 F. 686 (1918) in which the defendant was selling a homemade version of aspirin, but using the trademark "Bayer Aspirin." Due to Word War I, there was a shortage of medicines. The defendant argued, unsuccessfully, that his version was as good as the manufactured brand.

The FDA's power to regulate food and drugs was greatly expanded by passage of the Federal Food, Drug, and Cosmetic (FD&C) Act of 1938. Under the 1938 Act, the FDA was given the authority to require safety clearance on new drugs before distribution, to promulgate standards of identity for food containers, and to prohibit the addition of poisonous or harmful substances to foods.

The FD&C Act was passed after a disturbing incident. In 1937, the remarkable use of sulfanilamide as an antibacterial was discovered. A Tennessee-based firm decided to put the antibacterial on the market in liquid form, dissolved in diethylene glycol. The drug was called Elixir

Sulfanilamide. Unfortunately, the solvent, diethylene glycol, sometimes known as antifreeze, destroys the kidneys, and led to the death of more than a hundred persons, most of them children. The chemist who had devised the formula committed suicide.

Under the 1938 FD&C Act, the FDA was also given the authority to impose court injunctions, in addition to its power to impose seizure and prosecution. On July 1, 1940, the FDA was transferred from the Department of Agriculture to the Federal Security Agency (FSA). The FSA, in turn, became the U.S. Department of Health, Education and Welfare (HEW) on April 11, 1953.

Cases of actual drug counterfeiting in the United States are rare, although of serious concern. In 1955, the Salk polio vaccine was counterfeited. Although a few batches were found in the United States, much of the vaccine was unloaded abroad. In 1978, the FDA recalled more than 350 intra-aortic pumps, used to keep the heart beating during open-heart surgery. Investigations determined that a counterfeit $8 part in the $20,000 pump might have caused the pump to stall.[5] In 1995, a counterfeit-labeled version of the popular infant formula Similac was illegally distributed to a grocery store in Northern California.[6] The FDA issued an alert to consumers in fifteen states, after the counterfeit Similac was traced back to an operation in Kentucky.

In 1990, the FDA apprehended Javid Naghdi, the greatest pill pirate in history. When he was apprehended in London in 1990, Naghdi was selling counterfeits of the popular ulcer remedy Tagamet and Naprosyn, a nonsteroidal, anti-inflammatory drug that is principally used to treat arthritis. In a sensational four-week trial in the U.S. District Court for the Southern District of California, the thirty-year-old Iranian was convicted on nine counts of wire fraud in an attempt to sell counterfeit drugs.

During the trial, Naghdi offered a fantastic defense. He claimed that he was working for the Central Intelligence Agency, and using the drug scam as a cover for his part in the Iran-Contra affair. This was the type of grandiose defense one would expect from a twisted personality. Naghdi's lawyer attempted to subpoena corroborating documents from the Central Intelligence Agency (CIA), the Defense Intelligence Agency, and the National Security Administration. The lawyer also attempted to subpoena fifty-five high-ranking government officials, including Oliver North, to testify.

Judge Judith N. Keep quashed the subpoenas. Judge Keep described Naghdi as "a master of innuendo—glib, quick, and slippery."[7] The judge pointed out that Naghdi had provided no relevant information to support his claim that any of the witnesses were involved in a government conspiracy.

Naghdi was sentenced to fourteen years. The sentence was added onto a five-year sentence handed down in the Central District of California for running a pill counterfeiting operation. Naghdi had pleaded guilty in June 1987 in the Central District of California to charges of conspiracy in the manufacture and sale of Naprosyn and of trafficking in goods bearing counterfeit trademarks.

A trained chemist, Naghdi had easily obtained pill-pressing equipment and other supplies. He produced a batch of Naprosyn that was nearly indistinguishable from the real product. Neither FDA investigators nor representatives from Syntex, the legitimate manufacturer, could distinguish the counterfeit from the genuine by visual comparison. The counterfeit looked identical to the legitimate product, even down to the bar code that pharmacists scan electronically to verify a drug's authenticity. Only in a laboratory setting could the counterfeit, which contained mainly aspirin, be identified.

Naghdi was trying to pass off the drugs as overstock. He was offering the drugs at a discount over the retail price as a sales inducement. Fortunately, he was apprehended before he could unload the bulk of his illegal merchandise.

After pleading guilty, Naghdi was sentenced to five years. He jumped bail, and disappeared. Most fugitives on the run lie low—but not Naghdi. Within months, he was back in business.

In October 1987 Naghdi began sending American drug wholesalers and commodities brokers offers to sell eight million bottles of two drugs manufactured by SmithKline Beecham—Tagamet and Anspor, an antibiotic used to treat infections, and Naprosyn. The asking price was $485 million.

To complete the ruse of legitimacy, Naghdi used fraudulent shipping documents, a forged financial statement, a phony insurance policy, and numerous forged documents on fake SmithKline and Syntex letterhead. Naghdi told prospective buyers that he had obtained the drugs from Syntex and SmithKline and was storing them in a custom bonded warehouse in Tampico, Mexico.

One of the independent brokers whom Naghdi had approached was suspicious about the offer, and contacted SmithKline. SmithKline contacted the FDA. Together, SmithKline and the FDA quickly concluded that the offer was fraudulent and might consist of counterfeit drugs.

The FDA began to investigate and soon realized that the offerer was Javid Naghdi—the same Naghdi who had jumped bail three months earlier!

The FDA joined forces with the Justice Department, U.S. Customs Service, and eventually Scotland Yard to apprehend Naghdi, who had fled to London. The goal of the operation was to entrap and prosecute Naghdi and put him away for as long as possible.

Scotland Yard assisted in setting up a deal that would nab Naghdi. The deal took place on August 12, 1988 in the Dorchester Hotel in London. Naghdi met with Daniel Supnick, a U.S. Customs Service agent who was posing as a legitimate drug supplier.

No one expected Naghdi to be easily fooled. Supnick had been well coached by the FDA to complete his ruse as a legitimate drug supplier. Supnick's cover was that he was interested in purchasing a million 100-tablet bottles of Tagamet for $27 million. The deal was concluded in Naghdi's hotel room. Scotland Yard was waiting outside and arrested Naghdi as soon as he left the room. He was extradited to the United States to stand trial and was eventually convicted.

THE DRUG APPROVAL PROCESS

An organization of this size and power has its critics and its scandals. In 1995, the Republican-led Congress singled out the FDA for reform, as part of the Party's overall strategy of challenging unnecessary governmental regulation.[8] One area of controversy was the drug approval process. Although the Republicans ultimately left the FDA unchanged, the drug approval process in the United States has often been criticized for raising the research and development costs of new drugs, and for unduly preventing many valuable drugs from coming onto the marketplace. Mifepristone (better known as RU-486), the so-called French abortion pill, was banned from the United States, until public outcry virtually forced a reevaluation of the pill's merits. In 1996, the FDA declared mifepristone to be safe and effective, but required additional information on the product's manufacture and labeling before considering final approval.[9]

The 1962 Kefauver-Harris amendments to the 1938 FD&C Act raised the standard for approval of new drugs. The Kefauver-Harris amendments came in the wake of the Thalidomide tragedy. Thalidomide, a sedative, was introduced in 1958 by a German firm. With the exception of France and the United States, Thalidomide was widely accepted. A year after its introduction, incidents of phocomelia, a deformity marked by seal-like flippers in place of arms and legs, were reported in newborn infants. Use of Thalidomide by pregnant mothers was eventually found to be the cause. Eventually, 10,000 phocomelia-deformed babies were born in twenty different countries. In 1998, the FDA allowed Thalidomide into the market.

Since passage of the 1962 Kefauver-Harris amendments, other regulations and regulatory guidelines have added to the cost and length of time involved in the drug development process. Most drugs on the market today undergo arduous testing and approval by the regulatory authorities before being allowed on the market. As a result, the drug discovery and development process is a long, complex, and expensive venture. In the United States, the average pharmaceutical agent requires fifteen years of research and development, costs more than $350 million to bring to market, and has a one in 10,000 chance from the time of discovery to receive FDA approval.

Companies that are members of the Pharmaceutical Research and Manufacturers of America (PhRMA) spend 20 percent of their revenues in research and development as compared to 4 percent for the U.S. industry overall.

The major areas of the drug approval process are drug discovery and compound synthesis, preclinical laboratory and animal testing, three phases of clinical trials in humans, and FDA dossier review. For compounds that meet the safety and clinical standards in preclinical testing, a company files an Investigational New Drug (IND) application with the FDA; an IND becomes effective if the FDA does not disapprove of it within thirty days, after which it becomes an approved new drug application (NDA).

The approval process has led to what is known as the drug lag. A drug that is introduced in one country may not be introduced in another country for many years. This problem persists in all industrialized countries, because the drug approval process differs from one country to another. There is no easy way to weigh the negative effect of a regulatory provision that delays the approval of a good drug against the positive effect of a provision that delays or prevents the approval of a bad drug. Thalidomide is a good example. Its approval was held up in the United States due to suspicions over its quick approval in Europe. Dr. Frances O. Kelsey, the FDA drug investigator who kept Thalidomide off the shelves in the United States, was eventually given a medal by President John F. Kennedy.[10]

In an attempt to circumvent the lengthy drug approval process, companies have been accused of falsifying evidence, or resorting to bribes.

In 1988, the FDA investigated an alleged cover-up by Hoffmann-La Roche concerning the effects of its Versed, a liquid anesthetic that may have caused forty deaths.[11] A congressional subcommittee investigated evidence that tied forty deaths to breathing and heart problems associated with concentrated dosages of the drug.

In 1991, Britain banned sales of Upjohn's sleeping pill Halcion amid charges that the company had falsified evidence that would have linked the sleeping pill with paranoia and agitation. Upjohn was alleged to have omitted data from a 1972 summary of studies. Halcion was approved in the United States in 1982. The FDA set up a task force in May 1994 to investigate Upjohn, but the task force was disbanded in 1996 and concluded that Halcion is a safe and effective treatment for insomnia when prescribed and taken as directed in the current labeling.[12]

The drug industry was rocked by scandals involving the FDA's generic approval process in the late 1980s. After a patent on a drug has expired, another company may produce and market a generic version using the abbreviated new drug application (ANDA) route. The ANDA route usually does not involve animal or human trials, and is far less expensive than obtaining an NDA. For that reason, once the patent has expired on a popular drug, the competition to market a generic product is great.

In 1987, Mylan Laboratories in Pittsburgh hired private investigators to ascertain whatever evidence they could find about possible corruption within the FDA's Generic Division. Ray McKnight, who later testified before the Dingell Committee on the Generic Drug Approval Process, had felt for several years that his company was being unfairly treated by the FDA in respect to obtaining ANDAs for several drugs that the company wanted to market.

By sifting through the garbage of several FDA officials, private investigators came up with evidence of bribery. This evidence was turned over to the House Subcommittee on Oversight and Investigations, chaired by Congressman John Dingell. In May 1989, Dingell, working with the U.S. Attorney in Baltimore, held an executive session on the Generic Drug Approval Process.

The private investigators working for Mylan had sifted through the garbage of Charles Chang, supervisory chemist for the FDA's Branch III, which is one of three chemistry review branches in the division, and discovered that he had accepted gifts, including a round-the-world trip, from American Therapeutics of New York. Shortly after this evidence was presented before the Dingell session, the U.S. Attorney in Baltimore, the judicial district in which the FDA resides, charged Chang with two counts of interstate travel in aid of racketeering. Chang eventually was sentenced to one year in prison, fined $10,000, and ordered to perform 1,000 hours of community service.

In all, five FDA officials would be convicted of perjury and taking bribes to certify new drugs, and eight companies and twenty-seven executives convicted of adulterating drugs, or other testing and manufacturing fraud. The cases were pursued by Gary Jordan, the federal prosecutor who headed the Justice Department's Generic Drugs Task Force. Consumers around the country felt the impact when untold thousands of bottles of drugs were pulled from pharmacy shelves.

Several pharmaceutical companies appeared before the Dingell Committee in connection with fraud involving drug approval. In July 1989 Vitarene Pharmaceuticals, Inc. of Queens, New York appeared before the Committee. Vitarene had won approval for a generic version of Dyazide, a pill used for the control of high blood pressure. To win approval, Vitarene had filled capsules with actual Dyazide and submitted the capsules as generic versions.

A few days later, Par Pharmaceutical Inc. of Rockland County, New York was fined $2.6 million.[13] Quad Pharmaceuticals, a Par subsidiary, was also implicated and eight of its executives were indicted: the president and vice-president of Quad Pharmaceuticals resigned, after pleading guilty to bribing FDA employees.

Bolar Pharmaceuticals was fined $10 million for forging documents to win FDA approval of its generic version of Dyazide. This was the largest fine in FDA history. Bolar had to pull 159 drugs off the market, including its generic version of Thioridazine. Bolar had won approval for a generic version of Thioridazine, which was developed by Sandoz; independent testing later showed that the outer coatings of the Bolar tablets sent to the FDA covered the Sandoz logo. Eight of Bolar's key executives were eventually convicted.

It would take several years before the generic drug industry recovered from the "generic drugs scandal," as it is called. The scandal led to passage of the Generic Drug Enforcement Act of 1992, which was signed into law on May 13, 1992. The Act has five major elements: debarment, civil money penalties, suspension of the right to distribute drugs under ANDAs, temporary denial of ANDA approval, and withdrawal of ANDA approval.[14]

In 1993, the people of Italy were rocked by a similar scandal involving drug companies allegedly paying corrupt officials. Artificially elevating drug prices and drug approval were the charges in Italy. In "Operation Michaelangelo" payments made by pharmaceutical companies to doctors in the Florence area conducting clinical trials of their products were investigated. The allegations were that these payments were made to obtain preferential treatment of their products, and that ethics committee members also took payments for giving favorable opinions on proposed drug trials.[15] The government responded with an austerity drive that included reducing the drug budget, price cuts, product delistings, and extra taxes. Drug sales plummeted. In 1994, Menarini, Italy's leading pharmaceutical group, placed advertisements in the national press that threatened to move its manufacturing activities from Italy to Germany in response to the government's pricing policies.[16] In the general elections of April 1996, the new Prime Minister, Romano Prodi, promised to take a more active hand in the matter.

DRUG COUNTERFEITING IN THE THIRD WORLD

Historically, pharmaceutical inventions have received different intellectual property protection than other inventions.[17] European governments refrained from granting complete monopoly rights to pharmaceutical products on the ground that they serve an important public interest. Under the French patent law of 1844, a patent could be declared void if its holder did not subsequently use it for commercial purposes; such nonexploitation was considered an abuse of the patent holder's monopoly rights. The French law was modified over the years, and in 1968 was modified so that a compulsory license of right could be granted after a period of three years from the issue of the patent. Hence, if the patent owner had not worked his patent during a three-year period, a third party could be granted a compulsory license and could manufacture the drug upon payment of a royalty to the patent holder.

To prevent patentees from abusing their monopoly rights by not exploiting or working a pharmaceutical patent, the patent-law regimes of many countries allowed the relevant patent authorities to grant compulsory licenses of right to third parties. Under Section 41 of the British Patent Act of 1949, the Comptroller of Patents could issue a compulsory license for misuse of the patent; under Section 46, the government could import a patented product from sources other than the patentee.

Under a compulsory licensing arrangement, a manufacturer pays a royalty to the legitimate manufacturer for the use of its patent. The permission of the legitimate manufacturer is not required. As the costs to develop and market drugs have increased, most industrialized countries have done away with compulsory licensing of pharmaceuticals. Canada and New Zealand repealed their compulsory licensing provisions during the 1990s.

Compulsory licensing of patented inventions is not recognized by the United States. After passage of the Omnibus Trade and Competitiveness Act of 1988, which authorized the use of trade sanctions under the Special 301, the Office of the United States Trade Representative (USTR) focused its efforts on having countries recognize that importation of products was sufficient to satisfy the working requirement. The USTR has been successful in China, Thailand, Taiwan, and Korea, all of which amended their patent laws to allow importation of a patented product to fall within the definition of working a patent.[18]

Many developing countries in East Asia and in Latin America had no patent protection for pharmaceutical products until after the 1970s. Developing countries have been reluctant to grant patent rights to pharmaceutical products and other chemical compositions such as pesticides and fertilizers, because granting such rights caused the price to rise two- or threefold. Usually, as the local industries of the developing countries have grown, the importance of protecting useful inventions became apparent. In 1975, Japan granted intellectual property protection for pharmaceutical products and chemical compositions; Malaysia followed Japan's example in 1983, Taiwan followed in 1985.

Although the developing countries in East Asia gradually adopted a stronger legislative agenda in regard to protecting intellectual property, many countries went in the opposite direction. Under the Patents Act of 1970, India did away with product patents for food and medicines. Patents for any other inventions are valid for fourteen years. Acting in the public interest, the government retained the right to cancel or revoke patent licenses already in effect.

India's 1970 Patents Act was passed to end a near monopoly by foreign transnational companies in the pharmaceutical market. The result was that India became a haven to drug piracy.[19] By the end of the twentieth century, India was possibly the world's leading pharmaceutical pirate.

In December 1994 in response to the ratification of GATT, the Indian parliament proposed amendments to the 1970 Patents Act that would have brought India's patent law in line with the Trade Related Aspects of Intellectual Property (TRIPS). Under TRIPS, developing countries that did not provide patent protection for pharmaceutical and agricultural chemicals were given ten years to establish such protection. In the interim, these countries were required to establish a "mailbox" system to receive patent applications and to assign each application a priority date based on the date the application was filed. The "mailbox" provision was covered under Articles 70(8) and 70(9) of TRIPS. The Indian government issued provisional legislation to establish such a mailbox system, but Parliament refused to enact it on a permanent basis and the legislation expired.

In July 1996, the USTR requested World Trade Organization (WTO) dispute consultations with India regarding India's lack of compliance with Articles 70(8) and 70(9) of TRIPS. A panel was established on November 20, 1996. During the panel proceedings, India claimed that it was actually receiving mailbox applications through an unpublished administrative system, and that this system fulfilled India's obligations. The issue was eventually taken before the WTO's Dispute Settlement Body (DSB) and became the first TRIPS case in the WTO. The WTO ruled against India in 1997, and India eventually complied and set up a mailbox system through which companies could register patent applications that would be examined on their filing and priority dates for possible entry into force at the end of the transition period.

The absence of patent protection played a leading role in the development of a market for pirate pharmaceuticals in many countries. During the 1970s and 1980s many multinational drug companies pulled out of Latin America due to the lack of intellectual property controls. Lederle, Searle, and Squibb left Brazil in the 1970s. Eli Lilly, SmithKline, Upjohn, Searle, and Lederle left Argentina. Eli Lilly ended operations in Chile.

Brazil ended patent protection for pharmaceutical products in 1945, and amended its patent laws in 1969 to deny patent protection for pharmaceutical manufacturing processes. Brazil took these actions in an attempt to end what was considered to be multinational control of the domestic pharmaceutical industry. Other Latin American countries followed Brazil's lead.

In 1981, Pfizer had sales of $4 million for its arthritis drug Feldene in

Brazil. Within five years, eight other companies set up business selling Feldene and had taken half the market.[20] In Argentina, a local company launched its own copy of Feldene nearly a month before Pfizer entered the market. Throughout the mid-1980s, copies of Pfizer's Unasyn, an antibiotic, and Difulcan, an antifungal medicine, appeared in the Brazilian and Argentinian market.

"Who is robbing who?" asked the director of Sintofarmia, one of the Brazilian companies that was producing copies of Pfizer's Feldene.[21] According to the director, compulsory licensing is the only way that Brazilian patients can get the best possible buy.

In the early 1980s, FMC, an American company, lost an estimated $15 million in sales in Brazil to a competitor that stole its patent for an insecticide. Although FMC's carbofuran insecticide was covered by patents in Brazil, a domestic company began importing a similar active ingredient from Eastern Europe and began manufacturing and selling the insecticide in Brazil.[22] FMC was unable to enforce its patent in Brazil's courts.

In response to industry complaints, President Reagan ordered a 100 percent tariff on imported Brazilian paper products, consumer electronics, and certain Brazilian-made drugs. Despite an angry response from the President of Brazil, Brazil's congress began considering different versions of an intellectual property bill.

The threat of trade sanctions only aggravated what was becoming an untenable situation in Brazil. Brazil's experiment was backfiring. The domestic pharmaceutical industry that was supposed to develop never did. The lack of a domestic manufacturing sector led to an increased pharmaceutical trade deficit. Instead of developing a strong domestic pharmaceutical industry, Brazil developed a problem involving counterfeit and misbranded pharmaceuticals. The problem was aggravated by a lack of governmental regulation. In 1994, only six of the thirty-five companies with a market share of more than 1 percent were Brazilian national companies.[23]

For many years during the 1970s and 1980s, an estimated 20 percent of all the drugs in Brazil were counterfeit or of spurious origin, according to Professor Antonio Zanini, who was formerly in charge of health surveillance.

Zanini was born in São Paulo and obtained his medical degree from the University of São Paulo, and afterward received postgraduate training in the United States. In 1980, he became the director of health surveillance for the Ministry of Health. Zanini was in charge of all foods, drugs, cosmetics, and hygienic supplies, and he was in charge of all health inspection at Brazil's ports, airports, and borders.

As director of health surveillance, Zanini's duties were similar to those of drug administrations in many countries, with one crucial difference—

the absence of law enforcement. "We had governmental oversight, but only for regulatory affairs, not for law enforcement," Zanini explained.

Zanini found many troubles with the system for inspecting drugs. He found that there was no auditing of the drug inspectors, who have the power of the police and the judge. The drug inspectors were not required to file a report of any incidents; they simply issued a ticket. Hence, there was no official record of any infractions.

Despite their power, the drug inspectors were paid little and were often bribed. Some drug inspectors were involved in the counterfeit drug trade, even acting as unofficial salesmen for the illegal operations. The drug inspectors never informed on one another. Doing so would invite retaliation.

Often overlooked by the drug inspectors was the practice of using a clerk to dispense medicine. By law, a licensed pharmacist was supposed to be present in the pharmacy at all times, but many *dragorias* substituted a clerk to dispense medicine and paid a small sum to a pharmacist to lend his name. In Brazil, there are only a handful of drugs for which one needs a prescription. As in many countries, self-medication is widely practiced. Often, how reputable the *dragoria* is will determine what kind of drugs can be purchased without a prescription.

According to Zanini, the counterfeit market was an invisible business. The counterfeiters controlled just enough of the market, 20 to 40 percent, so that the legitimate industry could not complain. If the legitimate industry complained, drug sales in the region would plummet over fear of purchasing adulterated drugs.

Much of the counterfeiting involved adulterating and misbranding. A typical counterfeit drug did not conform to the ingredients on the label and was often misbranded, or the drug contained substances in addition to the formula. In one instance of misbranding, fake penicillin and tetracycline products were found to contain only a small portion of the labeled amount of the antibiotic. In another instance, psychoactive drugs were deliberately adulterated by the manufacturer in the misguided belief that he was making the drugs more effective.

One of the worst cases of drug counterfeiting occurred in 1981, when a small Brazilian company began manufacturing an ointment for use in treating virus infections of the eye. The ointment, Inter-IF, used interferon, a very expensive ingredient. Suspicious, Zanini had the drug analyzed at the National Institutes of Health (NIH) in the United States. The NIH reported that they could find no interferon in the ointment.

Zanini urged the government to set up a control system that would address some of the problems, but to no avail. Zanini had a staff of 150 men, of whom one-third were trained abroad and had experience in regulatory affairs. After a change of government in the early 1980s, that third of Zanini's force that had experience in regulatory affairs was let go by the government. Further cuts were made after President Fernando Henrique Cardoso assumed power. President Cardoso wanted full power over the Ministry of Health and soon the staff of health surveillance was cut to about thirty persons, an insufficient amount of personnel to tackle the country's drug problems. Zanini himself was eventually let go. The staff of health surveillance would eventually be restored to over 1,000 persons.

In April 1991 a draft bill regarding patent protection was introduced. In May 1993, the Chamber of Deputies, Brazil's lower house of Congress, approved an amended version with a "working" requirement that foreign inventors produce their patented products in Brazil. The bill never made it to the Senate, prompting the USTR to identify Brazil as a Priority Foreign Country. Brazil was removed from the list in June 1994, after the country promised to enact a new law granting patent protection.

On December 15, 1994 Brazil accepted the TRIPS provisions of the GATT. In May 1995 the Senate's Constitution, Justice, and Citizenship Committee significantly amended, then finally approved, the intellectual property bill.[24]

Like many of the developing countries in Asia, Brazil moved toward greater protection of intellectual property as its economy began to grow, halting what had become a downslide in the growth of the legitimate market and the emergence of a counterfeit market for pharmaceuticals. In 1997, Brazil was in an uproar when contraceptives manufactured by Schering AG's Brazilian subsidiary proved to have no active ingredient. Schering had manufactured placebo microvlar pills in January 1998 to test a new packaging machine.[25] The placebos were turned over to another company for distribution, but some of the packages were stolen and illegally sold. Schering was fined $2.5 million by the Brazilian government, and the Brazilian plant was temporarily closed. In response to the scandal, the Health Ministry announced that it intended to increase the number of drug inspectors from the current 1,500 to 10,000.

The situation in Latin American differs from that of Africa. Economic development has transformed most Latin American countries, but Africa remains stagnant. Constant warfare has debilitated many countries such as Sudan, the largest country in Africa. Sudan, which has 28 million people and 600 tribes, has been in a state of constant civil war since the early 1960s. Most of the medicines available are those supplied by international relief. One of the worst counterfeiting cases on record occurred in the country of Kenya, when counterfeit fertilizer was purchased. The counterfeit fertilizer arrived in canisters bearing the trademark of the legitimate U.S. manufacturer. Instead of fertilizer, the canisters contained chalk, and the country's coffee crop was destroyed. In South Africa, sanctions over the country's apartheid system led to increased instability and the pullout of many industries. As the legitimate industry left, a pirate market developed. Almost 75 percent of the over-the-counter medicines were estimated to be counterfeit or substandard at one time. "Today, many countries want to get back into South Africa and are trying to clean up the market," says Paul Carratu. Carratu International has maintained an office in South Africa for many years to monitor the drug situation in the African continent.

One of the largest sources for counterfeit drugs in Africa is Nigeria. Nigeria, with a population of over 88 million people, is the most populous nation in Africa and has long been known as a haven for counterfeit drugs. Nigeria is also one of the wealthiest countries in the world, with large reserves of oil, minerals, and farmland. Decades of military rule have left much of the country in poverty. Corruption is widespread. In June 1998 Ismaila Gwarzo, security adviser to General Sani Abacha, the self-declared dictator of the country, was arrested in connection with the disappearance of $2.45 billion from the Nigerian central bank.[26]

Not only was Nigeria having a problem with counterfeit pharmaceuticals, but it was labeled as a "problem country" in reports submitted to the USTR by the International Intellectual Property Alliance (IIPA) in 1985 and 1988. The piracy rate for motion pictures and sound recordings was 100 percent; and for books, 75 percent. The IIPA estimated losses due to piracy in Nigeria at $131 million in 1984. In 1986, the naira was allowed to float, resulting in a substantial devaluation. This led to diminished losses from product counterfeiting, although the actual rate of piracy remained high until enactment of an improved copyright law in 1988.

In the late 1980s, many African countries banned Nigerian drugs after the health minister declared that more than 70 percent of the medicines circulating in the country were fake.[27] According to the Pharmaceutical Society of Nigeria (PSN), the ban hurt the legitimate Nigerian pharmaceutical industry, which encouraged the counterfeiting industry. The counterfeit drug problem was spiraling out of control, due in part to the falling purchasing power of the naira and runaway inflation. Branded drug preparations and generic drugs were faked or adulterated routinely. Prices for the same drug differed markedly depending on where one shopped.

According to Professor G. E. Osuide, the Director-General for the National Agency for Food and Drug Administration and Control (NAFDAC) in Nigeria, a common form of counterfeiting involved the substitution of a cheaper product for one with a higher sales price. In one case, wheat flour was used as a substitute for antibiotics.

In 1990, over a hundred children died and several were hospitalized in Nigeria following consumption of paracetamol syrup, which was prepared using diethylene glycol instead of propylene glycol. Containers of diethylene glycol, which is used as antifreeze, had been mislabeled by the exporter. The label of a Dutch pharmaceutical company that no longer existed was used, and the mislabeled drugs had been purchased by a Nigerian wholesale pharmacist.

As Nigeria's economic and political situation deteriorated, the counterfeit market began to replace the legitimate market. Much of the counterfeit product was imported from surrounding countries. Product registration was insufficient, and pharmaceuticals coming into the country were not thoroughly analyzed and duly registered before being released for distribution and sale. Nigerian law had insufficient penalties to prevent pharmacists, who were legally the only persons allowed to import drugs, from distributing branded and counterfeit drugs. The Nigerian pharmaceutical industry, which might have been able to play a role in the situation, was unable to do much, largely because the companies acted independently of one another.

In November 1986 a Mediconsult Health Seminar entitled "Fake and Imitation Drugs in a Depressed Economy" was held that dealt with the social and medical aspects of fake and imitation drugs in Nigeria. The seminar was followed by the 1987 annual symposium of the Nigerian Association of Industrial Pharmacists, a powerful group within the parent pharmacy professional body, the PSN. The 1987 symposium topic was "Drug Adulteration—The Nigerian Experience."

In the early 1990s, Nigerian pharmacists estimated that more than a quarter of the nearly 4,000 different medicines in the marketplace were of questionable origin. According to the Health Minister, Olikoye Ransome-Kuti, one lot of antibiotics turned out to be talcum powder.[28]

In June 1993 presidential elections were supposed to change Nigeria from military to civilian rule, but they were annulled and General Sani Abacha assumed military control of the country. Shehu Musa Yaradua, a former general and vice president, sponsored a motion at a constitutional conference in 1994 to force General Abacha to hand over power. It was reversed after his arrest, and in a secret trial, Yaradua was convicted on charges that he plotted a coup, and he was sentenced to death.[29] The death penalty was eventually commuted to life imprisonment. In December 1997, Yaradua died in prison. Yaradua's death came after the Abacha regime nullified elections in March 1996, and security forces arrested or killed opponents, including legislators, and tortured suspects. In its 1996 annual report on human rights, the Clinton administration declared that the human-rights record of the military council headed by General Sani Abacha "remains dismal."[30]

For all its faults, the Abacha regime has addressed some of the country's problems. In November 1993, a new provisional ruling council was installed, and political stability has improved.[31] To combat corruption in government a law was passed mandating that public officers declare their assets. NAFDAC, a government agency fashioned largely after

FDA, regulates pharmaceutical business and is responsible for drug approval and licensing. NAFDAC was established in 1993. During a three-year period ending in 1997, NAFDAC assisted in the seizure of about 1.9 billion naira worth of fake drugs (the dollar exchange rate for the naira is eighty-three to one U.S. dollar). The seizures resulted because of a government crackdown on the problem of counterfeit drugs. Unregistered products were not allowed to be sold, factories were inspected, and samples were analyzed, including imported products. Governmental pressure may well have been the cause for the counterfeit drug donations to Niger that resulted in an estimated 3,000 deaths in 1995, either in an attempt to unload the drugs before they were seized or to embarrass the government.

The initial success of the government in tackling the problem of counterfeit drugs was dealt a setback in 1998, when General Sani Abacha died and the country was sent back into turmoil.

ASSISTANCE FOR THE DEVELOPING COUNTRIES

In a round table discussion held by ReMeD in Paris on October 21, 1997 many of the difficulties involved in addressing the medical needs of the Third World countries were discussed. Diseases like malaria and dysentery, not often encountered in Europe and North America, are serious problems in Africa and other Third World countries. The problem is becoming ever more serious, because strains of these tropical diseases have become resistant to the known drug therapies. More research is needed, but unfortunately, there is little monetary incentive for the drug industry to develop needed medicines.

The development of effective drug therapies is only one problem; the lack of adequate hospital facilities is another problem. In Africa, 80 percent of all children die in the home, largely due to the lack of hospitals and available medical supplies. Fifteen to 40 percent of those children who travel the long distance through the jungle to a hospital arrive too late to be helped.

The problem of improving world health cannot be undertaken by industry or by an industrialized country working in isolation. Several United Nations agencies are involved in addressing the diverse and complicated needs of the world's developing countries. Besides the World Health Organization (WHO), there is the United Nations Conference on Trade and Development (UNCTAD), the United Nations Industrial Development Organization (UNIDO), and the United Nations International Children's Emergency Fund (UNICEF).

Founded in 1948, WHO is an international body, funded by its member states. WHO functions as a secretariat, and is run by a directorate, general director, and assistant director general. WHO replaced a world health organization that was founded after World War I by the League of Nations.

WHO has enacted several programs and guidelines to assist the developing countries. The WHO guidelines for small authorities are for large developing countries that have a small and unsophisticated health ministry. The WHO Certification Program on the Quality of Pharmaceutical Products Moving in International Commerce was developed to assist developing countries that do not have a strong regulatory system in place. Among other requirements, the Certification Program requires the drug exporter to provide a declaration signed by the government of origin that the drugs were manufactured in conformance with good manufacturing practices (GMP) and to provide the country of registration.

At one time, many developing countries were flooded by drugs. The drugs were being aggressively promoted by the multinational drug industry. In countries where there were only a few dollars per head to spend, the vast array of drugs was a burden. To assist the developing countries, the WHO devised the Essential Drug List.

The Essential Drug List was pioneered by Dr. Halfidan Mahler, who was appointed by the director general of the WHO in May 1973. The Essential Drug List was introduced at the WHO/UNICEF International Conference on Primary Health Care held in Alma-Ata in 1978. To assist the health ministries of the developing countries, the WHO identified a selection of approximately 200 drugs that were considered to be "essential," or basic to supply the health needs of a population. The Essential Drug List was bitterly criticized by the established drug industry, but has proven its use in countries like Bangladesh and others.

After the 1995 Niger incident the WHO released new guidelines for drug donations during international emergencies. Unfortunately, many drug companies use the request for aid as an excuse for dumping unwanted drugs. The guidelines came in response to requests from relief organizations, which are sometimes overwhelmed with drug donations. One of the chief problems is that many of the drugs are nearing their expiration date. In 1988, 5,000 tons of drugs were sent to Soviet Armenia after an earthquake; it took six months to sort through the stock, by which time 8 percent had expired. In 1994, the WHO field office in Zagreb, Croatia estimated that 15 percent of the drugs received were unusable and 30 percent were not needed. In 1995, an incinerator had to be built in Bosnia to destroy 340 tons of expired drugs that had been sent. Among the recommendations in the WHO guidelines is that the drugs have a shelf life of at least one year.

During April 1–3, 1992 the WHO held its first workshop on counterfeit drugs. The workshop was held in Geneva and was a joint effort with the International Federation of Pharmaceutical Manufacturers Association (IFPMA). The workshop arose out of a conference held in Nairobi in 1985 concerning the growing problem of counterfeit drugs in Africa and the problem of parallel imports and drug safety. The Nairobi conference was followed by the adoption of resolution WHA 41.16 by the World Health Assembly in 1988. WHA 41.16 requested that "governments and pharmaceutical manufacturers cooperate in the detection and prevention of the increasing incidence of the export or smuggling of falsely labeled, counterfeit, or substandard pharmaceutical preparations."

"During the last decade, the number of reports of counterfeit medicines has increased considerably," said Dr. Hu Ching-Li, assistant director-general of WHO, in his welcome speech at the WHO/IFPMA workshop on counterfeit drugs.

> Indeed, the money involved is estimated to run into billions of dollars each year. However, it is the associated health risk that is of most immediate concern to WHO. Pharmaceutical products that are marketed without having passed the regulatory channels may not meet required standards. They may contain little or no active constituent. A patient suffering from a serious disease such as malaria or diabetes who receives such a product will be deprived of proper treatment. In these circumstances lack of therapeutic activity can be lethal. Counterfeit medicines may also contain unauthorized substances and excipients, different from those in the genuine product and are sometimes toxic.

The 1992 workshop was followed by a more comprehensive workshop that was held in November 1997 in Geneva. The workshop marked the end of a three-year project that was funded by the Japanese. It was a follow-up to the 1992 workshop and several workshops held by the WHO in Asia, which included one workshop for improving inspection procedures and another for improving analytical techniques. The 1997 workshop succeeded in establishing a network of contact persons in all the governing health ministries to monitor the growing trade in counterfeit drugs.

Dr. K. Kimura, project coordinator of the WHO drug safety unit, presented a breakdown of the WHO database. The results were compiled from questionnaires that were sent to pharmacists, pharmacies, and the health ministries around the world. The results were as follows:

- 751 cases of counterfeit pharmaceuticals have been received between 1982 and October 1997.
- 25 percent of cases were found in developed countries and 65 percent in developing countries.

- The majority of counterfeit products were discovered by visual detection.

- The reports embraced virtually all classes of products, but antibiotics appeared to be the most common.

The WHO workshops are unique in that they represent a worldwide effort to address the counterfeiting problem. The only other worldwide initiative is that being conducted by the Counterfeiting Intelligence Bureau (CIB) in London, which has organized a Countertech and Counterforce organization for tackling the international problem.

According to Dr. ten Ham, the workshop still had much to accomplish, but unfortunately, there was no more funding. Lack of funding has always been a problem for WHO programs, which are funded almost entirely by the developing nations. At the end of 1995, unpaid contributions from member states totaled $243 million, with the rate of collection during the year amounting to 53 percent, the lowest in WHO history. At its World Assembly, a resolution was passed "expressing deep concern" at the unprecedented level of outstanding contributions.[32]

NOTES

1. "African Fake Vaccines Debacle Hits Merieux, SB," *Pharma Marketletter*, September 2, 1996, p. 17.

2. Dixie Fairley, "Counterfeit Pills Buy Prison Time," *FDA Consumer*, December 1990, p. 35.

3. Christopher S. Wren, "U.N. Report Says Tens of Millions Use Illicit Drugs," *New York Times*, June 26, 1997, p. A12.

4. "Quelle Qualité pour les médicaments disponibles au Cambodge?" in the July 1997 newsletter of ReMeD, pp. 1–5.

5. "Heart Pumps," Associated Press, May 10, 1978.

6. Richard Turcsik, "Counterfeit Similac Found in California," *Supermarket News*, February 27, 1995, p. 35.

7. Marian Segal, "Drug Counterfeiter Sentenced," *FDA Consumer*, September 1990, p. 41. See also Gregg Williams, "Sting Operation Nabs Iranian Counterfeit Drug Dealer," *FDA Consumer*, April 1989, pp. 37–38.

8. Glenn Collins, "What if Congress Reforms the F.D.A.? Investors Should Think about It Now," *New York Times*, March 26, 1995.

9. See "US House Votes to Bar Abortion-Inducing Drugs' Approval," in the *Pharma Marketletter*, July 6, 1998, p. 12.

10. Saul Friedman, "Assault on FDA Would Be Bitter Pill, Agency Says," *New York Newsday*, February 23, 1995, p. A39.

11. Christine Gorman, "Special Report: Drug Safety. Can Drug Firms Be Trusted?" *Time*, February 10, 1992, pp. 42–44.

12. "Halcion a Matter for Justice Dept." in *Scrip* No. 2135, June 7, 1996, p. 17.

13. Michael Unger, "Generic Drugs on the Rebound," *New York Newsday*, November 9, 1992, pp. 29–30.

14. See Donald O Beers, *Generic and Innovator Drugs: A Guide to FDA Approval Requirements*, 4th ed. (Aspen Law & Business Publishers, 1995), Section 8.1.

15. See "More Pharma Firms Investigated in Italy," in *Scrip* No. 2044, July 21, 1995, p. 3.

16. Ian Schofield, "Italy's Very Public Price Wars," *Scrip Magazine*, September 1996, pp. 37–39.

17. See Zafrullah Chowdhury, *The Politics of Essential Drugs* (Zed Books, 1995).

18. Arthur Wineburg, "U.S. Trade Threats Spur Asian Laws on Intellectual Property," *National Law Journal*, July 13, 1992, International Law section, pp. 29, 35–36.

19. "India: Good for Manufacturing," in *Medical News*, August 1996, pp. 1, 36.

20. Faye Rice, "How Copycats Steal Billions," *Fortune*, April 22, 1991, p. 164.

21. "The Patent Pirates Are Finally Walking the Plant," *Business Week*, February 17, 1992, p. 12.

22. Earl V. Anerson, "Intellectual Property: Foreign Pirates Worry U.S. Firms," *Chemical and Engineering News*, September 1, 1988, p. 12.

23. "Brazilian Patents—What Effect?" *Scrip* No. 2043, July 18, 1995, p. 15.

24. Peter C. Schecter and Peter S. Ludwig, "Brazil's New Patent Law Becomes Reality," *Pharmaceutical Executive*, November 1996, pp. 92–94.

25. "Dummy Pill Fraud Closes Schering AG Brazil Plant," *Pharmaceutical Marketletter*, July 7, 1998; "Schering Hits Back after Brazil Suspends Sales," *Pharmaceutical Marketletter*, July 13, 1998.

26. Roger Cohen, "Nigeria's Pain Paradox of 'Self-Imposed Poverty,'" *New York Times*, August 23, 1998, p. 1.

27. E. E. Essien, "Drug Adulteration—The Nigerian Experience," *Trademark World*, February 1998, p. 48.

28. Tom Masland and Ruth Marshall, "A Really Nasty Business," *Newsweek*, November 5, 1990, p. 36.

29. "Dissident Dies in Nigerian Jail; Cause of Death Remains Unclear (Reuters)" in the *New York Times*, December 10, 1997, p. A6.

30. Steven Erlanger, "U.S. Report on Human Rights Faults China, Nigeria and Cuba," *New York Times*, January 30, 1997, p. A10.

31. Lere Baale and Olumide Akanmu, "Nigeria: Rx Marketing in a Depressed Economy," *Pharmaceutical Executive*, November 1995, p. 74.

32. See *Scrip* No. 2135, June 7, 1996, p. 19.

9

Nuts and Bolts

A 1990 report by the General Accounting Office (GAO) identified several government agencies using counterfeit and substandard fasteners. Generally, fasteners refers to nuts, bolts, and screws. Among the government agencies listed in the GAO report is the Department of Defense (DOD), which discovered nonconforming parts in radar, sonar, and communications systems, as well as in the guidance systems for aircraft, ships, and missiles. The Department of Energy (DOE), also listed by the GAO, found nonconforming circuit breakers in several of its nuclear weapons facilities.

The GAO report documented that counterfeit and substandard parts have been discovered in 72 of America's 113 nuclear power plants. In 8 percent of the nuclear power plants, the counterfeit fasteners formed part of the safety system used to prevent the escape of radiation during a nuclear accident. Other counterfeit parts included fuses, pumps, valves, and circuit breakers.

The U.S. military and other governmental agencies are often duped into purchasing counterfeit and substandard fasteners. The government awards its work to the lowest bidder, who underbids by manufacturing a substandard or counterfeit product. For example, in the late 1980s, the DOD accepted bids for genuine Chrysler replacement pistons that were to be used in the military's M880 troop carrier. When Chrysler learned that an unauthorized parts distributor in Florida had won the bid, Chrysler contacted the DOD and filed a bid protest. After examining the pistons the DOD purchased, Chrysler discovered that the items were counterfeit and estimated the maximum life at 15,000 miles. Chrysler eventually won a $275,000 judgment against the unauthorized distributor.[1]

Counterfeit transistors were discovered in parts destined for use in a test of the U.S. space shuttle in 1976. Substandard counterfeit parts were discovered among parts intended for use on the F-4 fighter plane and the Chaparral and Lance missile systems in 1978. In 1978, Bell Helicopter Co. discovered that counterfeit helicopter parts had been sold to NATO allies and American civilian helicopter fleets. Among the items palmed off were transmission parts and landing gear assemblies, which were discovered in 608 helicopters in the military fleets of several American allies, including: Britain, West Germany, France, and Belgium.[2]

According to a Bell Helicopter quality-assurance director, the same parts that can cause a fatal injury are the very same that the counterfeiters go after because they have to be replaced regularly. The counterfeits include fake rotor grips, tail-rotor drive shafts, and a variety of gears and bolts.

One of the biggest suppliers of counterfeit parts is the U.S. government. In 1991, Ray Robinson, special agent with U.S. Customs, was involved in Taskforce Lifesaver, an investigation into the trafficking of counterfeit aircraft parts. Many of the counterfeit parts that the Taskforce uncovered could be traced back to the U.S. government. Under the Defense Reutilization Marketing and System (DRMS), the DOD sells aviation parts by weight at pennies per pound. The scrap parts are usually near the end of their useful life. By altering the historical service record and refinishing the part, dishonest dealers could sell the scraps as "like-new" parts. Robinson also investigated a trail of aviation parts coming from Asia. Nearly all of the parts came from countries that have a large supply of U.S.-made military aircraft.

Fasteners pose the greatest hazard of all counterfeits. Even worse, the extent of the problem is unknown. Most fasteners are manufactured to specification and involve specific alloys. With modern, numerically controlled tools, counterfeiters can duplicate the precision of most fasteners. By scrimping on the alloys, heat treatments, and hardening, the counterfeiter can manufacture a product that is visually identical to the real product, but lacks the tensile strength or resilience required by the industry standard.

Because of their size and seeming unimportance, once the counterfeits are screwed or welded into position, they are likely to elude inspection. In many instances, counterfeit fasteners are a potential accident waiting to happen. In November 1987 the collapse of the Interstate Highway 10 bridge over the Calcasieu River in Louisiana was attributed to the failure of counterfeit fasteners in a bridge joint. Fortunately, no one was injured.

Not everyone has been fortunate. In 1994, after a five-year investigation, Norwegian investigators determined that the worst airplane crash in that country's history was caused by counterfeit bolts in the tail; the airplane was manufactured in the United States. In October 1985, a helicopter crashed in Peru, killing several people; a worn-out tail rotor blade, fraudulently palmed off as a Bell Helicopter Co. part, was the cause.[3] In Saudi Arabia, counterfeit automobile brake pads made of wood led to the death of a mother and her child.

Many counterfeits are never uncovered and pose a significant—although largely hidden—danger to the average consumer. Counterfeit fasteners have hit the U.S. auto and airline industries harder than the comparable industries in any other country. With nearly 200 million cars and trucks on the road, the United States is the auto capital of the world, making it the country of choice for counterfeit parts. About one-half of the counterfeit auto market is produced in the United States; East Asia and the Middle East account for much of the rest. The U.S. aviation industry was seriously weakened after passage of the 1978 Deregulation Act, and many airlines went bankrupt. Deregulation was a catastrophe for the industry. By 1992, the U.S. airlines had the oldest fleet in the noncommunist world. To supply the fleet with parts, a large and unregulated market of parts brokers emerged, some of whom dealt in counterfeit and substandard parts.

To help ensure the reliability of the fasteners sold in the marketplace, the Fastener Quality Act (FQA) was passed in 1992. The Act requires that certain fasteners bear an identifying insignia for traceability. Product inspection, testing, and certification is required, as well as record keeping and fastener recordation. The National Institute of Standards and Technology (NIST) has responsibility for all aspects of the law, except enforcement and recordation. The U.S. Patent and Trademark Office (USPTO) is responsible for recordation and the Bureau of Export Administration (BXA) is responsible for enforcement. All three agencies are subagencies within the purview of the U.S. Department of Commerce.

COUNTERFEIT AUTOMOBILE PARTS

On December 7, 1990, William E. Hoglund, GM Executive Vice-President, held a news conference at a GM parts facility in Pontiac, Michigan to announce the success of Operation Partsman. Operation Partsman was an undercover sting operation conducted by the FBI and the U.S. Attorney. The Operation led to forty raids in fifteen states and resulted in the seizure of car and truck parts.

As part of his opening remarks, Hoglund said, "Looking at the millions of dollars of confiscated goods here which won't be bought and used by the American public, I'd have to say our law-enforcement friends are very much in the business of customer satisfaction."

On display for the press was a sample of auto parts that had been seized. The counterfeit parts included: brake pads, wheel covers, floor mats, voltage regulators, and many other auto parts.

Prior to passage of the Trademark Counterfeiting Act of 1984, the FBI had no jurisdiction in trademark enforcement. Once the Act had been passed, Dan Elliott, chief of security for GM Parts Division, was anxious to get the federal agency involved in the car parts counterfeiting problem. By the end of 1984, GM was conducting a growing number of ex parte seizures, thanks to passage of the 1984 Act. GM was not alone. On November 28, 1984, three facilities were raided by U.S. Marshals on behalf of Ford Motor Company; $100,000 in spurious parts and 500,000 pieces of parts packaging were seized.

Elliott established an undercover operation using an AC-Delco (GM) warehouse distributor as a front for pursuing counterfeiters in the Detroit area. Because of the name recognition, Delco products are widely counterfeited. As Elliott's undercover operation expanded, the FBI was brought in. Operation Partsman became a huge sting operation, undertaken by the FBI, other law enforcement, and the Big Three automakers.

As part of Operation Partsman, FBI agents established an auto parts business that was in the market for counterfeit parts in 1988. Within two years, the sting operation had expanded into the wholesale and retail distribution chain at every level. In early 1990, the trap was sprung. The FBI carried out a coordinated raid that covered fifteen states. An estimated $50 million worth of counterfeit parts were seized. Dozens of persons were arrested; many were charged with a felony for the interstate transportation of counterfeit goods and for trademark counterfeiting under the Trademark Counterfeiting Act of 1984. Operation Partsman was the largest nondrug seizure in FBI history.

Shortly after Operation Partsman was concluded, GM installed a shredder at the AC Rochester Division's Dort Highway complex, now called the Delphi Energy & Engine Management Systems. The shredder began shredding, for recycling purposes, 100,000 counterfeit metal wheel covers that had been seized in Operation Partsman and other automotive seizures.

GM released the results of quality control tests that had been conducted on a sampling of the seized counterfeit automotive parts. The overall evaluation of the seized counterfeits was that they were of poor quality and posed a safety risk to the public. Car engines seized up after using counterfeit oil filters that failed after 200 miles. Inferior transmission fluid consisted only of a cheap grade of crude oil that had been dyed red to make it look like transmission fluid. Counterfeit gasoline caps leaked in a vehicle rollover situation. Poor-quality chrome and metal posed a significantly greater chance of serious injury in an accident. Of particular concern was that most of these defects were not noticeable to the average consumer. Ford Motor Company estimated that the average counterfeit part offers between 5 and 25 percent of the working life of a genuine part. Chrysler Corporation has come across replacement brake shoes so soft they could be scratched with a fingernail; counterfeit brake linings that wore out after one stop; antifreeze that corrodes cooling systems; and transmission fluids that solidify at low operating temperatures.

Prior to the 1980s, counterfeit automotive parts were rarely seen. The market for counterfeit automotive parts is a reflection of changing auto-buying habits. At one time, car owners rarely had to take their car in for repair services. On average, they traded in the car every other year, before most parts had worn out. Starting in the 1980s, car owners have been driving their cars an average of seven years before purchasing a new car. Many modern car owners cannot afford a new model car, which costs upward of $20,000, and settle for a used car. As a result, used car sales have been steadily increasing over the years. These changes in auto-buying habits have made servicing the automobile, particularly buying parts, an important part of owning a car.

The increased demand for auto parts led to an underground counterfeit market. Seizures of counterfeit automotive parts have included: ignition wires, voltage regulators, valves and valve listers, distributor caps, gasoline filters, disc brake pads and shoes, bearings, air-conditioning compressors, oil and air filters, starters and starter drives, shock absorbers, and many other parts.

In 1988, the Federal Trade Commission (FTC) estimated that approximately $3 billion in fake automotive parts were sold each year in the United States, and $12 billion worldwide. The FTC estimated that counterfeit automobile parts had resulted in the loss of 210,000 jobs in the auto industry. The FTC figures at the time were considered conservative by the Chrysler Corporation, which estimated that American consumers had bought $15 billion worth of counterfeit parts in 1986 alone.[4]

Experts at GM believe that over half of all counterfeit GM parts originate from inside the United States. Other source countries include Taiwan, Hong Kong, Thailand, Singapore, Malaysia, India, Guatemala, and Jordan.

The largest market outside the United States for counterfeit GM parts is the Middle East. This area has the largest concentration of North American–produced GM vehicles outside the United States. Because of the environment, automobiles and trucks require frequent service intervals for air, oil filters, and bearings. Additionally, the lack of legal protection for intellectual property, particularly trademarks, has made the Middle East a haven for counterfeit auto parts.

Information on counterfeit operations comes from a variety of sources, according to Rodney Kinghorn, director of investigations for GM Corporate Security. This includes the GM Awareline (800–244–3460), GM customers, GM licensees, and attending various trade shows and auto-related swap meets. Information obtained during an investigation of a counterfeiter often leads to the identification of other counterfeiters.

"There is no typical counterfeit operation," says Kinghorn, "other than to say that the most frequently counterfeited items are usually items in high demand and require replacement one or more times during the life cycle of the vehicle. Counterfeit product is seen primarily in the aftermarket."

General Motors first discovered that there was an underground market for counterfeit parts in early 1984, when a container load of counterfeit engines was discovered by a district manager in Saudi Arabia. The Saudi dealership had ordered a shipment of engines that were supposed to be Goodwrench Engines. The district manager became suspicious when he noticed that the engines were packed in containers that bore old Targetmaster logos. The engines turned out to be rebuilt engines.

Throughout 1984 and 1985 GM representatives, including the director of security for the former GM Warehousing and Distribution Division, traveled to Saudi Arabia and other Middle Eastern countries to investigate the counterfeiting of auto parts. With the help of government authorities in the Middle East, 126 raids were carried out in the United States and overseas, with $67.5 million in counterfeit auto parts seized and eventually destroyed.

Ronald Bliss, an attorney with the firm of Fullbright & Jaworski in Houston, conducted numerous seizures of counterfeit auto parts during 1984 and 1985 for General Motors and put one of the largest counterfeiting rings in the country out of business. Bliss got involved in investigating the widespread use of counterfeit auto parts in early 1984, when Dan Elliott, chief of security for GM Parts Division, contacted the law firm. Elliott had learned from informers that three cargo containers in the Port of Houston contained counterfeit automotive engines. The seatainers, which are twenty to thirty feet long and resemble freight cars, were destined for the Middle East. GM wanted the law firm to conduct a seizure of the counterfeit parts.

The seizure would ultimately lead to other investigations and seizures in Texas and New York. For the remainder of 1984, Bliss would be working with Elliott and GM security. As an associate, Bliss handled extensive investigations that would have taxed the most experienced attorney. He would later prove quite resourceful, something he may have learned as an Air Force Academy graduate and a fighter pilot in Vietnam. In 1966, he was flying an F-105 out of Thailand over North Vietnam, when he went down. He was imprisoned in the infamous Hanoi Hilton, where he spent much of the next six and one-half years (2,374 days, according to Bliss, who counted the days) as a prisoner of war. During this time, he was chained in leg irons and was often physically assaulted by his captors.

Bliss's initial problem in the counterfeiting investigation was how to obtain authorization to conduct the seizure. This was prior to passage of the Trademark Counterfeiting Act of 1984. There was little precedent for conducting a seizure for trademark counterfeiting. Bliss decided to seek legal relief under the general equitable power of the court and under the 1946 Trademark Act, otherwise known as the Lanham Act, which governs trademark law.

A seizure order, particularly an ex parte seizure order, which is a seizure that is conducted without giving notice to the defendant, was a relatively new legal remedy for trademark counterfeiting under federal law until enactment of the Trademark Counterfeiting Act of 1984. Some courts had granted ex parte seizures under Rule 65(b) of the Federal Rules of Civil Procedure. The leading decision was decided by the Second Circuit in 1979 in the case *In re Vuitton et Fils S.A.*, 606 F.2d 1 (2nd Cir. 1979). At the time, this was a landmark decision in the battle against trademark counterfeiting.

In ex parte seizure cases following *Vuitton*, the courts relied on other procedural mechanisms, notably Section 36 of the Lanham Act, which generally empowers a court to order the seizure and impoundment of articles that include infringements of federally registered marks.

Bliss opted for relief under the general equitable power of the court, which allows the court to fashion appropriate remedies at its discretion, and under the Lanham Act as well. Seeking relief under the general equitable power of the court is usually a tough argument for a lawyer, since the circumstances have to be very compelling before a judge will intervene. Bliss prepared the documents for a seizure and met in chambers before Judge Ross Sterling, a descendant of a former Texas governor. The stack of documents included the complaint, supporting affidavits, ex parte seizure order, and TRO. One of the affidavits was signed by Elliott of General Motors.

In the seizure order, Bliss argued that imminent and irreparable harm was about to occur to General Motors, as well as to the public, due to the likelihood of confusion between the counterfeit parts and the genuine. Bliss had carefully crafted his argument of irreparable harm to include the word "confusion," which, when referring to trademarks, means much more than bewilderment. Legally, confusion means actual harm to the distinctiveness inherent in a trademark.

The judge granted the seizure, but required that a large bond be posted. The bond was necessary, because the defendants had to be offered some monetary protection should the seizure fail. Should the seizure prove meritless, the defendants would have legal claim to the bond for damages incurred. The posting of bond caused some consternation by GM security. It was well into the six figures. The information about the sea-tainers had been obtained from informants, and could be false.

On the day of the seizure, Bliss, Elliott, and other members of the firm arrived by taxi and were met by U.S. Marshals and several regional managers from GM. They located the sea-tainers, which were wired shut and ready for shipment.

"Everyone was tense," Bliss recalls. "If we were wrong, GM stood to lose a sizable bond. There was dead silence when the Marshal snipped the wire and the container was opened. Honestly, the engines looked like the real thing. They were real knockoffs. The GM people looked inside an alternator box. Finally, one of them jumps up and says, 'We got 'em!' "

The parts were counterfeit. They were generic parts that were stamped "Made in Taiwan." The parts were otherwise identical to the Delco parts, but inferior in quality. The generic parts had been placed inside counterfeit boxes, then placed in containers bound for Saudi Arabia. Not until the boxes were opened would the buyer realize that the parts were fraudulent. To complete the ruse, the shipping documents showed that the merchandise came from the United States, not Taiwan.

At the time, this was the largest seizure of auto parts in history. The counterfeits, engines and alternators, were bound for the Middle East. But who was the shipper? An inspection of the shipping invoices and shipping documents revealed nothing; a nonexistent company was the supposed shipper. Nonetheless, using what little information they had, Elliott was able to extrapolate the radius from which the counterfeits had originated; the curve ran through Dallas.

Subsequent investigations by GM pointed to an operation on the northeast side of Dallas. Bliss sent in a private investigator, whose report confirmed that this was a counterfeiting operation.

Bliss knew that he had to act quickly. As soon as the counterfeiter was aware that the counterfeit shipment had been seized, he would begin dismantling the operation and destroying business documents. Bliss, Elliott, and U.S. Marshals soon conducted a seizure in Dallas and unloaded a warehouse that was packed from floor to ceiling with generic engines and auto parts. One of the Marshals rented a front-end loader forklift, and began loading the merchandise onto a truck.

After this raid, the full extent of the counterfeiting operation was uncovered. The Dallas company had dealt with a number of companies in New York and New Jersey that were also shipping auto parts to the Middle East. Bliss realized that he would have to travel to New York to investigate. Through local counsel in New York City, Bliss subsequently contacted Harper Associates, a private investigation firm in New York City.

terfeit auto parts market in the New York area. At one point, Leech and his investigators began to canvass all of the auto distributors in the area using the Yellow Pages. Dozens of operations were uncovered.

Leech investigated a parts manufacturer that was counterfeiting fuel injection lines for marine engines. The fuel injection lines were manufactured by a subsidiary of Delco Marine. The counterfeiting operation was a small exporter, who was exporting the counterfeit fuel injection lines into Haiti.

The exporter was doing a lively business. Because of a balance of trade deficit with Haiti, the U.S. government was providing tax incentives to export to Haiti. Additionally, the exporter had struck a deal to consolidate its shipments to Haiti with Delco, and was shipping free on side (FOS) to save money.

Over the years, the exporter had purchased a considerable inventory of Delco merchandise. At one point, instead of exporting to Haiti, the exporter began selling the merchandise in the United States. Taking advantage of the tax incentive offered by the U.S. government, the exporter was able to undercut the market.

The exporter was engaging in diversion. Diversion occurs when merchandise is sold outside the normal distribution chain. Success was the exporter's downfall. Demand had become so great that the exporter could no longer keep up. He began to use counterfeit fuel injection lines to keep up with the demand, and interspersed the counterfeit fuel injection lines with the legitimate product. The exporter could not resist the easy profits and began to expand his inventory of counterfeit goods.

When Delco Marine got wind of the operation, Leech was dispatched to investigate. The exporter was housing the counterfeit merchandise in a huge warehouse. When the warehouse was raided, Leech discovered a multi-million-dollar operation involving marine and auto parts. There were even counterfeit ship transmissions. The shoddily built transmissions were designed for a ship engine, but subsequent tests revealed that they were unsafe. It took days to inventory and remove the counterfeits.

Automotive experts recognize several types of counterfeiting. *Direct counterfeiting* involves duplicating the part and packaging. *Passing off* occurs when the manufacturer tries to substitute a part as a factory item by packaging it in a generic box with actual part numbers. *Parts diversion* occurs when the parts are sold outside the normal distribution chain. Parts diversion may involve refurbishing old parts and trying to sell them as new. *Simulated parts* give the impression of being another company's part without using the company's trademark.

During a six-year period, Ford Motor Company filed eighteen legal actions for simulations of its Motorcraft packaging. Ford Motor Company has a line of automotive products sold under the trade name Motorcraft®. The simulated parts were sold under the trade name

Motorcare. The packaging, or trade dress, was similar in design to Ford's Motorcraft line. More than forty corporations in California, New Jersey, Arizona, Minnesota, New York, and Washington, D.C. were sued for using simulations of the Motorcraft trade name.

In the mid-1980s CR Industries discovered imitations of its Scotseal product. The look-alike seals were being imported into the United States from Japan, Korea, and Taiwan. The counterfeiters were trying to pass off the seals, which were very close in appearance to the genuine seals. The fraudulent seals experienced significant leakage within less than 20 hours, compared to an average 2,000 to 4,000 hours for the real Scotseal.[5]

Parts diversion is a problem in the vintage or classic car market. Many parts offered for sale in the classic car market are sold through mail order or are offered for sale by other enthusiasts or at car shows. Many of the parts are refurbished parts.

In an effort to ensure the quality of the parts in the restoration market, the Big Three automakers continue to manufacture some of the parts for the more popular antique cars. Chrysler Motors publishes *Mopar Performance News*, a publication that covers the restoration scene, and has a national parts locator program, which is a satellite-based electronic information system that is capable of matching thousands of Chrysler Motors dealers with millions of parts through inventory information exchange. Chrysler's policy concerning restoration parts is that if there is sufficient demand for parts among their dealers and the original tooling can be located (much of which was lost many years ago), special production runs will be made to accommodate the demand.

General Motors Service Parts Operations (SPO) has a GM Restoration Parts Licensing Program, which provides the restoration enthusiast with original equipment quality parts and accessories. GM Restoration Parts are manufactured to specification by approved, licensed manufacturers from original blueprints and, when available, with original GM-owned tooling. With more than 5,000 parts licensed under the Program, customers can purchase official products to restore their vintage GM vehicles, with parts that fit almost every model from muscle cars to trucks. Some of the more popular GM vehicles restored include Corvettes, Camaros, Chevelles, '55 to '57 Chevys, and GMC Motor Homes.

Most counterfeiting operations involve a medium-sized distributor of auto parts. The counterfeiting operation employs ten people or less. The counterfeiters either build the fake parts themselves or clean up old parts and package the items in new cartons. Most counterfeiters concentrate on one or two parts and sell in quantity to other distributors and jobbers. A usual scam line used by counterfeiters is that a large quantity of parts was purchased on a production overrun at a terrific price; or that he purchased more than he can distribute and is looking to unload some of the inventory at a discount over the usual price.

In several instances, counterfeiting operations have been uncovered due to the alert action of an authorized automotive distributor. In 1987, Chrysler uncovered a counterfeiting ring that was trying to palm off used turbochargers as new Mopar components. The counterfeiters approached a Chrysler dealer and offered him a deal. Although the packaging looked authentic, the dealer became suspicious and sent one of the turbochargers to Chrysler. Engineering analysis discovered that although the turbochargers appeared to be new, the turbine blades were coated with soot. The soot was exhaust soot, and not easily detected.

After the counterfeiting ring was put out of business, Chrysler modified the graphics on its Mopar packaging to make reproducing the trade dress more difficult. The red, white, and blue packaging and graphics were too easy to duplicate. To foil counterfeiters, Chrysler used a cutaway line drawing as part of its package graphics.

In 1990 Mogul Corporation won a large settlement against the distributors of counterfeit oil seals. An auto parts store had been duped into purchasing a quantity of counterfeits. Mogul began an investigation when the store owner complained of substandard quality and tried to return the oil seals. Thousands of boxes of counterfeit oil seals were eventually seized.

Fortunately, few fatalities have been caused by counterfeit auto parts. Authorities in Saudi Arabia have been able to document that a mother and child were killed in an auto accident when their brakes, which were made of wood, failed. Although no fatalities have been attributed to counterfeit parts in the United States, the death of a construction worker in Tennessee during the construction of a Saturn automobile plant was caused in part by the failure of a counterfeit bolt. A particularly dangerous counterfeit was uncovered by the Framm Company in the mid-1980s. An investigation uncovered an operation in Southeast Asia that was selling Framm filters at a bargain price. The filters were tin cans that had been cleverly painted.

To foil the counterfeiters the Big Three have begun using holograms on their packaging. GM uses holograms on the packaging of its Middle East–bound brake shoes, electronic ignition modules, and air-conditioning compressors. According to Kinghorn, the counterfeiting situation has changed very little in the ten years since Operation Partsman was concluded.

For many years beginning in the early 1990s the Big Three automakers have waged a battle against "knockoff" replacement parts manufacturers who provide parts to the auto body shop. The replacement parts manufacturers do not produce counterfeit parts, or otherwise try to engage in palming off their product as genuine. They produce substitute or "generic" parts that are meant to be used in place of the genuine body part, usually a fender, grille, or door side.

The knockoff manufacturers are widely backed by the insurance industry, which prefers that its customers use the less expensive "generic" parts. In December 1990 Ford was forced to cut the price of many replacement parts.[6] GM tried placing advertisements in leading publications warning about the dangers of the "imitation" and "fake" replacement parts, and issued a warning to consumers that the "fake" parts are not manufactured to specification, with the result that the quality, alignment, and corrosion resistance are impaired.

During the 1980s, a popular knockoff in use among car enthusiasts was the customized auto kit. Using one of these kits, a car enthusiast could remove the siding of a Corvette and replace it with siding that would make his car look like a Ferrari. The legality of the customized car kits was decided for the plaintiff in *Ferrari S.p.A. Esercizio Fabbriche Automobili E Corse v. McBurnie Coachcraft Inc.*, 10 USPQ2d 1278 (1988).

In 1984 the producer of the television show *Miami Vice* entered into an agreement to lease two "Mardikian" vehicles for use on the show. The "Mardikian" was a replica of the Daytona Spider, which was produced by Ferrari S.p.A. Esercizio Fabbriche Automobili E Corse from 1969 until 1974. In all, Ferrari manufactured 127 Spiders, of which 69 were sold in the United States.

Several years after the Daytona Spider model was discontinued, Albert Mardikian reproduced the body design in a fiberglass mold. The reproduced design was used with a Corvette, which is made from fiberglass. In 1980, Mardikian entered into an agreement with Thomas McBurnie to produce Ferrari Daytona Spider replicas for McBurnie's company, McBurnie Coachcraft, Inc. The replicas were very popular and would later be known as the McBurnie California Daytona Spider.

By 1983, McBurnie had ended his business relationship with Mardikian, who was near bankruptcy. Starting in 1984, McBurnie began producing the first of his own McBurnie California Daytona Spiders. McBurnie sold his product in kit form, and ran advertisements for the kit.

In 1986, McBurnie was hit with a lawsuit by Ferrari, which had discovered the replica car on the *Miami Vice* show. Universal Studios and Ferrari N.A. entered into an agreement under which Ferrari agreed to lease two Ferrari Testarossas to Universal Studios for promotional consideration. Universal City Studios agreed not to use any Ferrari replicas during the term of the lease.

Attorneys for Ferrari argued successfully that the defendant infringed the trademark and trade dress of its automobile body style. Defendants counterclaimed and alleged that Ferrari was instituting a sham trade dress litigation. The counterclaim failed, in part because McBurnie had tried to palm off his car as a replica of the Ferrari Daytona Spider—even going so far as to call the car the McBurnie California Daytona Spider and using the Ferrari trademarked name and "prancing horse logo" in his advertising.

COUNTERFEIT AIRCRAFT PARTS

Mary Schiavo's stormy tenure as Inspector General (IG) of the U.S. Department of Transportation and the publication of her 1997 book *Flying Blind, Flying Safe*, with its charges of incompetence and indifference within the FAA, caused a furor.

A former prosecutor known as "Maximum Mary," Schiavo was appointed in 1990, and began to investigate counterfeit parts and to question aviation maintenance practices. Her appointment came on the heels of a sixty-count indictment of Eastern Airlines charging the carrier with neglecting important repairs and faking maintenance documents. Eastern Airlines, which was then in bankruptcy, became the first airline against which criminal charges were filed. Prosecutors asserted that the faulty repairs were not the work of a few employees, but part of a much broader agenda involving pressure and intimidation from top managers to cut costs.[7]

Armed with a search warrant, federal investigators entered Eastern's office in New York City and carried out boxes of documents and computer records. Evidence uncovered in the seizure eventually involved strings of violations that stretched from 1985 to 1989 at New York's La Guardia and Kennedy International airports. The violations included forged and fake signatures from repair logs, a practice known as "pencil whipping."

Pencil whipping occurs when a form is filled out claiming work has been completed, when in fact the work was not completed. The FAA has established a hot line for reporting pencil whipping, and relies on safety-conscious employees to report the practice. In February 1993, USAir's senior vice-president for maintenance operations sent a letter to all maintenance supervisors warning them against engaging in pencil whipping. The warning came after USAir supervisors at two airports were caught falsifying records to cover plane repairs that were not done. In one incident, a USAir maintenance supervisor in Charlotte, North Carolina acknowledged that he allowed a jet to fly with a defective warning system and said he did so to save the airline money; the supervisor was suspended and demoted. In the other incident, disciplinary actions were taken against two foremen in Indianapolis for pencil whipping.[8]

Over the years, Eastern's shoddy maintenance had reached a dangerous state. Other carriers that had bought jets from Eastern, which was liquidating its inventory to raise capital, found them in exceedingly poor condition. One Federal Express official said that his workers found corrosion in the belly skins and cracks in the main beam of the wingspan in aircraft purchased from Eastern. These are problems associated with progressively poor maintenance.[9]

The July 1990 indictment of Eastern was the most visible sign of an industry in deep trouble. During the five-year period 1990 through 1994, the airline industry lost a staggering $13 billion; $10 billion was lost in three years from 1990 to 1992. In 1992 industry losses approached $5 billion. To add to the industry's woes, the airlines were hit with two tax hikes in 1990, when ticket taxes were hiked to 10 percent and cargo taxes were raised to 6.25 percent.

Airline safety has always been a catalyst for change in the airline industry. When two large passenger planes collided in midair in 1956, killing 128 people, airline safety came under national scrutiny. The 1956 collision was preceded by several midair collisions. Public outcry for government involvement eventually ushered in the modern era of airline safety. In 1958 the Federal Aviation Agency, later renamed the Federal Aviation Administration (FAA), was created.

Under its federal mandate, the FAA was given the dual task of ensuring safety in the airline industry and promoting air commerce. The dual mandate was designed as a national industrial policy to foster commercial aviation. Unfortunately, the dual mandate posed a potential for conflict of interest. The aftermath of the crash of ValuJet Flight 592 in 1996 brought FAA administrators themselves to insist that the FAA's mandate be changed.[10]

The FAA became part of the Department of Transportation (DOT), which was created in 1966 and replaced the Civil Aeronautics Board (CAB). The National Transportation Board (NTSB) was created as part of the DOT. The FAA is part of the DOT and is the decision-making regulator of aviation safety for the U.S. government.

The Airline Deregulation Act of 1978, which was signed into law by President Carter, was a disaster for the airline industry. The CAB, which controlled prices, routes, and the purchase of airplanes, was phased out.

The premise of deregulation was that actual and potential competition could be relied upon to maintain adequate service and reasonable fares. However, as competition weakened, deregulation began to strangle the industry. Numerous "no-frill" airlines competed with the larger, established airlines for the most profitable routes. Price wars erupted. Few of the "no-frills" lasted, but the price wars took a toll on the established carriers.

The airline industry's problems had been predicted. A book written by Ralph Nader and Wesley J. Smith, *Collision Course: The Truth about Airline Safety*, which was published in 1994, warned of the effect of deregulation on aviation safety and the ineptitude of the FAA.

Between 1990 and 1991, the market shares of the financially distressed airlines fell from over 30 percent in 1990 to less than 25 percent in 1991.

During this two-year period, Eastern ceased operations, while Pan Am, Continental, Midway, and America West filed for bankruptcy protection, and TWA defaulted on its loan obligations.

A GAO report, "Airline Competition: Industry Competitive and Financial Problems," published in 1991 outlined many of the problems caused by deregulation. Among the problems cited were: reliance on debt financing, which made the airlines more vulnerable to market fluctuations; federal law that restricted U.S. airlines' access to foreign capital; and barriers to competition that distorted the distribution of consumer benefits.

A federal commission that was appointed by President Clinton to devise a plan to save the industry proposed a number of steps, including privatizing the FAA, which was frequently criticized for failing to modernize the air traffic control system. Billions of dollars were estimated to be lost through flight delays. In a draft report, the commission called for removing much of the FAA's power and creating an independent federal corporation to take over many of the FAA's more important responsibilities.[11]

In 1993, the FAA employed approximately 53,000 people with a $9.4 billion budget. In 1993, FAA specialists performed 30,000 security inspections and assessments, hosted more than 5,000 safety seminars, and conducted 300,000 safety inspections of airlines and aviation activities. Despite these impressive statistics, there were indications that the FAA was understaffed and was lax in its safety inspections. The FAA has a 2,500-person safety inspection force that has the immense task of monitoring 3,500 airlines. In 1995, the FAA's director of Flight Standards Service announced that the agency planned to add 600 inspectors within the next three years.

Deregulation put pressure on the airlines to remain competitive, and several cut costs by skimping on maintenance. The Eastern Airlines incident was the most serious in a string of incidents. "We overdid deregulation," said one law professor. "We went to sleep, and we're now paying for it."[12]

Several airlines were fined or cited for safety violations beginning in the mid-1980s, including United Airlines, which paid a $1.5-million fine in 1985 for poor maintenance practices.[13] In 1992, without admitting any wrongdoing, Express One International, Inc., which operates a small airline out of Dallas, signed a consent order with the FAA and agreed to pay $379,000 in penalties for alleged maintenance and other violations.[14] In 1996, Mesa Air Group, the largest independently owned commuter airline in the United States, signed an FAA order requiring the carrier to improve its operations and pay a $5,000 fine. Mesa had long been known for its mechanical problems, overbooking, and poor personnel.[15]

One of the worst violators was Arrow Airlines. The airline came under fire after the December 1985 crash of an Arrow Air DC-8 charter in Newfoundland in which 256 persons, many of them soldiers headed home for Christmas, were killed. Arrow had been fined in 1994 for putting off repairs and using inadequate training manuals. Although investigators never determined the cause of the crash, they discovered numerous maintenance violations, the most serious being that adhesive tape had been used to hold shut some windows and panels. In the nine years after the accident, the FAA cited Arrow twenty-four times for operations and maintenance violations. In 1995, acting on a tip, the FAA again investigated Arrow and discovered numerous maintenance problems. An airlines official called the airline's violations the worst he had seen in sixteen years with the FAA.[16]

Deregulation played a major role in the aging of the U.S. fleet, and this, in turn, increased the demand for servicing and parts. In 1989, the U.S. fleet average of thirteen years of service per plane made it the oldest in the noncommunist world.[17] The increased demand for servicing came at a time when the number of air mechanics was in decline. A 1989 Air Transport Association (ATA) survey of twenty-one major airlines found that carriers were unable to find mechanics for 4,000 vacancies out of a total of 69,000 positions. The ATA report also reported a significant decline in the number of applicants.[18]

The increased demand for aircraft parts beginning in the late 1980s swelled the number of parts brokers to an estimated 20,000. In 1994, 26 million aircraft parts were changed. The parts brokers benefited by the shakeout of the airlines industry that resulted after deregulation of the industry in 1978. A mountain of spare parts became available, after many major airlines went bankrupt. A major source of substandard parts was put out of business in 1989, when the FBI raided a subsidiary of the Fairchild Corporation and seized its inventory of substandard fasteners. Millions of dollars worth of substandard fasteners were estimated to have been sold around the world by the subsidiary.

Between 1991 and the middle of 1996, the Office of the Inspector General (OIG) was responsible for or assisted in 133 convictions and the handing down of $8.8 million in fines. Many of the investigations and convictions involved parts brokers. Investigations were conducted around the country by seventy-eight agents, principally in south Florida, Texas, and California, and on the East Coast.

Two of the most serious investigations occurred in 1991, shortly after Eastern was indicted. One of the cases involved counterfeit bearing seal spacers that were for installation in the Pratt & Whitney JT8D engine, and the other involved an investigation into Classic Aviation, an aircraft parts brokerage in south Florida.

The counterfeit Pratt & Whitney JT8D seal spacers had passed through several safety inspections, and might have been installed except for the alertness of Richard Newmann, a United Airlines mechanic working in United's giant maintenance base in San Francisco.[19] Newmann opened a box that contained bearing seal spacers and became suspicious when he noticed that the spacer's edges were too rough and appeared to lack certain coatings. It appeared to be a mistake of some kind, Newmann recalls. He noticed that the Pratt & Whitney logo of the soaring eagle was flying in the wrong direction—it was flying into the ground. He opened other boxes that were part of a shipment from a parts broker in Connecticut. The spacers failed a Rockwell hardness test that was conducted by a United quality assurance official.

The spacers were counterfeit. The engine parts were sent back to Pratt & Whitney. Subsequent tests performed by Pratt & Whitney showed that the spacers had a useful life of less than 600 hours of flying time, instead of the normal 20,000. Tests by the FAA indicated the spacers would have resulted in failure of the No. 4 ½ bearing and fracture of the low-pressure turbine shaft. The parts might have been installed in a Boeing 727 or 737 or a MacDonnell-Douglas DC-9.[20]

The FAA issued an airworthiness directive, the agency's most powerful tool, directing airlines around the world to check their inventories for the counterfeit spacers. At least fifteen airlines around the globe had taken the fake parts into their inventory. The counterfeits were traced back to Gary Shafer, a parts broker in Connecticut, who had the parts duplicated at a machine shop and tried to palm them off as legitimate by listing the spacers in a nationally recognized inventory of aircraft parts. United had first checked with Pratt for spacers, and when it found that Pratt was out of stock, bought the spacers from Shafer.

Another major seizure involving a parts vendor occurred in the spring of 1991, at nearly the same time as the discovery of the counterfeit Pratt & Whitney spacers. Harry Schaefer, a special agent with the OIG, executed a search warrant for Classic Aviation, an aircraft parts brokerage in south Florida. Rodney Kostoff, the owner of Classic Aviation, was engaged in widespread "stripping and dipping," which involves the illegal cosmetic treating of spent parts and retailing them as new or fully reconditioned.[21]

Schaefer confiscated gears, starter parts, and complete starter units, which were later found to have been fabricated with substandard and repaired scrap parts. Kostoff had already sold 600 of the starters to repair stations for installation on commercial airliners and cargo carriers. The FAA issued an airworthiness directive, requiring operators of six types of Boeing and McDonnell-Douglas airliners to track down the Classic Aviation starters and to remove them. Classic Aviation, it was later uncovered, was the center of an operation involving as many as twenty-five FAA-licensed repair stations, which had supplied and bought from Classic or had been hired by Kostoff to build starters and to certify the work as an FAA-approved overhaul. In November 1994, Kostoff was convicted and sentenced to thirty-three months in prison and fined $6,000.

"Classic Aviation really opened our eyes up," Schaefer says. After the Classic Aviation seizure, Schiavo declared that investigating substandard and bogus aircraft parts would hereafter be her number one priority. Subsequently, Schaefer began giving a seminar for industry people on how to identify suspicious parts. Pratt & Whitney developed a similar seminar, which is given to suppliers and distributors.

In 1991, Ray Robinson, special agent with U.S. Customs, was involved in Taskforce Lifesaver. This was a joint investigation with the FAA and the DOT into the trafficking of counterfeit aircraft parts. Robinson had an ideal background for such an assignment. He was a helicopter pilot in Vietnam from 1962 until 1970, and after joining U.S. Customs, he was involved in investigating the illegal trade in implements of war to terrorist nations such as Iran and Libya. Throughout the 1980s, Robinson was involved in several reverse undercover operations (RUOs), which involved establishing a corporate cover as a shady aircraft parts broker.

Taskforce Lifesaver discovered that one of the biggest sources of aircraft parts was the Department of Defense. Under the Defense Reutilization Marketing and System (DRMS), the DOD sells a variety of engines, blades, and other aviation parts for scrap metal. The parts are sold intact by weight at pennies per pound. In most cases, the scrap parts are near the end of their useful life, but by altering the historical service record and refinishing the part, an unscrupulous dealer can try to sell the parts as "like-new" parts with "time remaining."

The Taskforce probe centered on two brothers who were operating in California. The two brothers were selling "powered-down" helicopter blades all over the world. These were blades that had been altered and their service record doctored.

"When a main rotor blade fails or a tail rotor blade fails on a helicopter, it is nearly always termed a 'catastrophic failure,'" says Robinson. "In other words, that helicopter is going down, along with everybody aboard."

Initially, the U.S. Attorney did not want to prosecute the case. At the time, there was not a specific statute governing the sale and resale of military scrap. Finally, Robinson convinced the U.S. Attorney to file the case under the 1984 Trademark Counterfeiting Act for palming off the military scrap blades as Bell Helicopter blades. They won, but the brothers got only a minimum sentence of six months.

In 1992, the Taskforce investigated several companies in Texas. One company was selling hydraulic fittings to all the major airlines, including General Dynamics, which manufactures the F-16. "This guy was going down to True Value Hardware and buying hydraulic brass fittings, stamping them with the DOT specifications, and selling them as the real thing," says Robinson. "After the seizure was conducted, the FAA issued an airworthiness directive, and all the aircraft and F-16s around the world were checked to see if they had bought from this company."

The Taskforce also executed a search warrant against a company in Wheatland, Texas. The company had sold incorrectly machined swashplate support assemblies for Bell 205 and 212 helicopters. The swashplate support assemblies had been made under contract for Bell Helicopter-Textron, which had rejected them. The Wheatland company sold the rejected swashplates to other companies.

Robinson investigated a virtual pipeline of parts coming in from overseas, notably from the Asian countries of Korea, Vietnam, and Thailand. These countries have a large supply of U.S.-made aircraft, and many of the parts were being sold back to U.S. parts brokers. "We lost about 5,000 helicopters in Vietnam," says Robinson. "Many of them were most likely seized by the North Vietnamese when the country was reunited. People overseas with the right contacts can bribe their way into Vietnam and ship the parts from Thailand past U.S. Customs."

Throughout her career IG Schiavo was at loggerheads with the FAA. One of her first assignments was to investigate whether FAA officials had leaked confidential agency and grand jury documents to Eastern, including secret investigation reports. The New York U.S. Attorney's office during its investigation of Eastern became suspicious of the FAA, which was uncooperative during its investigation, and notified the Attorney General in Washington. The matter was referred to Secretary of Transportation Samuel K. Skinner, who referred the matter to Schiavo.

The IG set up a meeting with lawyers from the Justice and Transportation Departments. FAA Deputy Administrator Barry Harris and junior field officers who regularly worked at Eastern and had seen the suspicious maintenance records attended. The meeting was meant to review and resolve the complaints. Instead, as Schiavo recalls, FAA Deputy Administrator Harris issued a forceful defense of Eastern Airlines, saying that whatever evidence there was of poor maintenance or falsified records was groundless. Harris said that he flew home every week on Eastern, and Eastern was a safe airline.[22]

Harris's forceful defense of Eastern cut short the meeting that Schiavo had arranged, and little was accomplished. The FAA subsequently removed itself from the investigation into Eastern. FAA complicity in leaking documents of any kind to Eastern was never proven. Ultimately, Eastern pleaded guilty to conspiring to prevent the FAA from determining that its maintenance records were falsified, as part of its fifty-three-count indictment.

The Eastern incident proved to be the beginning of increasingly acrimonious relations between the IG and the FAA. Schiavo conducted a series of audits that evaluated the safety oversight programs of the FAA and found many deficiencies. For example, a 1992 review of the FAA's inspection system by DOT investigators found that numerous inspections were not performed; an insufficient number of safety inspectors was cited as the cause.

Schiavo's audit of fourteen FAA-certified repair stations concluded that 43 percent of the new parts on the shelves and 95 percent of the parts obtained from parts brokers came with insufficient documentation. Based on the audit, the IG concluded that most of the parts purchased by repair stations from distributors did not have reasonable evidence of FAA production approval status. Another audit by Schiavo of the FAA's parts inventory discovered that 39 percent of the Agency's parts inventory for its planes were uncertified.

The IG's audits came during a time of increased public fear over safety in the skies. There were several air crashes during 1994, which was one of the worst years on record for fatalities. On November 17, 1994, shortly after the crash of two commercial aircraft, *ABC PrimeTime Live* aired a segment on airline safety. A three-month investigation by ABC News Chief investigative correspondent Brian Ross showed how the tagging of airline parts for safety is haphazardly done, and may involve fraud.

After the December 14, 1994 crash of an American Eagle Jetstream 31 turboprop regional airliner, Transportation Secretary Federico Peña announced a three-pronged campaign to address airline safety. The campaign consisted of a comprehensive review by the FAA, the hiring of another 300 safety inspectors, and an industry-wide safety summit, which was held on January 9, 1995. The theme of the airline safety summit was "Zero Accidents: The Challenge."

On February 27, 1995, as a result of the IG's audits, the FAA approved an enhanced enforcement policy in the *Federal Register*. The FAA policy granted a three-month amnesty period to all parts manufacturers, distributors, parts brokers, and airlines to file applications for FAA approval without the information contained in the application being used in an enforcement action against the filer of the application.

"The FAA was called to the carpet, and they responded by saying that they were going to enforce the Federal Aviation Rules (FARs) to the letter," says Bill Matievich, director of technology for SPS Technology, a midsized manufacturer of fasteners located in Pennsylvania. "The problem is that by enforcing the rules to the letter, the action placed a huge quantity of parts into the unapproved category—parts that were previously treated as approved."

Much of the problem, according to Matievich, is that nearly all fasteners are considered to be standard parts and exempt from the FAA's Parts Manufacturing Approval (PMA). The PMA is for critical parts and larger assemblies. The PMA uses specific tags during production that make the part traceable. Manufacturers that operate with a Type or Production Certificate are called Production Approval Holders (PAH). There are several kinds of Type or Production Certificates besides the PMA, including the Approved Production Inspection System (APIS), Production Certificate (PC), Technical Standard Order (TSO), and others.

Installing parts under the PMA is required under Federal Aviation Regulation (FAR) Section 21.303, which makes it illegal to produce a modification or replacement part for sale on a type-certified aircraft engine or propeller, unless that part is produced pursuant to a Parts Manufacturer Approval. Parts that do not have documentation establishing their production records are one type of suspected unapproved part (SUP). SUPs sometimes involve fraud. For example, if a part is sold as being produced with an FAA approval, when no approval has been issued to the manufacturer, a fraud has been committed. Maintenance personnel are required to notify the FAA of any SUPs, and the FAA, which does not have the search-and-seizure power of law enforcement agencies, is required to report all SUPs to the DOT IG, which makes every report a potential criminal investigation.

The enhanced enforcement policy required repair stations to report any unapproved parts and required that they use only approved parts. Unapproved parts in the aviation industry are usually parts that are sold by suppliers to the aftermarket without written authorization by a PAH. The usual pipeline for parts is that the supplier sells the parts to the PAH holder, who has the FAA license to manufacture the airplane, and the PAH holder sells any overages to the parts brokers. However, if a subcontractor or parts broker needs a part, and none are available, the only recourse is to seek out the supplier—even if the purchase constitutes purchase of an "unapproved" part. Such a sale is in violation of FAR 21.303; however, the rule was never enforced rigorously by the FAA, because enforcing the FAR would slow down maintenance. David R. Hinson, Administrator of the FAA, criticized Schiavo's findings and said that the unapproved parts problem was largely a paperwork problem.

A part offered for sale without an FAA production authorization is an unapproved part; however, some parts may be produced without the authority—including standard parts and parts produced by owners or operators for their own use. Manufacturers like SPS were required to manufacture only standard parts that were defined under national standards, which were defined under the FARs as government standards and standards set by the National Standards Organization. This narrower, by-the-book definition left out parts that are bought under vendor parts numbers, which constitute the bulk of the fasteners in use by the industry. With a stroke of the pen, most of the fasteners in use were lumped into the same category as unapproved parts. For the most part, the fasteners meet the criteria for airworthiness, but under the enhanced enforcement policy, suppliers were either going to have to drop their vendor parts numbering system, an impossible task, or devise a paper trail under the PMA.

Schiavo had her supporters and detractors within the FAA. One of her most notable detractors was Anthony J. Broderick, FAA associate administrator for regulation and certification. He often questioned Schiavo's competence on matters of airline safety. In retaliation, Schiavo accused FAA headquarters of doing everything it could to minimize the dangers of SUPs. Schiavo was supported by a statement from the Professional Airways Systems Specialists, a union representing more than 10,000 FAA employees, to the effect that there had been significant attempts by the FAA to hinder the SUP investigative process, to mitigate the findings, and even to cover up such investigations.

Matters came to a head on May 24, 1995 when a Senate Subcommittee held a hearing entitled "Aviation Safety: Do Unapproved Parts Pose a Safety Risk?" The hearing, which was broadcast on cable television, took place one week before the end of a limited amnesty period for parts manufacturers to file applications for FAA approval of their parts.[23]

Senator William S. Cohen (R-Maine) and Senator Carl Levin (D-Mich.) chaired the Subcommittee. Both senators delivered opening statements on the growing problem of unapproved parts. In his opening statement, Senator Cohen noted wryly that not even the Presidential helicopter is exempt from SUPs and faulted the FAA for dismissing the problem of unapproved parts as a paperwork problem.

FAA executives who testified disagreed with the conclusions drawn by IG Schiavo. For its part, the FAA said that the number of bad parts and the safety threat were greatly exaggerated. After the IG delivered the results of the audit during her testimony before the Senate Subcommittee, relations between the FAA and Schiavo grew so fractious that Transportation Secretary Peña said that he intended to bring FAA officials and Schiavo together to iron out their differences.

After the three-month amnesty period, the FAA cracked down. Many companies billed as OEMs were targeted. These self-designated companies did not have the FAA authorization to produce and sell parts in the aftermarket. Other companies like SPS were forced to devise a production authorization for use with their parts. In 1998, the FAA allowed bearings and fasteners to be approved under the Technical Standard Order (TSO) process.

The friction between Schiavo and the FAA came to a head with the crash of ValuJet Flight 592 on May 11, 1996. All 110 people aboard the jet were killed when the jet crashed into the Everglades. Anthony Broderick, the FAA's associate administrator for regulation and certification, resigned in June 1996, after the FAA came under fire for its poor oversight of ValuJet,[24] and Schiavo resigned two weeks later.

ValuJet was touted as a success story of deregulation. Founded in 1993 and based in Atlanta, it was one of many small, no-frills airlines that went head to head with the bigger airlines. Few of the no-frills lasted long, although they enjoyed a few good years of high revenue. Like many no-frill start-ups, ValuJet bought used or reconditioned jets. ValuJet kept capital expenses to a minimum, paid its pilots only for flights they completed, and its maintenance was divided up among fifty different contractors at eighteen companies.

ValuJet's safety record steadily deteriorated. In 1994, ValuJet pilots made fifteen emergency landings, and in 1995, its pilots were forced down fifty-seven times. From February through May 1996, ValuJet would have an unscheduled landing on average every other day. Schiavo, who was receiving the reports about ValuJet's mishaps, was concerned that the FAA had reviewed ValuJet's planes over the last three years and had never reported any significant problems until March 1996 when FAA inspectors recommended grounding ValuJet. Unfortunately, the FAA did not ground ValuJet.

Immediately after the crash of ValuJet Flight 592, Transportation Secretary Federico Peña assured the public that the airline was safe. The FAA began an investigation of ValuJet to determine the cause of the accident and found numerous problems. One plane repeatedly flew with a hole in the engine cowl, which would have reduced the effectiveness of the fire extinguishers if there had been a fire. A plane was returned to service uninspected after being struck by lightning. An unqualified technician was performing X-ray examinations of critical aircraft parts.

A consent decree was signed with ValuJet, under which Valujet agreed to pay $500,000 immediately and $1.5 million within sixty days. In return the FAA agreed not to pursue any civil penalty for violations described in the agreement, except for violations of regulations on hazardous materials and civil aviation security.

On July 8, 1996, Inspector General Schiavo resigned. Her decision to resign was voluntary, she declared. Nonetheless, her resignation may well have been prompted by a guest essay that was published in *Newsweek* shortly after the ValuJet crash. She wrote that she had had long-standing concerns about ValuJet and blamed the FAA for the crash. Long criticized for her outspokenness, her criticism of the FAA prior to any investigation of the crash was unprecedented and inappropriate.[25]

NOTES

1. Howard Todd, "Counterfeit Controversy," *Hot Rod*, June 1988, p. 103.

2. "Bogus Helicopter Parts Scheme Alleged," *Washington Post*, February 12, 1977, p. A1.

3. Weiner O'Donnell, "The Counterfeit Trade: Illegal Copies Threaten Most

Industries and Can Endanger Consumers," *Business Week*, December 16, 1985, p. 67.

4. Todd, note 1, p. 102.

5. Kim M. Magon, "The Counterfeit Crisis," *Truck Parts and Service*, November 1990, pp. 22–23.

6. "Body-Part Heat: Ford vs. Independents," *Business Week*, December 17, 1990, p. 30.

7. Eric Weiner, "Criminal Charges against Managers Send a Message on Airline Safety," *New York Times*, July 29, 1990.

8. "Fake USAir Repairs," *New York Newsday*, March 25, 1993, pp. 35–36.

9. "The 'Final Nail in the Coffin'?" *Newsweek*, August 6, 1990, p. 46.

10. Carole A. Shifrin, "Ex-FAA Official Urges Agency Autonomy," *Aviation Week and Space Technology*, August 5, 1996, p. 40.

11. Paul Tharp, "Airline Aid Urged by Federal Panel," *New York Post*, July 20, 1993, p. 26.

12. Weiner, note v.

13. Ibid., note vi.

14. "The Legal Storm Swirling around Express One," *Business Week*, November 28, 1994, p. 100.

15. "Fly Right (The FAA Moves to Clean Up the Mess at Mesa Air)," *Time*, October 17, 1996, p. 76.

16. Adam Bryant, "F.A.A.'s Lax Inspection Setup Heightens Dangers in the Sky," *New York Times*, October 15, 1995, p. 1.

17. "Tarnished Wings," *Time*, March 13, 1989, p. 41.

18. "Needs Work (Too Few Jet Mechanics, Too Many Breakdowns)," *Time*, August 21, 1989, p. 43.

19. Glenn Kessler, "A Twisted Trail of Fake Jet Parts," *New York Newsday*, June 15, 1993, pp. 33, 37.

20. James Ott, "U.S. Indicts Broker in Alleged Parts Scam," *Aviation Week and Space Technology*, April 5, 1993, p. 36.

21. Triplett, "Search and Destroy: The War on Counterfeit Parts," *Air and Space*, November 1996, p. 23.

22. Mary Schiavo, *Flying Blind, Flying Safe*, Avon Books, 1997, pp. 55–57.

23. Matthew L. Wald, "Counterfeit Airline Parts Are Said To Be Often Used," *New York Times*, May 25, 1995, p. A18.

24. "The FAA's About-Face," *US News and World Report*, July 1, 1996, p. 49.

25. Adam Bryant, "Outspoken F.A.A. Critic Quits Transportation Post," *New York Times*, July 9, 1996. See also "The Mouth of 'Maximum Mary,'" *Business Week*, June 24, 1996, p. 40.

10

Piracy in Cyberspace

In November 1996 segments from "Discoteque" and "Wake Up, Dead Man," two cuts from an upcoming U2 album, showed up on the Internet. The thirty-second cuts were believed to have been lifted by hackers from video cables during a recording session in a Dublin studio.[1] Thinking this was part of U2's publicity campaign, several radio stations downloaded the segments and began broadcasting them.

The Internet segments appeared at nearly the same time that bootleg CD copies of the upcoming U2 album were being sold in Ireland and Britain. As U.K. authorities tracked down the bootleggers, Island Records, U2's label, asked the stations to cease broadcasting the segments.

Shortly after the U2 bootlegging incident, the International Federation of the Phonographic Industries (IFPI) held a seminar in London on the role that interactive technologies, such as the Internet, are having on the spread of music piracy. The Internet involves the storage and distribution of digital codes, rather than physical products. A sound recording or computer program downloaded from the Internet is a nearly perfect digital copy.

The Internet has opened up a gate to virtually unlimited copyright piracy (see Figure 10.1). A person who uploads a computer program or a sound recording has made the product available to anyone connected to the Internet. Currently there are an estimated 45 million people connected to the Internet in ninety countries.

Many of the pirates are college students and teenagers, who are part of a movement that believes that the Net differs from the established commercial marketplace. In one respect they are right: the Internet is a unique marketplace. As anyone who is connected to the Internet knows,

Figure 10.1
Sources for Internet Software Piracy

- USENET Newsgroups
- E-Mail
- Telenet
- Internet Relay Chat (IRC)
- Web Pages

Source: Business Software Alliance.

there are thousands of products—computer programs, games, and music—that can be downloaded for free. In some cases, the products are being offered by upstart companies or hopeful musicians. In some instances, as an inducement to purchasing the product by credit card, book publishers offer book excerpts and record companies offer thirty-second cuts of an upcoming album.

There is also an incredible underground network of software and music pirates. Anyone who does a search for "warez" (pronounced "wares"), "hackers," or any of a number of search names can be introduced to this network. There are many programs, like hacks and cracks, that can be downloaded and will assist in obtaining pirated software. Hacks and cracks has the serial numbers for all currently available software and is updated regularly. Although the BSA and other software companies shut down the Web sites offering this program, others appear with regular updates.

"I've never bought any legitimate software" boasts a New York City web designer, who obtains all of his software programs for free on the Internet. Many software updates and new programs are pirated and appear on the Internet, before the legitimate companies have had time to offer them through normal commercial channels.

During 1997, upcoming albums for Madonna, Van Halen, Pearl Jam, and Eric Clapton were prereleased on the Internet without authorization. "These were not bootlegs," says D'Onofrio of the RIAA. "Somehow they got hold of a copy of the album before the official release date."

According to D'Onofrio, these prereleases pose a serious problem. Major recording artists are losing control of when and how to market their recordings. The legitimate industry puts hundreds of thousands of dollars, even millions, into recording and marketing a sound recording. When someone puts the album on the Internet for a worldwide audience to download, the buildup and marketing pitch preceding the release of a major recording is damaged. Future sales of the recording are affected adversely.

What is baffling about the Internet pirates is that money is usually not their main concern. "It is like a subculture," says Allen Schubert, an Internet investigator for the BSA. "Some of them don't like particular companies—like Microsoft, which is the industry leader. Their main motivation is not money. They do it to undermine the established order of things. Some of the sites have a certain look to them and involve considerable creative effort."

Schubert surfs the Net full-time searching for pirated software. Some pirates are easily caught, says Schubert, who turns them over to the legal department. Some naively advertise in Internet newsgroups and supply their home address and telephone number. Schubert tries to determine their identity, if possible, and also their service provider. Other maneuvers involve using billboards that direct the viewer to locations in other sites. According to Schubert, the sheer number makes it difficult, even impossible, to track them all. Moreover, many pirates switch providers frequently to hinder detection.

"Detection is getting more difficult," says Schubert. "What many are doing is remote downloading. Although it appears that you are downloading from a certain site, you are mirroring a site somewhere else— and the site could be anywhere in the world."

Many pirates on the Internet are not even aware that they have committed a crime. A student at Iowa State University thought it would be a wonderful idea to put *Winnie-the-Pooh* on the World Wide Web. The student received a cease-and-desist letter from E. P. Dutton, the publisher of A. A. Milne's work, and *Winnie-the-Pooh* soon exited the Internet.

"Most of the book pirates are pirating short books, usually children's books," says Carol Risher of the AAP. "Fortunately, people are not scanning and putting up 600-page books, although we have seen some Web sites using journal and other scholarly literature without authorization."

The technology is available to "scan" any two-dimensional work, such as a book or illustration, into digital form and, from this digital version, create an exact copy that can be disseminated onto the Internet. One pirate site contained the complete texts of Douglas Adams' popular *Hitchhiker's Guide to the Galaxy* series.

Many of the pirates operate under a cyber philosophy whose underlying proposition is that the Internet will erode and ultimately transform the value of intellectual property. One leading proponent is Esther Dyson, president of Edventure Holdings, a company focused on emerging information technology. In her book *Release 2.0*, Dyson argues that because computers and the Internet have made it almost cost-free to reproduce content, and to send or retrieve it anywhere in the world, intellectual property will undergo a change. Individual creators, Dyson argues, will not have the means to protect their copyrights or to exploit them commercially. Instead, creators will be forced to give away their works, and to accept remuneration in other ways for their creativity.

What kinds of information should be free on the Internet is the subject of considerable legal and ethical debate. For example, in May 1998 Carl Malamud, president of the Internet Multicasting Service, a nonprofit organization, sent a letter to Vice President Al Gore and Commerce Secretary William M. Daley. In his letter, Malamud challenged the federal government to make the nation's patent and trademark database available for free on the Internet—otherwise he would do so himself.[2] This was not a crank threat. In January 1994, Malamud began posting the full text of many SEC documents and several years of the patent database on the Internet. Only lack of funds prevented him from continuing.

Malamud is apparently motivated by humanitarian ideals. Malamud, who is a visiting professor at the Massachusetts Institute of Technology Media Lab, hopes that by making the entire patent and trademark database available, he will touch off an explosion of creative ways in which to utilize the nation's science and technology storehouse. To carry out his vision, he must raise enough funds to acquire the information from the U.S. Patent and Trademark Office (USPTO). The USPTO has objected to Malamud's idea, because it will deprive it of an estimated $20 million yearly in fees that it charges for making copies of the information. Malamud's campaign is just one in a continuing dispute between those who advocate widely distributing government databases that are created at taxpayers' expense and the private information industry that makes a living selling information.

The Internet has evolved in such a way that no one agency or organization is responsible for overall management of the Internet. This decentralization has provided the needed flexibility for the Internet's continuing growth and evolution. On the other hand, who polices the content of the Internet is a concern of law enforcement agencies and governments, as well as private enterprise.

Fraudulent offers abound on the Internet. America Online and CompuServe have an attorney who spends about half of each day monitoring what is offered on the Internet.[3] A "campfire mentality" among Internet browsers leads many consumers to trust claims they might otherwise reject. Pyramid schemes, which lure people into an ongoing line of payments, are illegal, but many web surfers fall for them. Claiming a health product cures something when it does not is illegal; nonetheless, scam artists can skirt the law by merely suggesting their product will cure a disease or by teasing consumers into sending money for more information. Several states, including Minnesota, North Carolina, and Georgia, have been patrolling the on-line services for scams.

The Internet began as an experimental, prototype network called Arpanet, which was established in 1969 by the Department of Defense's

Defense Advanced Research Projects Agency (DARPA). Through Arpanet, DARPA sought to demonstrate the possibilities of computer networking based on packet-switching technology, which is a technique for achieving economical and effective communication among computers on a network. A loosely organized web of interconnected networks, starting with Arpanet and including many local and regional networks, developed to support a growing community of researchers, including computer scientists, physicists, mathematicians, and others. The term cyberspace was coined by the author William Gibson and denotes a world of networked computers and the people who control them.

Use of the Internet was free to individuals engaged in government-sponsored research. One function that was widely used was electronic mail (e-mail), which provided a means of sending person-to-person messages almost instantaneously. Responsibility for managing and securing host computers was given to the endusers—in most instances, the college campuses and the federal agencies that owned and operated the computer networks or host site. The host site functioned as a service provider or company network that provided access to the Internet and used a domain name to identify itself. Most persons on the Internet today use an Internet service provider (ISP), which can be either a local or a national provider.

A host site may contain any number of computers. In a corporate setting, the host site is controlled by the systems manager. A systems manager performs a variety of security-related functions, including: establishing access controls to computers by use of passwords; security checks to detect and protect against unauthorized use of computers; configuration management, which enables them to control the versions of the software being used and how changes to that software are made; software maintenance to ensure that software flaws are repaired.

A typical security device for a host site is a firewall, which limits entry into the network, using either a packet-filtering router or a proxy server. A hacker is someone who enters a host site without authorization, either bypassing security, like a firewall, or exploiting a flaw in the software.

Hackers are a real menace. In November 1994, hackers penetrated the firewall of General Electric Company and accessed GE systems that contained proprietary information.[4] Although there was no apparent damage to the information, GE shut down Internet access for seventy-two hours as a precaution. Hackers have hacked into bank databases to obtain the financial information of the bank's clients, and frequently try to hack into defense computers. In 1995, a GAO report said that as many as 250,000 attempts may have been made to penetrate military computer networks and 65 percent (162,500) were successful.

In 1994 two hackers hacked into computers of the Air Force command and control research facility in Rome, New York, more than 150 times.[5]

To avoid detection, the hackers went through international telephone lines, passing ports in South America, Seattle, and New York to reach the Air Force computer systems of NASA, Wright-Patterson Air Force Base, defense contractors around the country, and South Korea's atomic energy center. One of the hackers was a sixteen-year-old from the United Kingdom with the computer nickname "Datastream Cowboy." Datastream Cowboy broke into the Rome system, virtually shut it down, and, at least temporarily, raised fears of an international incident with North Korea, when he accessed a computer in either North or South Korea and downloaded information on atomic research into the Rome laboratory. In doing so, he raised fears that North Korea might think the United States was committing an act of aggression. Understandably, defense installations have stiffened the firewalls and access codes needed to enter their computers since the mid-1990s.

One early hacker was Bill Gates, founder of Microsoft.[6] In 1969, Gates was in the ninth grade and shared a common interest in computers with Paul Allen. Both teenagers introduced themselves to the engineers at Computer Center Corporation (CCC). CCC's founders were just out of college and were taken with the boys' enthusiasm. Eventually a deal was made between CCC and the teenagers. The engineers were trying to work out the bugs in their PDP-10 software. In exchange for computer time, the boys agreed to test out CCC's software and compile a list of bugs. Gates soon found a way to bypass CCC's password protection and obtained authorization to information held in the computer's memory. His prank caused the system to crash. Gates himself would have his first brush with pirates only a few years later. He had developed a computer program called BASIC, which was Microsoft's first product. BASIC was widely pirated by computer hobbyists, who obtained copies at computer club meetings and from each other. The end-user piracy nearly put the fledgling Microsoft out of business.

The Domain Name System (DNS) arose because of the growing number of people and businesses with an Internet address. At one time, there were only a few computers linked to Arpanet. They were located in a file named hosts.txt, which was a master list of each computer's address and its host name. Increasing numbers of Internet users wanted their computers on Arpanet, but they had to wait for NIC to update hosts.txt. In late 1987, Paul Mockapetris outlined the Domain Name System (DNS).[7]

DNS functions as a White Pages for computers. Instead of maintaining a single database, elements of DNS are distributed across thousands of name servers, each of which contains information about one branch of the Internet. The DNS resembles a tree: at the top are the root name servers that contain information about the contents of the top-level domains (TLD), such as ".com," ".net," and ".org," coupled with the second-level domain (SLD) requested by the party seeking the domain assignment (e.g., Microsoft.com).

Generally, domain names are assigned on a first-come, first-served basis. In the United States, the vast majority of domains are assigned by Network Solutions, Inc. (NSI), which is under contract from the National Science Foundation. Situations arose involving the intentional "pirating" of someone else's domain name. One case, *MTV Networks v. Adam Curry*, 867 F.Supp 202 (S.D.N.Y. 1994), involved a former MTV "video jockey" who, while employed by MTV, had registered "mtv.com" under his own name with his employer's approval. The video jockey established a large following, but when he left MTV, he refused to give up the domain name. MTV filed suit, and eventually obtained control of the disputed domain.

Cyber-squatters, as they are called, who attempt to profit from the Internet by reserving and later reselling or licensing domain names back to the companies that own the trademarks, began to proliferate. Many companies with well-known marks paid thousands of dollars to gain the rights to domain names that matched trademarks that they own.

To thwart cyber-squatters, NSI adopted a policy that allowed an applicant only one domain name; later the policy was rescinded. NSI then imposed a fee for obtaining or renewing a domain. This was intended to put an end to the cyber-squatters' practice of grabbing multiple domains containing well-known company trade names or trademarks for the sole purpose of selling the domains back to the companies that own the marks.

Charging fees did not stop the cyber-squatters. Eventually, NSI adopted the Domain Name Dispute Policy, which went into effect on November 23, 1995. Under the Dispute Policy, the owner of a trademark registered in the United States or in a foreign country could challenge use of the "identical" second-level domain by submitting the registration certificate to NSI. NSI continued to register domain names on a first-come, first-served basis, but did not perform any trademark searches or otherwise investigate whether the applicant had rights to the requested domain name.

NSI's dispute resolution policy conflicted with traditional trademark principles, and was widely criticized.

"The problem with the NSI dispute resolution is that it fails to take into account that trademarks are entered onto the Principal Register by class," says Jeffrey Samuels, who was formerly an Assistant Commissioner with the USPTO. "If you go to the Principal Register and look for Sterling®, you will likely find several companies using it—Sterling Bank, Sterling Drug, and possibly others. Because they're registered in different classes on the Principal Register, there is no conflict; however, on the Internet, there can only be one Sterling.com."

The NSI dispute resolution policy has been amended several times since 1995. Last amended in early 1998, the policy provides that a trademark holder whose mark was registered prior to the issuance of a domain name could submit the registration certificate to the NSI, and the NSI would put the domain name on "hold"—which effectively prohibited anyone from using it. For obvious reasons, this amendment proved unsatisfactory.

"In the end, the legitimate trademark holder is forced to take legal action against the cyber-squatter, unless a deal of some kind can be made," says Samuels. "There are many cases involving cyber-squatters that have been filed and resolved. Invariably the court has ruled in favor of the legitimate trademark owner, and ordered the NSI to transfer the domain name to the legitimate trademark holder."

According to Samuels, the NSI is sometimes brought into the suits involving domain name piracy, but thus far has avoided being found liable for contributory negligence. NSI primarily serves as a register and provides an infrastructure for that register.

NSI's contract with the National Science Institute expired in March 1998 and a two-year extension was granted. The Clinton administration issued a green paper on the domain name registration system and proposed a number of changes, including the recommendation that more top-level domain names be added and that there be a series of private nonprofit entities in charge of each of the registers on a not-for-profit basis.

The Clinton administration's proposals were not greeted warmly. On June 5, 1998 the Commerce Department issued a white paper proposing that a nonprofit corporation be established to handle the registration of domain names. Many trademark holders are choosing to register their domain names with the USPTO, which does allow the registration of domain names on the Principal Register, if they are used in connection with the sale of goods.

Because it usually does not involve profit, copyright piracy initially baffled the courts. One of the first cases involved a Massachusetts Institute of Technology (MIT) student who uploaded hundreds of computer programs: *U.S. of America v. David LaMaccia*, 871 F. Supp. 535 (D. Mass. 1994). LaMaccia, a student at MIT, used the school's computer network to gain access to the Internet. Using pseudonyms and an encrypted address, LaMaccia set up an electronic bulletin board and encouraged correspondents to download popular software applications like WordPerfect 6.0. LaMaccia's piracy is estimated at $1 million, the largest amount by a single individual.[8] However, in its 1994 decision, the court cleared him of the criminal charge of wire fraud, in part because he had not sought monetary gain for his actions.

LaMaccia was legislatively overruled in December 1998, when President Clinton signed the No Electronic Theft (NET) Act into law, making it a crime to possess or distribute multiple copies of on-line copyrighted material, for profit or not. Dubbed the "LaMaccia bill," because it closed a loophole in the copyright law, the NET Act was meant to address the posting of copyrighted material on the Internet, whether for profit or not. Even without seeking monetary remuneration, music and software that is given away for free on the Internet causes considerable loss of revenue to the legitimate copyright holders.

The NET Act tightens the criminal infringement provisions of the Copyright Act, amending the Act's definition of "private financial gain" to include the barter of illegal copyrighted works, and redefining criminal infringement to include willful infringement that, while it may lack a commercial motive, still has a substantial commercial effect. Under the NET Act, the penalties include fines of up to $250,000 and five years in prison.

After the *LaMaccia* ruling, many industry groups began to monitor the Internet for signs of piracy. The BSA and the RIAA, both headquartered in Washington, D.C., maintain a group of Internet detectives who monitor the Internet for offerings of pirated software and recorded music. Simon & Schuster, the publishing giant, and other publishers browse the Web for pirated books.

Although there are few laws governing intellectual property on the Internet, an on-line service provider can be held liable for the acts of its subscribers. One of the earliest counterfeiting cases on the Internet was *Sega Enterprises Ltd. v. Maphia*, 857 F.Supp. 679 (N.D. Cal. 1994), in which the court entered a preliminary injunction and seizure order against the owner of a computer bulletin board system (BBS) who had knowingly solicited the uploading and downloading of unauthorized copies of Sega's video games.

In the case *United States Religious Center v. Netcom On-Line Comm. Serv., Inc.*, 907 F.Supp. 1361 (N.D. Cal. 1995), both Netcom and the BBS sought to be relieved of liability for copyright infringement, after a former member of the Church of Scientology went on-line and posted messages that were critical of the founder, L. Ron Hubbard.

The court noted that although the Internet service provider and BBS did not create, copy, control, or monitor the contents of the church's information, they could both be liable for contributory infringement, if they were found at trial to have failed to cancel the messages and stop the worldwide distribution of the copies. The court required the plaintiffs to establish at trial such contributory infringement, an issue of fact that required knowledge of the infringement and substantial participation in it. The case was settled in the summer of 1996.

"This case makes it clear to companies like Netcom that they cannot turn a deaf ear to third-party complaints, as a way of avoiding contributory liability for infringing material that subscribers post on their systems," says Carole Aciman, an attorney in New York City who teaches a class on the Internet at New York University's School of Continuing Education.

"Although many Internet Service Providers (ISPs) already require their subscribers to adhere to some terms and conditions—notably with respect to copyright infringement—the outcome of this case has encouraged ISPs to follow Netcom's lead and establish protocols to handle intellectual property disputes and strict policies for the posting of copyrighted material through their services."

Netcom was a landmark decision in fighting computer and music piracy. ISPs and universities that have customers or students on-line have had to pay closer attention to the content being put onto the Internet. In 1996, America Online shut down Tape Traders Central Web site, because of potential liability of copyright infringement. Tape Traders Central was a Web site where music fans posted offers to exchange bootleg tapes. When it became apparent that some of the bands may not have consented to be included on the site, America Online pulled the plug.[9]

Starting in 1997, the RIAA began to shift its antipiracy focus to deal with a barrage of music piracy on the Internet. Music piracy involving analog cassettes had been steadily decreasing over the past five years, and beginning in 1997, 80 percent of the RIAA's antipiracy effort turned to protect members' copyrighted sound recordings on the Internet, and to deal with a new form of CD piracy, the CD-Recordable (CD-R).

CD-Rs look like compact discs. CD-Rs are usually gold on one side with a greenish tint on the nongraphic, or "read-only," side. Currently, CD-Rs are not currently being used by the major record companies for retail releases. To produce a CD-R requires a CD-R burner, which is commercially available for about $400; the blank discs cost around $1. During the first half of 1998, the RIAA confiscated 23,858 unauthorized CD-Rs, as compared to 87 in the same period in 1997.

Unlimited music piracy on the Internet became possible with the invention and widespread use of a data compression technology called MPEG-1 Layer 3, otherwise called MP3 or MPEG.[10] Prior to the invention of MP3, the only obstacle to unlimited music piracy was enhanced digital compression and faster modems. Audio and sound files are very data intensive, and take a very long time to download.

MP3 uses a technique known as "lossy compression," which is a special software program that decides what parts of the sound you won't be able to hear and eliminates it. A file format capable of compressing a fifty-megabyte song is used for storing sound digitally and allows users to download hundreds of full-length songs. The songs can be stored, either on a computer hard drive, ZIP disk, or CD-R. Most of the Internet pirates are college students, who have free computer and Internet access provided by the university. The university site may also provide band-width as high as the commercial Internet service providers, which allows for the creation of Web pages, as well as the uploading and downloading of a significant amount of sound. The higher bandwidth also allows for the uploading and downloading of near-CD-quality music.

Many of the MP3 sites, which are also called music archive sites, encourage people to upload recordings in exchange for being able to download music. Some of the sites are open to all, but others have a password. Some of the MP3 sites even have a commercial aspect to them—they have banner ads where they're getting some monetary benefit from having the sites.

"In many instances, they are not necessarily getting any overt monetary benefit," says D'Onofrio, "but the record company's and the artist's choice on how, when, and where to market their product is taken away by others who have no right to do so."

The RIAA has responded to the infringing acts in the law courts. On May 5, 1997, the RIAA filed two suits. One in the U.S. District Court for the District of Arizona in Phoenix was filed against Arizona Bizness Network, a Phoenix-based Internet service provider. The ISP's home page linked to another ISP page that offered a "song of the week." The second suit was filed in the U.S. District Court for the Western District of Washington in Seattle against a music archive site that offered more than 1,100 songs for downloading. The site also permitted users to request songs not found on the site. The owner of the Washington State music archive site had sought to be relieved of copyright liability by posing a disclaimer that read: "Please be aware that currently you must own the copyrighted material you download here in some form." D'Onofrio explained that disclaimers, such as this, do not immunize site operators from prosecution.

In June 1997 the RIAA filed civil lawsuits in federal court in New York, Texas, and California against three Internet music archive sites and their operators. The archive sites were reproducing copyrighted songs without authorization from the copyright owners. The RIAA was awarded over a million dollars in damages in each case. The archive site owners entered into consent judgments with the RIAA. In the judgment, the RIAA agreed to forgo collecting any monetary damages on the condition that the defendants never again engage in music piracy.

Throughout 1997, the RIAA sent cease-and-desist letters to hundreds of Internet sites informing them that they were infringing member companies' rights. The majority of sites were located on college campuses and were promptly shut down; in some instances, the sites were shut down within a few hours. The few remaining sites sought proper licensing or removed the unlicensed recordings. The University of Evansville in Evansville, Indiana revoked one student's computer privileges for a specified period of time as punishment. Other students were suspended.[11]

After the RIAA sent a cease-and-desist letter to Rice University, two student Web sites were removed by the University. Like many universities, Rice has a copyright policy for the students to adhere to, although the University does not police student Web pages. After the Web sites were removed, a group of Rice faculty decided to revise the copyright policy to better cover on-line publishing issues.[12] Like many of the universities that had copyright situations involving music archive sites, Rice sought the assistance of the RIAA in devising a better code. After Rice and other universities requested assistance, the RIAA developed Soundbyting, an educational program including a teaching module that covers the legal and ethical copyright issues on the Internet.

"In 1998, we test-marketed the educational campaign in ten major universities, where we've found the most archive sites," says D'Onofrio. "The universities dialoged us regarding the problem. As a result, we developed the Soundbyting program. Soundbyting talks about the morality and the ethical issues involved in taking intellectual property. It also discusses the civil and criminal ramifications of Internet copyright infringement."

Students still trade music using the university intranet. This is a minor problem compared to the growing market for pirate and bootleg discs being sold on the Internet. "The Internet is actually becoming a marketplace for the sale of pirate goods," says D'Onofrio. "It's like a worldwide flea market or mail-order business."

By the end of 1997, the IFPI, BPI, and RIAA were engaged in projects to survey the extent of the unauthorized use of music on the Internet. Using automated web crawlers, the initial search indicated that at any one time there could be up to 80,000 infringing MP3 files on the Internet. However, the actual number of servers on the Internet hosting these infringing sites was estimated at 2,000, based in thirty countries. The majority were located in the United States, with a high proportion found in Australia, Sweden, and Canada.

As part of the pilot project, IFPI alerted the national music groups in the countries where illegal sites were located. Immediate action was undertaken. IFPI Sweden contacted about 100 MP3 sites with warning letters. Nearly all of the sites situated in Sweden closed down, but about half of the sites were deep-linked to File Transfer Protocol archives in the United States. IFPI Sweden has also encountered an increasing number of sites that are selling or swapping CD-Rs containing hundreds of MP3 files. The piracy situation was caused in part by Swedish computer magazines that had published articles explaining how to make MP3 files and where to find illegal MP3 sites on the Internet. The IFPI survey uncovered a small underground market in Taiwan involving college students. Taiwanese students were marketing CD recordings of songs downloaded from their school's File Transfer Protocol servers.

Because of the Internet, music and software piracy is evolving from a crime involving high-speed duplicators to one that involves an individual and a computer. Faster modems and enhanced technology for downloading and uploading information have facilitated the piracy. To stem the piracy losses, IBM, Microsoft, and other companies with a portfolio of assets protected by copyright are working on developing anticopying technologies. In 1999, the music industry hired Leonardo Chiariglione, one of the inventors of MP3, to help set standards for encoding digital music. Encoding may involve use of a digital watermark.

A digital watermark is an inaudible, usually unerasable message that contains copyright information. Watermarks can be hidden anywhere on the product. In February 1996, NEC Corp. introduced a watermark system that relies on spreading a bit pattern through the file to stamp it without disrupting the image, sound, or video in the process. A graphics file with a watermark can be printed, photocopied, and faxed without distorting the watermark.

Watermarks may offer a solution to the difficulty of identifying infringers on-line. Nearly everyone on the Internet masks his identity, and so who is really on-line and where he is located are a mystery.

By use of watermarks, record companies and software companies can automatically scan the Internet and discover which of the many products and services being offered might be pirated. Products purchased on-line may have a watermark embedded that contains the name and credit number of the purchaser of the product. Examination of the watermark may make it possible to trace pirated products discovered on-line back to the purchaser.

To facilitate and protect the flow of copyrighted information on the Internet, the AAP and the Corporation for National Research Initiatives, a nonprofit organization funded by private industry and government, have developed the digital object identifier (DOI). DOI, which is meant to be used with a watermark, will identify the author and provide appropriate copyright information, which in turn will facilitate document retrieval, clearinghouse payments, and licensing. The DOI system was launched at the 1997 Frankfurt Book Fair and was enthusiastically endorsed by the publishing industry.

The International Standard Recording Code (ISRC) is an identification code that may be used with a watermark to identify sound recordings. IFPI is the registration authority for the ISRC. The ISRC enables record producers to identify an individual recording. Each track of music on a CD or a DCC can be given its own unique coded identification number, which is encoded in the digital recording and does not physically appear on the product.

According to Aciman, powerful industry groups are likely to exercise some pressure on ISPs to promote the use of such copy-protection devices. Aciman cites the example of the Software Publishers Association (SPA), which, in its ISP Code of Conduct (http:/www.spa.org/ piracy/code.htm), defines copyright infringement to include not only the distribution of protected software, but the provision of cracker utilities and any other information that can be used to circumvent manufacturer-installed watermarks.

Another way of protecting information transmitted on-line is through encryption. The technology to intercept anything transmitted over the Net, or to gain access to a computer hooked up to the Net and download files, is widely available. In most instances, intercepting or accessing information on someone's computer or e-mail is illegal, but discovering the identity of the hacker may prove difficult and, if the hacker or pirate is in another country, exercising legal jurisdiction may be impossible.

Encryption may be the only way to provide security for property—intellectual property, credit card numbers, and "electronic cash"—that is entered or can be accessed in the electronic commerce on the Internet. Encryption is part of the field of cryptography, the science of secure and secret communications. Using a secret key, the sender can transform information into a coded message. Only the sender and receiver have the secret key, which allows the authorized receiver to decode and decipher the hidden information. Unauthorized receivers will not be able to decode the message without the key. The problem with traditional encryption is that it relies upon both the sender and receiver of an encoded message having access to the key. The danger always exists that an unauthorized person will obtain access to the key.

In April 1993 the Clinton administration proposed a new standard for encryption technology developed with the National Security Agency. The technology was known as the Clipper Chip, because it used a secret algorithm called Skipjack to encrypt information.

The Clipper Chip was considered impossible to crack and, as proposed by the Clinton administration, was to be installed on all telephones, computer modems, and fax machines to encrypt voice communications. The Clipper Chip caused an uproar because it would have had government master keys built in—specifically, a law enforcement access field (LEAF), which would be transmitted along with the user's data and contain the identity of the user's individual chip and the user's key. With a court order, government or law enforcement could access the encrypted information using LEAF.

The Clipper Chip was supposed to be the answer to the individual's concern for data security and the government's concern for law enforcement. Private citizens would have access to the encryption they need. Criminals would be unable to use encryption to hide their illegal activities. Despite political opposition, Clipper technology is being used by government agencies for unclassified communications, and by some corporations.

Encryption is a controversial topic in other countries, as well as in the United States. In France, you need a license to use encryption, and it is primarily used by banks and credit card companies. In 1997, Britain circulated a proposal that would allow private use only of cryptography that was officially licensed. The proposal was to ensure that the software used a code that law enforcement could crack. In Germany, encryption remains a divisive issue; the Interior Ministry has supported the need for encryption restrictions of some sort, but the Justice Ministry and the Economics Ministry have both signaled their opposition.[13]

Another way of protecting products offered on the Internet is through stronger protection of the underlying intellectual property. On December 20, 1996 delegates from 160 nations met in Geneva, Switzerland at the World Intellectual Property Organization (WIPO) and ratified several international treaties for the protection of intellectual property in the digital age.

The United States offered three proposals to protect literary and artistic works, music recordings, and databases from unauthorized use. Two of the proposals were adopted and a compromise was reached on the third proposal, which would have extended copyright protection to computerized data and would have treated temporary copies downloaded from the Internet as possible violations of international copyright law.

The first treaty included provisions for computer software and databases; distribution of copyrighted materials over networks and in tangible formats; legal protections for anticopying technology; and guarantees for a new means of on-line licensing of copyrighted materials. The second treaty brought protection for sound recordings into closer accord with the protection available for other creative products, such as books, movies, and computer software.

The legislation to implement the WIPO international copyright treaties (H.R. 2281) was approved in February 1998 with only minor amendments by the House Judiciary Subcommittee on Courts and Intellectual Property. The Subcommittee action led to passage of the Digital Millenium Copyright Act (DMCA) in October 1998.

The DMCA makes it a crime to circumvent antipiracy measures built into most commercial software and outlaws the manufacture, sale, or distribution of code-cracking devices used to illegally copy software.

Passage of the Digital Millenium Copyright Act was a victory for President Clinton, who has always been a strong advocate of the Internet. In his first policy statement on the Internet, released July 2, 1997, President Clinton mapped out a vision of the global computer network as a largely unregulated and untaxed electronic marketplace.[14] The nonbinding report was the result of fifteen months of work by a task force made up of government officials and representatives from the Internet industry. The task force advocated a laissez-faire commercial environment as the best means for the Internet to develop. Although some critics lamented the tax-free environment, all were unanimous in support of the task force's recommendations that industry and government work together to develop further protection of intellectual property on the Internet.

NOTES

1. Robert Dominguez, "Online Bootlegging a Net Loss for U2," *New York Daily News*, November 19, 1996.

2. John Markoff, "U.S. Is Urged to Offer More Data on Line," *New York Times*, May 4, 1998, p. D6.

3. Kirsten Danis, "Hoboken Man Roots Out On-line Fraud," *Jersey Journal*, November 21, 1995.

4. Clinton Wilder, "How Safe Is the Internet?" *Information Week*, December 12, 1994, p. 13.

5. See "Defense Computers Prove an Easy Target for Host of Hackers," *Star-Ledger*, May 23, 1996.

6. See Daniel Ichbiah and Susan L. Knepper, *The Making of Microsoft*, Prima Pub., 1991, chapter 2.

7. Tim Barkow, "The Domain Name System," *Wired*, September 1996, p. 84.

8. Philip Elmer-Dewitt, "Nabbing the Pirates of Cyberspace," *Time*, June 13, 1994, p. 63.

9. Robert Levine, "ABC Television Boots Concert-tape Traders off its America Online Site," *Rolling Stone*, September 5, 1996, p. 25.

10. Jason Chervokas, "Internet CD Copying Tests Music Industry," *New York Times*, April 6, 1998, p. D3.

11. Jennifer Nally, "Student Accused of Internet Violation," *Crescent*, October 1997.

12. Greg Norman, "Student Web Pages Break Copyright Laws," *Rice Thresher*, December 5, 1997.

13. Philip Manchester, "Anomalies across International Borders," *Financial Times*, November 6, 1996, pp. 35–36.

14. McAllester and William Douglas, "Clinton's Ideal Internet," *New York Newsday*, July 2, 1997, pp. A3, A33.

11

Public Education

CONSUMER DEMAND

Pamela L, a vice-president at a residential real estate company in New York, has a genuine Rolex and a counterfeit Rolex. She is happy with the counterfeit—a cheap quartz watch bearing the Rolex® trademark. "It tells time accurately," she says. She is one of countless satisfied consumers, who view the counterfeit garments and watches as a type of discount merchandise.

Huge consumer demand is the principal reason for the market in counterfeit goods. The demand is based on a simple fact. Although most manufacturers will never admit it, many counterfeit goods are a bargain. For someone who does not have the money to buy a genuine Rolex, the counterfeit may be considered a good purchase. The counterfeit offers something of value, although the value is an intangible one—the goodwill and quality associated with the trademark. The theft appears harmless, since it does not involve an actual theft of the legitimate manufacturer's inventory of goods.

At the end of the twentieth century, digital technology has accelerated the demand for pirated products. Digital copies are nearly identical to the legitimate product. Pirated computer software, music, and motion pictures sell for a fraction of the cost of the legitimate product. The compilation CDs that were for sale in the streets of many Chinese cities in the mid-1990s sold for $10 to $20 and contained hundreds of computer programs. The actual retail cost of the pirated software was between $10,000 and $20,000, a bargain too great to resist.

For the most part, the business community is the primary victim of commercial counterfeiting. Individual businesses and industry trade groups and coalitions have responded by lobbying for stronger legislation and seeking legal redress under civil and criminal law. Responding to industry complaints, governments have responded by enacting stronger legislation and using the threat of trade sanctions against developing countries whose intellectual property laws are insufficient. Nonetheless, at the end of the twentieth century, product counterfeiting has become the most visible and prevalent business crime in the world. Counterfeit T-shirts, pirate music cassettes, and motion pictures cassettes are sold on the streets and in small retail establishments in nearly every large city in the United States. The counterfeiting situation is worse in many developing countries.

Advances in technology and the globalization of the economy are likely to make the crime even more of a problem in the twenty-first century. Jim Moody, head of the FBI's branch on organized crime and drugs, calls product counterfeiting "the crime of the twenty-first century."[1]

PUBLIC EDUCATION

To combat the seeming indifference of the public, many trade groups have begun using public education campaigns in an effort to change public attitudes. This is a formidable task. Public information campaigns are used to educate people about the dangers of drugs. Yet, while no one would deny the harm that drugs do, many people are not as understanding when it comes to the dangers of product counterfeiting. Many pirates are obstinate and justify their transgression under a guise of freedom. It is an old line, one used by James Frederick Willets, the music pirate of the late 1800s in England, who operated under the lofty goal of offering music to the masses at a cheap price.

Many rap artists, incensed at the high prices charged for music CDs, have deliberately pre-released their own works on the Internet. Like Willets, the pirate king, their goal is to bring music to the masses at a cheap price by offering their own music for free in defiance of the legitimate music industry. In late 1998, the rap group Public Enemy posted tracks from an unreleased album on the Internet using MP3 technology, and in early 1999, rapper Chuck D released his upcoming album *Bring the Noise 2000* on the Internet. In both instances, attorneys for the legitimate music publishers demanded that the music be removed from the Internet.

Many pirates do no jail time, which encourages them to become repeat offenders. According to Henry Hack, vice-president, telecommunications services New York metro area for CableVision on Long Island, some people who get caught hooking up illegally for cable television are repeat offenders who hook up again and again. About one-half of 1 percent of the piracy cases investigated by CableVision involve people who have hooked up illegally before and been caught. Only when criminal penalties are threatened will the piracy cease.

"It's like a kid going into the candy jar—he'll continue to do it, until you slap his hand," Hack says. "Sometimes you get a scofflaw—the type of person who runs red lights and never pays his bills."

Hack says that he encountered one individual in Cleveland who was a repeat offender. The individual had a ground connection, and had broken into the underground vault holding the cable wires. His neighbors turned him in, because he was interfering with their cable service. When CableVision contacted him, he wrote a letter claiming that there was a 1924 law[2] that made the airwaves free space, and he further stated that if CableVision wanted to pursue this, he was prepared to fight in court. The offender did try to defend himself in court and lost.

Because the theft involves an intangible product, the average consumer is little concerned. Because they are stealing from a large corporation or successful designer, many pirates rationalize the crime. They may become vindictive; their justification is that they are "getting back" at a product or service that they feel is overpriced.

Changing people's attitudes and otherwise educating them is the final frontier, and the ultimate solution to commercial counterfeiting. It is a daunting task, in part because people buy counterfeits for reasons other than monetary value. For example, imitation plays an important role in society. Even people of wealth and fashion recognize the value of imitation. Coco Chanel, the famous French dress designer, never wore her jewels in public, but had replicas of her jewels made for everyday wear. Jacqueline Kennedy, widow of President John F. Kennedy, wore imitation jewelry. At the auction of her personal possessions after her death was a string of fake pearls.

The average consumer very likely has misconceptions about what is right and wrong, because intellectual property law is complex. For products protected by copyright, the crime is hazy because certain types of copying are legal for purposes of home copying, parody, fair use, and as authorized by other legal doctrines under copyright law.

Copying is widespread in the garment industry. In the music industry, many music fans are encouraged to copy. The Grateful Dead is one band that allows and even encourages fans to tape their live performances, which likely encourages people to tape the live performances of other performers.

The need for public information campaigns was never more evident than during the trade dispute between China and the United States. By 1995, the pirate market based in China had shut out the legitimate market in much of Asia and was making inroads into Europe and Russia. One obstacle that the U.S. negotiators faced in resolving the problem

Watch crushing. *Photo courtesy of Cartier, Inc.*

Cartier, Inc. President & CEO Simon J. Critchell at a watch crushing, New York 1991. *Photo courtesy of Cartier, Inc.*

was the erroneous explanation offered by the Chinese negotiators that the problem was overstated and that the piracy situation was the result of a cultural tradition of copying the teachings of the masters. In fact, copying is a universally used teaching tool; school children worldwide are taught the alphabet by rote. Yet, for a national government to offer such an explanation during bilateral trade discussions demonstrated that misconceptions about the nature of commercial counterfeiting are embedded at the highest government levels. Nor is China the only government to turn a deaf ear to complaints about product counterfeiting. During the 1800s the U.S. government paid little heed to the complaints by English publishers of book piracy by American book publishers. To force the governments in Asia and Latin America to pay attention to the piracy problem in their own country, the United States enacted legislation that granted the USTR the political power to impose trade sanctions, if necessary, to prompt them to take action.

In the 1990s, many corporations began to realize the value of using public education as part of their antipiracy campaigns. As part of its settlement agreements for companies that engage in book piracy, the Association of American Publishers (AAP) requires that the defendant print a public apology. According to Carol Risher of the AAP, the use of public apologies has worked well in Asia. The apologies are usually one-quarter to one-half page in length and printed in the local newspaper. In Latin America, the companies take out an advertisement and pledge to work with the AAP to ensure that copyrights are enforced.

In 1995, a U.S. collaboration with China television proved quite successful in educating the general Chinese public about the importance of intellectual property. A sitcom, *My Computer Family*, featured famous Chinese actors who demonstrated the value of intellectual property. In one typical episode, the mother's manuscript is illegally copied and sold via computer.

To combat music piracy on the Internet, the RIAA launched a public education campaign in 1997. Many of the Internet music pirates are college students. To educate the students, the RIAA developed and began distributing Soundbyting, which is a program and teaching module that discusses the ethical issues involved on the Internet, the penalties for engaging in music piracy, and other pertinent issues.

The Business Software Alliance (BSA) has developed several public education campaigns. The campaigns are targeted toward preventing end-user piracy.

End-user piracy occurs when someone takes a legitimate computer program and installs it over and over again. Individuals engaged in end-user piracy are violating the shrink-wrap licensing agreement. Corporate clients are violating the commercial licensing agreement that allows for a specified number of installations of the program. Although end-user piracy is punishable by up to $100,000 per violation, it is the most prevalent form of computer piracy.

In 1995, the BSA launched a nationwide campaign in cooperation with Egghead Software, a leading U.S. retailer. The BSA provided software management information to the retailer's customers in more than 160 stores across the country. The educational campaign consisted of posters and educational flyers that were distributed at the point of purchase. When visiting an Egghead store, customers can fill out a mail-back card to ask for free BSA software management resources, including the *Guide to Software Management*.

According to a May 1995 *Computerworld* survey[3] of information systems professionals, 47 percent of the respondents admitted to copying commercial software illegally. To combat widespread corporate piracy, the BSA initiated a "Nail Your Boss" campaign in 1996. The program encourages people to take a stand against computer piracy, especially in situations where they know that a crime is being committed.

"People don't want to be known as snitches or whistleblowers," says Karine Elsen, director of marketing for the BSA. "We encourage people to try to discuss the situation with management and try to get them to turn over a new leaf."

In the corporate setting the piracy is sometimes unintentional and due to a management flaw. Management may be unaware that it has exceeded the number of programs allowed under the licensing agreement. Other times, an information systems employee is distributing the programs to other employees.

The BSA's Anti-piracy Hotline One (1–800–688–BSA1), which is accessible in the United States and Canada and Euro-Net Anti-Piracy Hotline (44–71–491–1974) have proven to be a very successful antipiracy tool. The BSA operates hot lines around the world for callers seeking information about piracy or to report suspected incidents (see Figure 11.1). Between 1988 and 1994, the BSA filed nearly 600 lawsuits that began from information received from the Hotline. In 1994, the BSA handled 7,272 calls. The BSA brought a total of 499 new actions in 1994, had 366 end-user cases pending, and executed 133 cease-and-desist notices.

Indifference to the crime of trademark counterfeiting is shared not only by the public, but also by law enforcement. Generally, prosecutors do not pursue commercial counterfeiters unless the organization is large. Commercial counterfeiting is a business crime, and unless the organization is large, engaged in interstate transportation, or otherwise engaged or connected to other types of illegal activity, prosecutors are not likely to pursue them.

Local law enforcement agencies often do not pursue the counterfeiters. In many large cities, the primary offenders are street peddlers. Even when complaints are filed, local law enforcement may not respond. Even

Figure 11.1
Business Software Alliance (BSA) Worldwide Hotlines

Argentina
0.800.9.7638

Australia
1.800.021.143

Belgium
32.2.361.54.44

Brazil
0800.11.00.39,
inside Brazil
5511.800.11039,
outside Brazil

Canada
800.263.9700

Chile
56.2.800.260020

Finland
09.644.141,
inside Finland
338.9.664.141,
outside Finland

France
33.1.43.33.9565

Germany
44.130.171801
toll free

Greece
30.1.363.0717

Hong Kong
852.2865.3318

Hungary
36.1.322.4891

Mexico
52.5.662.7257

Netherlands
06.899.8566 toll free
32.30.691.5267

Norway
80080055 toll free

Panama
507.265.3894

Peru
511.2410057

Philippines
63.2.811.5897

Poland
48.22.661.5512

Taiwan
886.2.757.6638

Thailand
662.618.5155

Turkey
90.212.272.22.39

United Arab Emirates
800.4828

United Kingdom
44.0800.510510

Uruguay
0800.2130

Euro-Net
44.71.491.1974
44.71.499.4733 fax

254

China
800-8100036
or 010-65992683

Colombia
257.5763
9.800.12575

Costa Rica
506 258 0811

Czech Republic
42.2.232.34.89

Denmark
80.34.00.00

Dominican Republic
809.535.5090

Ecuador
09.724.300

Egypt
20.2.302077

India
091.11.611.4971

Indonesia
021.522.2158

Israel
972.3.5403202

Italy
39.2.2056.2345
167.241.751 toll free

Japan
81.120.79.1451

Korea
080.022.3975 toll free

Luxembourg
800.3993

Malaysia
800.3875 toll free

Portugal
0.800.200.520 toll free

Puerto Rico
754.0989 San Juan

Saudi Arabia
800.124.8999

Singapore
65.266.0196

South Africa
0800.110.447

Spain
34.00.211.048
900.211.048 toll free

Sweden
46.8.677.5475

Switzerland
0800.812.121

United States
1.888.NO PIRACY
toll free
202.872.5500

Venezuela
58.800.33272

when the situation demands action, the police are unsure of what course of legal action to pursue.

"Local law enforcement often says, 'It's a federal violation, not a state matter,'" says Frank Creighton of the RIAA. "They are unaware that the RIAA has lobbied to get antipiracy statutes on the books for them to use."

To assist law enforcement, the RIAA meets on a regular basis with law enforcement agencies in cities throughout the United States. The RIAA works with the Organized Crime Investigative Division (OCID), which has multijurisdictional capabilities, and other agencies around the country. The RIAA trains law enforcement and customs inspectors on how to identify counterfeit products, how to get in touch with the RIAA, and what legislation and statutes apply to music piracy.

"We meet regularly with New York's Chief of Police," says Creighton. "In 1994, the RIAA presented Mayor Giuliani with a gold record for his support of our effort." Outreach training programs in which industry trains and establishes connections with law enforcement are meant to assist in the overall effort of fighting product counterfeiting. Such programs are used overseas as well. The MPAA reduced video cassette piracy in Japan partly by instituting an educational program.

Working with the IACC, General Motors regularly attends educational forums for educating U.S. Customs officers on the extent of the auto parts counterfeiting problem. Like most of the companies and trade groups mentioned in this book, General Motors has a public education campaign on the Internet.

Many industries are embracing the idea of using educational and outreach programs as a means of working closer with law enforcement, which is often hampered by lack of manpower and funds. Working with law enforcement can be frustrating. The largest seizure of counterfeit products in U.S. history took place on September 27, 1995, when U.S. Customs announced the success of Operation Pipeline. The success of Operation Pipeline was due in no small part to efforts of Chanel, Inc., which put up nearly $1 million toward the covert operation, and marked years of sometimes frustrating effort.

Operation Pipeline began as a joint operation between Chanel and U.S. Customs in 1992. By the early 1990s, Chanel's growing counterfeiting problem had become a concern for in-house counsel Veronica Hrdy. Much of the counterfeit merchandise was coming from Korea, and Hrdy initially decided to set up a storefront in Chinatown to penetrate the clandestine trade. A counterfeiter who had been arrested was used as an informant. The counterfeiter was known as Randy K.

Randy K was to introduce an undercover U.S. Customs agent and a Chanel investigator to other counterfeiters. The undercover investigators' cover line was that they had a means of bringing counterfeit goods into the United States and avoiding U.S. Customs. To complete the ruse, Chanel put up $50,000, so that Randy K could induce others to invest in the undercover business. Soon shipments were coming into the United States through Miami. In the spring of 1993, U.S. Customs in Miami decided that they could not work on the case anymore, and Hrdy decided to shift the operation to U.S. Customs in New York. New York Customs agreed to assist for one year.

Operation Pipeline became a gigantic sting operation, with Chanel funding surveillance equipment, hotel rooms, and private investigators. After a year, the sting operation was still going strong, and Hrdy met with the Assistant Attorney in Newark, New Jersey to obtain additional assistance should New York Customs decide to drop out of the investigation. Hrdy would eventually contact several state senators, the Justice Department, and several state and federal law enforcement agencies to see what assistance could be obtained. When the seizure finally took place, U.S. Customs agents seized $27 million worth of South Korean-made merchandise bearing over thirty trademarks, including Chanel, FILA, Guess?, Louis Vuitton, Reebok, and many others. Forty-three individuals were indicted.

Chanel's frustrating experience during Operation Pipeline is a reminder that enacting stronger legislation is insufficient; an effective intellectual property program requires adequate enforcement and public education.

NOTES

1. David Stipp, "Farewell, My Logo," *Fortune*, May 27, 1996.

2. There is no 1924 Act. The Wireless Ship Act of 1910 applied to use of radio by ships, but the Radio Act of 1912 was the first domestic law for central control of radio. Early broadcasting was experimental, but the number of stations broadcasting grew rapidly. The Radio Act of 1927 created a five-member Federal Radio Commission to issue station licenses, allocate frequency bands to various services, assign specific frequencies to individual stations, and control station power. The FCC was created under the Communication Act of 1934 and began operating on July 11, 1934. The FCC started regulating cable TV in April 1965, adopting rules for CATV systems served by microwave.

3. Mitch Belts, "Dirty, Rotten Scoundrels," *Computerworld*, May 22, 1995.

Selected Readings

Chowdhury, Zafrullah. *The Politics of Essential Drugs*. Zed Books, Atlantic Highlands, N.J., 1995.

Copyright and Home Copying. Office of Technology Assessment, Washington, D.C., 1989.

Economic Report of the President, transmitted to the Congress, February 1994, U.S. Government Printing Office.

Johnston, Donald F. *Copyright Handbook*, 2d ed. R. R. Bowker, New York, 1982.

Kane, Siegrun D. *Trademark Law, A Practitioner's Guide*. Practicing Law Institute, New York, 1987.

Melrose, Dianna. *Bitter Pills*. OXFAM Publishers, Oxford, England, 1982.

Morgan, Hal. *Symbols of America*. Viking Penguin, New York, 1986.

Patent, Trademark and Copyright Laws, 1985 ed. (edited by Jeffrey M. Samuels), Bureau of National Affairs, Washington, D.C.

Patterson, L. Ray and Lindberg, Stanley W. *The Nature of Copyright*. University of Georgia Press, Athens, Ga., 1991.

Schiavo, Mary. *Flying Blind, Flying Safe*. Avon Books, New York, 1997.

Seagrave, Sterling. *Lords of the Rim*. Originally published in Great Britain by Bantam Press, a division of Transworld Publishers Ltd. 1995.

Index

About the Author

PAUL R. PARADISE is a journalist and a freelance writer on a variety
of topics, particularly the law and law enforcement. The former editor
for a major publisher of law and law-related materials, Paradise is a
frequent contributor to law enforcement periodicals, and a staff writer
for T.F.H. Publications.